G000230065

ELIZABETH GASKELL: AN INDEPENDENT WOMAN

ANNA UNSWORTH

MINERVA PRESS
MONTREUX LONDON WASHINGTON

ELIZABETH GASKELL: AN INDEPENDENT WOMAN
Copyright © Anna Unsworth 1996

All Rights Reserved

No part of this book may be reproduced in any form,
by photocopying or by any electronic or mechanical means,
including information storage or retrieval systems,
without permission in writing from both the copyright owner
and the publisher of this book.

ISBN 1 86106 179 X

First Published 1996 by
MINERVA PRESS
195, Knightsbridge
London SW7 1RE.

Printed in Great Britain by
Antony Rowe Ltd., Chippenham, Wiltshire

ELIZABETH GASKELL:
AN INDEPENDENT WOMAN

"I am myself and nobody else, and can't be bound by another's rules."

ELIZABETH GASKELL

CONTENTS

My thanks to Alan Shelston for permission to reprint some of the material which has already been published in The Gaskell Journal.

PREFACE

It is not possible to identify and thank all the individuals who have helped, encouraged, criticised and provided me with information and suggestions in the writing of this book. I must, however, give special thanks to Dr John Beer and Professor Angus Easson who read earlier versions; Professors J.A.V. Chapple and Arthur Pollard for their edition of The Letters of Mrs Gaskell (1966) of which I have made such extensive use. I also express my gratitude to the Manchester University Press and Mrs Trevor Dabbs for permission to use Mrs Gaskell's letters and portrait. The Revd Roger Thomas helped me with the history of Presbyterianism; Dr Alec Vidler with the subject of Christian Socialism; Mr C.R. Bennet with the History of Knutsford; Dr Horst Müller with German Romanticism; Dr Andrew Morton with the identification of a Gaskell article; and more recently Mr Alan Shelston, editor of the Gaskell Society Journal has given me help and suggestions with the articles he has published in the Journal which are based on chapters from this book. My husband John Unsworth, a Unitarian minister, has been indispensable, especially in the construction of the complete Holland family pedigree, from which that given as an appendix at the end of the book has been extracted. I am grateful to the John Rylands University Library, Manchester College, Oxford Library, the Bodleian Library, the Gloucestershire County Library and the National Library of Scotland, all of which provided the books and photocopies of manuscripts and printed articles which make up my bibliography. I hope that some readers will not find the two chapters on the history of the Holland family, and of Puritanism, tedious, but their omission would have made it impossible to understand fully Mrs Gaskell's background, in which they are both so much intertwined and both of which played such a vital part in the making of her personality and so her life, her writing, her social work and her involvement in social reforms. Finally, I think I should take the opportunity of pointing out that I have approached my subject as a social scientist and social historian rather than as a literary critic, though literature has by no means been neglected. I must thank the Hibbert Trust for the grant without which the research for this book could never have taken place.

ABBREVIATIONS

GL: *The Letters of Mrs Gaskell*: ed. A. Pollard and J.A.V. Chapple, M.U.P., 1966.

HHS: *Mrs Gaskell: Haunts, Homes and Stories*: Mrs E. Chadwick, Pitman 1910.

Holt: *The Unitarian Contribution to Social Progress*: R.V. Holt, Allen and Unwin, 1938.

DNB: *Dictionary of National Biography*.

Sharps: *Mrs Gaskell's Observation and Invention*: J.G. Sharps, Linden Press, 1970.

UHST: Transactions of the Unitarian Historical Society.

ILLUSTRATIONS

CHAPTER 1

"No congregation should expect to control the time of the minister's wife"

When Elizabeth Gaskell arrived in Manchester in 1832, on her twenty-second birthday and five years before the accession of Queen Victoria, she came as the newly-wedded wife of a young dissenting minister, five years older than herself, assistant minister of Cross Street Chapel and the son of a well-to-do manufacturer of sail-canvass in Warrington. A Unitarian, as was his young wife, he was a Master of Arts of Glasgow University and portraits show him to have been tall, slim, and with finely-chiselled but rather cold features. In later years he was to become senior minister at Cross Street and remained there for the rest of his long life, much honoured by both congregation and city.

Known locally as 'the carriage-way to Heaven' because of the long line of carriages to be seen outside the chapel on Sunday mornings, Cross Street was frequented mainly by the rich, self-made manufacturers, merchants and business-men who were to provide Manchester with a large number of its Members of Parliament and municipal officers after the passing of the first Reform Act which occurred in the same year as the young Mrs Gaskell appeared on the Manchester scene. Whether she already had a conscious dislike of this transfer of political power from the landed aristocracy to men such as these we cannot say. What we can say is that one of her first actions on her arrival in Manchester was to make an announcement that 'no congregation should expect to control the time of the minister's wife' and that whatever she did would be 'of her own free will and not because she felt compelled.' This seems to have caused a considerable stir, for we find it still remembered in 1910, the centenary of her birth.[1]

We have to ask ourselves what gave the young Mrs Gaskell the confidence, one might almost say arrogance, to make such a statement in her circumstances. She had no private income which might have given her the independence of mind and action enjoyed by some women of her own and even earlier generations. In fact, at the time of her marriage she was penniless, entirely dependent on the relatives who had made themselves responsible for her welfare and education.

William Gaskell may have inherited a little from his father who was dead by the time William married, but all the evidence is that the young couple lived in very straitened circumstances in their first rented home, 14 Dover Street, off Oxford Road, which was then the main shopping street in Manchester.

Elizabeth had been born Elizabeth Cleghorn Stevenson, the second child of William Stevenson who, though of a sea-faring family at Berwick-on-Tweed, was a restless intellectual. He was, in turn, a travelling tutor on the continent to a young Englishman; a Unitarian minister in the Manchester area; failed farmer of a small-holding near Edinburgh as partner to Cleghorn, a Scottish experimental agriculturist (whose name he was to give to his, as yet unborn, daughter); a university 'crammer' and journalist in Edinburgh; and, finally, Keeper of the Treasury Records in London for the last twenty three years of his life.

It was at his London home, 3 Beaufort Row, Chelsea, that Elizabeth was born on 22nd September 1810, her mother being the former Elizabeth Holland of Sandlebridge, a farm some five miles from Knutsford in Cheshire. Elizabeth Holland's upbringing in the peaceful, secure countryside of Cheshire cannot have prepared her for the restless, insecure existence that marriage to William Stevenson entailed. But whatever the reason for her decline in health, she died in 1811 when her baby girl was only fourteen months old.

The motherless baby was taken up to Knutsford, some sixteen miles from Manchester, where she was reared by her mother's sister, Hannah Lumb, a widow of moderate means, in a pleasant Georgian house called Heathside. Within a few years, William Stevenson had re-married and fathered another son and daughter, and John Stevenson, Elizabeth's own brother, twelve years her senior, who had gone to sea like his Berwick forebears, disappeared about 1828 on a voyage to India; how or where it has been impossible to ascertain. The young Elizabeth seems to have seen her father about once a year in London and her brother when he was in England in between his voyages, which lasted up to two years. She remained devoted to both, exchanging affectionate letters with her brother and returning to her father's household after her brother's disappearance, by which time she was seventeen. Her father was by then already in poor health and no doubt this was accentuated by the loss of his son. Elizabeth helped to nurse him until his death two years later. The time spent in London was an unhappy one for her and after leaving London she didn't see her step-mother again for twenty-five years.

The Hollands of Cheshire therefore, were, in effect, Elizabeth's family: doctors, yeoman farmers, lawyers, and dissenting ministers mainly settled in the Knutsford area. The young Elizabeth was turned into an excellent housekeeper by her 'Aunt Lumb', whose small domain on the edge of Knutsford Heath was almost self-sufficient. Allowed to 'help' her in the mornings, it was in the afternoons that, with her aunt, she had her first lessons from old-fashioned text-books that the latter had used in her own youth. Various other 'old uncles and aunts who had all old books and very few new ones' also took a hand in her early education. Knutsford possessed a Young Ladies' Seminary patronised by the local tradespeople, but Elizabeth never attended it. French and dancing she learned from a French émigré aristocrat who was much respected in the town.

Each Sunday she accompanied Aunt Lumb to Brook Street Chapel and is believed to have taught in the small Sunday School, which was probably held in the chapel gallery; but at the early age of twelve she was sent to a boarding school, one which was first situated at Warwick, then at Barford, and finally at Stratford-upon-Avon. Elizabeth was a pupil (Ruskin's wife, Effie Grey, was to be another) for five years. The removals of the school were necessitated by expansion, for the school was an excellent one, giving what was probably the best available education in England at that time for a girl. It was conducted by the eight Byerley sisters, all of whom taught there at some time, returning periodically after their marriages with news of the world outside. Extremely cultured and well-informed but impecunious women, they were the daughters of Thomas Byerley, nephew and adopted son of the first Josiah Wedgwood, the famous potter, amateur scientist, and Unitarian, like the Hollands with whom the Wedgwoods were intermarried. Byerley got into financial difficulties and the second Josiah Wedgwood, who was interested in education,[2] financed the School where Elizabeth Gaskell spent five years.

After the two-year interruption, when she was in London caring for her father, her education was resumed in the household of Revd William Turner, a highly respected and scholarly minister, another family connection of the Hollands and one who, like her father, coached students for the Scottish universities. He also taught young workers at evening classes (Robert Stephenson of 'Rocket' fame among them) and was official lecturer to the Newcastle Literary and Philosophical Society. Turner was a widower with an unmarried daughter, Anne, some years older than Elizabeth. Meta (Margaret Emily), Mrs Gaskell's second daughter, always indignantly denied that there was ever any intention of her mother becoming a governess, but it seems reasonable to suppose that the Holland family intended to set her up in her own school as Josiah Wedgwood had established the Miss Byerleys. The intention certainly seems to have been that Elizabeth should spend at least the two winters of 1829-30 and 1830-31 in Newcastle and the summers in visits to relatives which were such a feature of the social life of the times. During the second winter, however, a cholera epidemic broke out in Newcastle and the two girls, Elizabeth and Anne, departed for Edinburgh.

The choice of Edinburgh may well have had a greater significance than that of a healthy resort, for the city was a centre of dissenting intellectual society, revolving round the university and various ladies who held 'evenings'. The most famous of the latter, Mrs Fletcher,[3] had known Mr Stevenson, and though by the time the young Elizabeth arrived there, the older woman had departed from the city, her father was still remembered there and it was not long before the two girls were drawn into the kind of social life which Mrs Gaskell was to describe in her introduction to *Round the Sofa* (1859): "In came Edinburgh professors, Edinburgh beauties, and celebrities..." and "people did not in these parties meet to eat, but to talk and listen." Here then Elizabeth enjoyed an informal 'finishing' and at twenty-one was a highly educated and polished young lady.

Any need to become a teacher, however, if such had been the intention, was forestalled by her marriage. Anne Turner's sister was married to the Revd John Gooch Robberds, senior minister at Cross Street Chapel, Manchester. It is generally believed that it was on summer visits to the Robberds that Elizabeth had met William Gaskell who, as his assistant for the past three years, was naturally in the house a good deal. It seems to have been something of a whirlwind romance, for Gaskell only met Mrs Lumb for the first time in March 1832 when he was already engaged to Elizabeth and the marriage took place on 30th August that same year at Knutsford parish church, as was then the law. In place of a dowry the young bride was promised a bequest from her aunt which would ensure her £80 a year (Mrs

Lumb died five years later) and the wedding reception was held at the house of her uncle, Dr Peter Holland, a Knutsford doctor.

To all appearances, therefore, Elizabeth Gaskell was, on the day of her arrival in Manchester, wife to the equivalent of an Anglican curate, living on little more than her husband's small stipend, a member of a respected but obscure provincial dissenting family, well-educated and well-mannered since Unitarians were noted for their interest in education. But none of this prepares us for the quality of temperament and character which enabled her to announce on her arrival at Cross Street Chapel to this congregation of rich, self-made men (and their wives) that they must not expect to control her time and that whatever she did would be done 'of her own free will and not because she felt compelled'.

Reports of Mrs Gaskell's physical appearance and manners have an intriguing flavour about them, again not what one would expect of a dissenting or as we would say, nonconformist, minister's wife. In Edinburgh she seems to have been accepted as one of the 'Edinburgh beauties' for during her stay there a miniature of her was painted by William John Thomson, an exhibitor at the Royal Scottish Academy, and a marble portrait bust executed by David Dunbar. This seems to have been a most unusual proceeding, for there could have been no question of the artists receiving a fee, and these two works of art seem also to have been presented to her for they are now in the John Rylands Library in Manchester, presented by her daughters. The miniature shows Elizabeth in true Romantic style, glancing from over a bare shoulder, back-hair piled high in braids held by a Spanish-style comb and side-hair falling on one side in one carefully-careless curl; while the bust-portrait, done in the Grecian style and again with draped bare shoulders, shows unusual serenity and dignity for her age. Such was the impression these two Scottish artists had of Elizabeth Stevenson shortly before her marriage.

Catherine and Susanna Winkworth, the Anglican daughters of a Manchester and Macclesfield silk-manufacturer, described her as she was in 1847, 'before she became celebrated', as 'a noble-looking woman with a queenly presence' and a 'high, broad, serene brow and finely cut, mobile features.'[4] Eliza Lynn Linton, an authoress and literary personality not renowned for the large-heartedness of her reminiscences and writing forty years later, has left a memorable picture of her as she was in 1858, by then a famous literary personality:

> The gracious and feminine dignity of Mrs Gaskell powerfully impressed me. She was so sweet and conscious. Her fine arms and neck were bare and destitute of ornament, and I remember the exquisite line of her throat and shoulders and the shape of her hands and arms. Her manner to me at an 'evening' when both Carlyle and Emerson were present was perfect. I was a young beginner and she was at the zenith of her fame; but she neither snubbed nor patronised ... and I have always loved and cherished her memory for the graciousness of her attitude and the kind words she spoke to me that evening.[5]

These four widely separated impressions of Mrs Gaskell seem almost to have a flavour of royalty, or at least of the highest and best type of aristocracy, which at first sight seems absurd. But research into the early background of the Holland family shows it to have been one of the oldest in the north of England. And not only old but colourful, romantic, aristocratic in the extreme and one very close to the throne.

In 1917, Bernard Holland, a nephew of one of Mrs Gaskell's cousins, published a history of the family, *The Lancashire Hollands*,[6] based on a vast number of early sources and also drawing on an earlier, privately printed work by Swinton Holland, *The Family of Hollands of Mobberly and Knutsford* (1902). Bernard Holland begins his book with a quotation from the Lancashire antiquary, Langton:

> There has existed no family in Lancashire whose career has been so remarkable as that of the Hollands. Playing an active part in the most picturesque period of English history, they figured among the founders of the Order of the Garter, allied themselves with the royal family and attained the highest rank in the peerage.

Sir Thurstan de Holland held land in Upholland, Lancashire, in the reign of King John, and his grandson, Sir Robert de Holland, came to a tournament in 1307, in 'the fields of Stepney', bearing the arms of the lion and lilies which henceforward, says Bernard Holland, were

18

the arms used by all the branches of the family. Sir Robert was the protégé of the great feudal lord of the north, Thomas, Earl of Lancaster, and their fortunes rose and fell together. As a result of a rebellion against Edward II, Lancaster was beheaded, Holland was imprisoned, lost his estates and the office of Chief Justice of Chester, and, though his estates were restored to him by Edward III, was killed by a personal enemy, probably to prevent his re-possessing them.

This violent death set the seal on the Holland family history. Again Bernard Holland says:

> The vicissitudes of their fortunes were great. If they rose to the heights, they also tasted of the depths. Most of the chiefs of the race, from the time of Edward II to that of Edward IV, came to violent ends, as befitted an ambitious and fighting family in stormy English times, when politics was a game played with lives for stakes.

The basis of the Hollands' climb to power was their prowess as fighters. Sir Robert had accompanied Lancaster on various military expeditions and his second son, Sir Thomas, fought in Flanders, Spain, Prussia and Gascony. He and his brother, Otho, were, according to Froissart, "esteemed the bravest in Christendom." It was also in Sir Thomas that the Holland family reached the peak of its fortunes, for it was he who married Joan Plantagenet, 'the Fair Maid of Kent', granddaughter of Edward III and a cousin of the Black Prince. She bore Holland four children: Thomas, John, Joan and Maud and, assuming his wife's title since her father and brothers were dead, he became the Earl of Kent. Appointed jointly with Philip of Navarre as lieutenant and captain-general of all English possessions in France and Normandy, on his death and by special dispensation of the Pope owing to the blood-relationship, Joan then married the Black Prince and became the mother of Richard II.

Both contemporary and modern historians have been in general agreement that Thomas and John Holland, Richard's half-brothers, were an evil influence on him. Holinshed accused John of 'having trained up the King in vice and evil customs from his youth' and Walsingham, in his Chronicles, accused the Hollands of sympathy with the Lollards, a movement towards what later came to be called Protestantism, while the Catholic and conservative Norman aristocracy called the Hollands upstarts and adventurers. Hard facts on the fourteenth century are not easy to come by and that the Hollands were on the losing side may well have caused them to be described as worse than they were when, in fact, they may have been no worse than their enemies. If they were a bad influence on Richard II, it was loyalty to him that led them to their death. The last great festivity of Richard's reign on St George's Day at Windsor was the Banquet of the Knights of the Garter at which the Hollands and their women-folk, now Ladies of the Garter, were present, together with the whole of the English nobility including the immortal Hotspur, Sir Henry Percy. Within nine months, Richard and the Holland men were dead, the Hollands beheaded for their part in a hopeless plot to put Richard back on the throne after his deposition by Bolingbroke. And again Walsingham calls Richard's supporters "friends of the Lollards", as well as "deriders of images", and the first Parliament of Bolingbroke, now Henry IV, passed the first statute in English history, De Haeretico Comburendo, authorizing the burning of heretics, as a reward to his Norman supporters.

Pedigrees show that the Holland family married into the houses of Lancaster, Plantagenet, Mortimer, York, Beaufort, Neville, Wilton, and Stuart, ancestors or ancestresses of Edward IV, Richard III, and Henry VII. It was the Wars of the Roses, that terrible struggle between the houses of Lancaster and York, which finally deprived them of their fortunes, removed them from the centre of power, and turned them into doctors, lawyers, yeoman farmers, and dissenting ministers.

The Winkworth sisters who wrote of the young Mrs Gaskell's 'queenly presence' in 1847 may have known of her ancient lineage, for their home at that time was Alderley Edge, within reach of Manchester yet well into the Cheshire countryside. But Eliza Lynn Linton, a struggling young author in London, described her in much the same terms. Perhaps a remark of Göethe's, made of a young German aristocrat who had visited him in 1832, may be thought appropriate here: "... in his mien and manners he was something by which the nobleman is seen at once. He could as little dissemble his descent as anyone could deny a higher intellect; for birth and intellect both give their possessor a stamp no incognito can conceal."[7]

Be that as it may, Elizabeth Holland's daughter, at the age of twenty-two, was not in the least over-awed by Manchester merchants and their ladies. In 1857, after twenty-five years in Manchester and after a first visit to Oxford, that most mediaeval of English cities, she wrote to an American friend, Charles Eliot Norton: 'I believe I <u>am</u> Mediaeval – and <u>un</u>Manchester, and <u>un</u>American ... I like Kings and Queens, & nightingales and mignonette(s) & roses...'[8]

To the same correspondent she wrote in the following year: 'I don't believe from what I hear of your looks that a Republic agrees with your health; do try a little aristocracy, and as a step to it try a visit to us, who are admirers of that 'effete institution.' '[9]

21

CHAPTER 2
The Holland Family

Though we find no reference to the long history of the Holland family in Mrs Gaskell's letters – she would have thought it inexpressibly vulgar to refer to it in any case – there is no lack of evidence that she and the rest of the Hollands knew and were proud of it. The name Thurstan, first recorded in the thirteenth century, occurs in several generations as that of the eldest son and it was Thurstan Holland, eldest son of Mrs Gaskell's cousin, Edward Holland of Dumbleton Hall, Evesham, who, in 1866, married Marianne, Mrs Gaskell's eldest daughter. Mrs Gaskell's letters also make it clear that both before and after her marriage, she mixed on equal terms with the old aristocracy of Cheshire and South Lancashire. Moreover, in Mrs Gaskell's novel *Ruth*, Miss Benson, talking of names, says of her brother, a dissenting minister that he was called Thurstan "because my father wished it; for, although he was what people called a radical ... he was very proud in his heart of being descended from some old Sir Thurstan, who had figured in the French wars."[1]

The county of Cheshire was originally much larger than it is today, taking in that part of Lancashire south of the Ribble which includes Warrington, and also part of North Wales. After the Norman Conquest, it was ruled by its own Earls for two hundred years and in 1237 became a County Palatine almost independent of the Crown, Sir Robert de Holland (d.1304) being in charge not only of the Castle at Chester but also those at Rhudlaw and Flint in North Wales. It is through his brother William (d.1314) and his grandson Thurstan de Holland, living in 1368 and known as 'of Denton', that the Hollands could trace their direct descent from Robert de Holland, living in 1241 and Lord of Upholland and Matthew de Holland, his father, who died in the same year. Bernard Holland writes of Denton Hall that it stood about five miles south-east of the old town of Manchester. The manor remained in the possession of Thurstan de Holland and his lineal male descendants from 1330 to 1686 – over three hundred years. These Hollands always held the position of a county family on the higher level and married into like families in Lancashire and Cheshire. In fact, it was a Sir Richard Holland (1498-1543) of Denton and Heaton who married Ann Fitton of Gawsworth, the sister of Mary Fitton (believed by some to have been Shakespeare's 'Dark Lady') and Gawsworth, a splendid black and white Elizabethan mansion, may have been a house where Shakespeare's company presented his plays.

Again according to Bernard Holland:

> The Hollands were never so obscure before or since as in the eighteenth century. They had lived at Mobberly in a quiet way, much as substantial yeomen, farming their own land, their younger sons becoming nonconformist ministers or provincial lawyers or the like. They were, however, in virtue of their descent from a manorial family described as 'gentlemen' in legal documents and they steadily used on their seals the old Upholland crest of the lion rampant grasping a fleur de lys which was borne by Sir Robert de Holland in 1307 on his banner at the Stepney tournament.

It was William Holland, son of a Manchester merchant, who acquired Dam Head House at Mobberly, near Knutsford, in 1650. One of the small halls of Cheshire, built of a warm red brick, it still stands on part of what is believed to have been, in the seventeenth century, a hundred and fifty acres of agricultural land. It had a stream which was dammed to give power for a small mill manufacturing crêpe for widow's weeds (hence its curious name). And it was William's great grandson, John Holland (1690-1770), who, by his marriage to its heiress, Mary Colthurst, in 1718 brought into the Holland family the small hall which was to play such an important part in the life of Elizabeth Gaskell, namely, Sandlebridge, also near Knutsford. It was, in due course, inherited by her grandfather, Samuel Holland (1734-1816), and was her mother's home. She herself was to return to it again and again and it appears several times in her fictional writings. After Samuel Holland's death, when she was six years old, it passed to his grandson, Sir Henry Holland, a wealthy London physician. He greatly added to its land and it was occupied by other Holland cousins. It was finally demolished about 1962.

Towards the end of the nineteenth century, Sir Henry's son, Henry Thurstan Holland, became a member of the Liberal Government and was created Viscount Knutsford and in 1955, when the College of Arms granted Armorial Bearings to the town of Knutsford, it adopted the motto 'Respice, Aspice, Prospice,' 'Look to the Past, the Present, and the Future', the motto which, at some time during its long history, the Holland family had added to its Coat of Arms.

After the Norman Conquest, large feudal estates had been established in the Knutsford area (the boundaries of which can still be traced today) and Knutsford itself had come into being as the natural meeting-place and trading centre for these estates. By the twelfth century it was a township which had already developed a certain independence, many of its inhabitants being freeholders, unlike the villages and hamlets on the estates which were wholly dependent on and dominated by the lords of the manors. Knutsford's independence may be thought of as symbolised by the unusually large area of common land (still a prominent feature of the town) known as the Heath. Elizabeth, according to Thackeray's daughter, Lady Ritchie, 'in her hours of childish sorrow and trouble ... used to run away from her aunt's house across the Heath, and hide herself in its green hollows.'[2] Other symbols of Knutsford's importance, as the years rolled by, were the magnificent Assembly Rooms attached to the George Inn, where the county balls were held, and the Sessions House where, from 1575, Quarter Sessions had been held. William Webb's 'Itinerary of Cheshire' described the town in 1621 as 'extraordinarily well-traded, which I have been induced to think hath risen from this, that it is on every side beset and environed with gentlemen's houses...' Even the Civil War had no great impact on Cheshire and by the eighteenth century, with its population steadily growing and prospering and the great family estates surrounding it at the height of their wealth and importance, Knutsford, in the Georgian period, entered upon what has been called by a local historian, 'the halcyon period of its existence.'[3]

Once the great estates had been settled on the original Norman families, younger sons had had to be provided for, and the ownership of the whole or parts of estates had also changed hands over the centuries. To the Fitz-Nigels, Tattons, de Masseys, de Tableys, de Meres, de Mobberlys, Mainwarings, Leghs, Leycesters and Cholmondeleys were added the Egertons, Shuttleworths, Stanleys, Davenports, Brookes, Deanes, Colthursts, Holfords, Duckinfields, and, of course, Hollands. The result was a profusion of historic houses for which Cheshire is now famous. Some of these were left in ruins when the owners built more fashionable houses on another part of their estate, some were demolished and new houses built on the same site, some were preserved in essentials and added to as generation succeeded generation. Very many of the small halls have been demolished, or have become known as 'Farms', as in the case of William Holland's Dam Head.

That the aristocratic families of Cheshire and South Lancashire were well known to Mrs Gaskell, and she to them, is clear. It is also clear that she was almost obsessed not only by the old families and houses but also by the customs of 'old England' in general even from her schooldays. Very few of the aristocratic names I have listed above are absent from either her works or her letters or their names from the grave-stones in the Knutsford Unitarian Chapel grave-yard (probably the oldest of its kind in the country). In one of the earliest of her surviving letters, written in May 1836, which contains an idyllic picture of Sandlebridge in early summer, we learn that she lunched at 'Mr Davenports at Capesthorne [Hall]', and the following day she and her husband had a ride, 'Mr Deane mounting and accompanying' them both. The Egertons, who lived at the vast Tatton Park, are the inspiration for the Cumnors of Cumnor Towers in Mrs Gaskell's last novel, *Wives and Daughters*; Mrs Mainwaring is one of the ladies of Cranford who practised 'elegant economy'; Legh is the name given to an admirable working class scientist in *Mary Barton*; and Mr Brooke appears in *My Lady Ludlow*. Lord Holford is the heir to Cumnor Towers. The Stanleys of Alderley, a branch of one of the great families of the north of England, were well known to her. Arthur Stanley, eventually Dean of Westminster, and his mother, Catherine, formerly a Leycester of Toft Hall, one of the original estates near Knutsford, became her close friends. Lady Kay-Shuttleworth, heiress in her own right to the estate of Gawthorp, about ten miles on the Lancashire side of Haworth, was also a friend and it was at her house in the Lake District that she first met Charlotte Brontë. It is the Deanes, Colthursts, and Duckinfields who lie beside the Hollands in the Knutsford Chapel grave-yard.

Mrs Gaskell's first extant piece of literary writing is found in a letter to Mary Howitt who, with her husband William, edited *Howitt's Journal*, a popular literary periodical. In 1838, she wrote from the humble parsonage in Manchester:

> Near the little, clean, kindly town where ... I was brought
> up there was an old house with a moat within a park called

Old Tabley, formerly the dwelling-place of Sir Peter
Leycester, the historian of Cheshire, and accounted a very
fine specimen of the Elizabethan style. It is beautifully
kept by its owner who lives in a new house built about
half a mile off, the velvet lawn up to the deep windows
being mown most regularly, and the large laurels and the
magnificent beeches trimmed with most excellent care.

And she goes on to describe summer picnics there with 'a merry
young party' and the impressions made on her youthful imagination by
this old hall with its chapel belfry, the bell of which could still be
rung, the gallery with its 'old armour hung up', its 'painted window
from ceiling to floor' and 'the strange sound our voices had in that
unfrequented stone hall!'[4]

A few months later she wrote, again to Mary Howitt, a similar
piece on old halls and customs, especially those in the Knutsford area,
and in 1840 William Howitt published her account of a visit to
Clopton Hall in Warwickshire, written from memory but probably
based on an essay written when at school in Stratford-upon-Avon. It
appeared as by a 'fair lady' in Howitt's *Visits to Remarkable Places:
Old Halls, Battle Fields, and Scenes Illustrative of Striking Passages
in English History and Poetry*. Already this piece showed what Mary
Howitt called, in her own autobiography,[5] 'powerful and graphic
writing' as well as an extraordinary memory and powers of
observation, historical accuracy combined with a vivid imagination
and an instinct for the poetic. It has also been said of Mrs Gaskell by
a modern critic that 'whatever interested her impressed itself upon her
mind.'[6] If so, the life and what still remained of 'old England'
interested her very much indeed. It is also obvious that, from her first
coming to industrial Manchester, the great contrast between the old
life and the new was continually before her eyes and in her mind.
Innumerable examples of this can be found in her writing but perhaps
one of the most evocative is the long account at the beginning of her
Life of Charlotte Brontë in 1857 of the background against which
Charlotte's own life had been lived. Of the Roe Head district, about
twenty miles from Haworth on the Lancashire-Yorkshire border, was
the school where Charlotte had taught for a period, and of Roe Head
Mrs Gaskell wrote:

26

in the broad green valleys below, traces of the old Plantagenet times are to be met with everywhere – the grey pile of buildings, formerly a 'House of Professed Ladies'; the mouldering stone in the depth of the wood, under which Robin Hood is said to lie; close outside the Park an old stone-gabled house now a roadside inn but which bears the name of the 'Three Nuns' ... is frequented by fustian dressed mill-hands from the neighbouring worsted factories ... round which future villages gather. In no other part of England, I fancy, are the centuries brought into such close, strange contact ... All round the lands held by the farmer who lives in the remains of Howley Hall are stone houses of today, occupied by people who are making their living and their fortunes by the woollen mills that encroach upon and shoulder out the proprietors of the ancient halls. These are to be seen in every direction, picturesque, many-gabled, with heavy stone carvings of coats-of-arms for heraldic ornament, belonging to decayed families, from whose ancestral lands field after field has been shorn away, by the urgency of rich manufacturers pressing hard upon necessity. A smoky atmosphere surrounds these old dwellings of former Yorkshire Squires, and blights and blackens the ancient trees that overshadow them; cinder-paths lead up to them; the ground round them is sold for building upon; but still the neighbours, though they subsist by a different state of things, remember that their fore-fathers lived in agricultural dependence on the owners of these halls; and treasure up the traditions connected with the stately households that existed centuries ago... (chVI)

The mature Mrs Gaskell's writings exhibit an unusually extensive knowledge of both English and European literature, its foundations laid during her five years of tutelage under the Miss Byerleys, the last three of these at Avonbank, the beautiful Tudor house which stood on the bank of the river Avon near the parish church. The house is believed to have been owned by a cousin of Shakespeare's, and, the Byerleys being dissenters of the Presbyterian persuasion, there is nothing unusual in the fact that pews were rented for the school in the parish church. Elizabeth Stevenson must, therefore, have seen Shakespeare's bust and tomb Sunday by Sunday during her impressionable years of fourteen to seventeen. Moreover, English literature was a major subject at the school and was taught by Catherine Byerley, to whom her grateful pupils had a plaque put up in the parish church in 1844. Mrs Gaskell's works show a detailed knowledge of Shakespeare's plays and quotations abound in them, often from memory and sometimes without acknowledgement as though they had become part of her own mind.

It is difficult to believe that Catherine Byerley, a family connection of the Hollands, could have been unaware of the Holland family history. She herself had some claim to gentility, her father being descended from Lord Wharton, and she had possibly held, at some time, a post in the household of Queen Charlotte, one of the clients of the Wedgwood show-rooms in London, of which Thomas Byerley was manager and where he lived with his family 'over the shop.' That Catherine was interested in the subject of the aristocracy is evident by the fact that, under the name of Grace Wharton, she published several works, among them *The Queens of Society*, *The Wits and Beaux of Society*, and *The Literature of Society*. It is highly unlikely that she could have refrained from mentioning to the young Elizabeth that the character named first as 'Kent' and then 'Surrey', in Shakespeare's *Richard II*, was none other than Thomas Holland, the king's uncle and a distant relative of hers.

In 1838, Mrs Gaskell wrote to Mary Howitt in her letter on the old customs of Cheshire:

> One of the customs, on any occasion of rejoicing [in Knutsford] is that of strewing the ground before the houses of those who sympathise in the gladness with common red sand, and then taking a funnel filled with white sand, and sprinkling a pattern of flowers upon the red ground. This is always done for a wedding, and often accompanied by some verse of rural composition. When I married, nearly all the houses in the town were sanded...[7]

At the time of her marriage, the population of Knutsford was nearly 3,000. She was a penniless girl of twenty-one who had spent the major part of her life away from the town, her father had been unknown there, her mother dead twenty years, her relatives a modest family of dissenters. Yet on her wedding-day 'nearly all the houses in the town were sanded.' One may feel that this could only be a tribute to the ancient lineage of the Holland family and its former greatness. Country memories are long ones.

When the young Mrs Gaskell came to Manchester, therefore, in 1832, it was as something of a 'great lady', partly in fact and partly in her own romantic, emotionally-compensating imagination. We have seen the extraordinary statement made to the congregation at Cross Street Chapel in 1832, and we know that she was writing romantic accounts of 'old England' in the 1830s. We have seen the description by the Winkworth sisters of her manner and appearance in the 1840s before she 'became celebrated'. In 1848, she began the preface which her publisher had persuaded her to write to the first edition of her first novel, *Mary Barton*:

> Three years ago I became anxious (from circumstances that need not be more fully alluded to) to employ myself in writing a work of fiction. Living in Manchester, but with a deep relish and fond admiration for the country, my first thought was to find a framework for my story in some rural scene; and I had already made a little progress in a tale, the period of which was more than a century ago, and the place on the borders of Yorkshire, when I bethought me how deep might be the romance in the lives of some of those who elbowed me daily in the busy streets of the town in which I resided.[8]

What the young Mrs Gaskell had felt 'compelled' to do when she first came to Manchester was to teach at the Mosley Street School, which had been founded by Anglicans and Unitarians (later carried on by Unitarians alone owing to denominational difficulties), to give some education to the cotton workers, and also to act as a district visitor for the Salford Provident Society which was founded in 1833. In her letters we see her getting on extremely well with working people, yet also capable of great 'hauteur' towards anyone who tried to be 'something they were not.' This included many of the Cross Street Chapel congregation and anyone whom she felt had behaved with an offensive familiarity towards her, as in the case of, for example, George Lewes, the eventual companion of George Eliot[9]. The best type of rural gentry had always felt a deep responsibility for those in their employment and for the poor in the villages on their estates. Mrs Gaskell wrote in 1837, once again to Mary Howitt: 'my

cousins ... know the ins and outs of every poor family in Knutsford...'
and they also taught in the Knutsford Chapel Sunday School. The
young Mrs Gaskell in Manchester, therefore, was only carrying on
and developing what her family had always taken for granted, though
it was now in vastly more discouraging and complex circumstances.
Again she says in her preface to *Mary Barton*:

> The more I reflected on (the) unhappy state of things
> between those so bound to each other by common
> interests, as the employers and the employed must ever
> be, the more anxious I became to give some utterance to
> the agony which, from time to time, convulses this dumb
> people; the agony of suffering without the sympathy of the
> happy, or of erroneously believing that such is the case ...
> the woes which come with ever-returning tide-like flood to
> overwhelm the workmen in our manufacturing towns ...

Mrs Gaskell's friends after her marriage, therefore, remained her
own and her husband's relatives, the old county families she had
known from childhood, and anyone with whom she came into contact
through their common efforts to improve the quality of life of the
working-classes. This included, in Manchester, the Anglican
Winkworths as well as the intelligent workers themselves. Like all
true aristocrats, she was as much at home with a Welsh cottager and a
Lancashire mill-worker as she was with the Duke of Devonshire, with
whom she became a great favourite. It is not surprising, therefore,
that in 1848, after criticism by the senior Unitarian minister's wife in
Manchester, Mrs J.J. Tayler, regarding her discussing Scott's
Kenilworth with her Sunday School class on a Sunday, she concluded
her account of the incident to Catherine Winkworth with the words: 'I
am myself and nobody else and cannot be bound by another's rules.'[1]

CHAPTER 3
Manchester in the 1830s and '40s

In the first half of the nineteenth century, Manchester was a dangerous place for all but the robust, the rich, and the aggressively ambitious. As early as 1808, the town had been described by a visitor from Rotherham as 'abominably filthy, the Steam Engine is pestiferous, the Dyehouses noisome and offensive, and the water in the river as black as ink or the Stygian lake.' And such things got worse rather than better.

In 1835, De Tocqueville, a French aristocrat wrote of the town as

> a collection of little hills, a narrow river ... two streams ... [and] three canals unite at the same point; Thirty or forty factories rise on top of the hills ... Their six stories rise up [and] the wretched dwellings of the poor are scattered haphazard around them... Some of the roads are paved but most of them are full of ruts and puddles into which foot or carriage sink deep: Heaps of dung, rubble from buildings, putrid stagnant pools are found here and there among the houses ... Who can describe the interiors of these quarters set apart, homes of vices and poverty ... one story houses whose ill-fitting planks and broken windows show them up as the last refuge a man might find between poverty and death. Below some of their miserable dwellings are cellars to which a sunken corridor leads. Twelve to fifteen human beings are crowded pell-mell into each of these repulsive holes...the huge palaces of industry...keep air and light out of the human habitations which they dominate; they envelop them in perpetual fog...a sort of black smoke covers the city... Under this half-light 300,000 human beings are ceaselessly at work... [and] from this filthy sewer pure gold flows.

This was three years after Mrs Gaskell had come to Manchester and all within walking distance of her home.

In 1842, the town authorities spent £5000 a year on cleansing the streets; those of the first class were cleansed once a week, the second class every fortnight and the third class once a month, while the courts and alleys were disregarded altogether. Eighteen thousand people lived in the insanitary cellars with no clean water supply; one observer called the streams mentioned by De Tocqueville 'liquid manure'; various fevers, particularly typhoid and cholera were continually breaking out, and 'more filth, worse suffering and moral disorder than Howard describes as affecting the prisoners is to be found among the cellar population of the working people.' House-building was left almost entirely to speculative builders and mill-owners with, but for a few exceptions, horrific results.[1] Mrs Gaskell faithfully records this industrial scene in her fictional writing. It is in *Mary Barton*, begun in 1845, that two working-men picked their way down one of these streets to bring succour to a friend dying of typhoid on the oozing earth-floor of a cellar-dwelling.[2] In *North and South*, (1854) she wrote of the 'deep lead-coloured cloud' which hung over the city, the 'hopeless' streets of working-class dwellings, the black 'unparliamentary' smoke (due to the ineffective Town Improvement Causes Act of 1847) which issued from the 'great oblong many-windowed' factories,[3] and in 1860 she begged the American, Charles Eliot Norton, to send her

> all manner of information and plans about your blocks of dwellings for working men...I don't know what you call them in America – great conglomerate sets of rooms in one vast building – erected according to laws of health ... in fact every evidence on your side of the water about lodging the working-people well, economically, and healthily. I shall be very glad of this information as soon as possible, and very willing to pay for its quick transmission![4]

But it was possible to live in Manchester without ever seeing (especially if one did not want to see) the filthy holes that were the habitations of the poor, and Isabella Banks, a journalist and antiquarian who was born and lived in the city until the 1840's, nowhere in her writings mentions them.[5] In *Mary Barton*, Mrs Gaskell shows the wife of one of the 'masters' getting out of her carriage and entering one of the luxurious shops in the Oxford Road, where the windows were like 'Aladdin's garden of enchanted fruits', unaware that she is being watched by one of the starving strikers.

By the 1830's, life in the industrial cities had come to be based on entirely different principles from those of 'old England'. The pressures of rapidly increasing numbers of people, the introduction of new industrial techniques and new ways of organising work had destroyed the old social relationships. Thornton, in *North and South*, at the beginning of the novel neither knows nor cares what any of his 'hands' do when they leave his factory gates and knows scarcely any of them by name.

Not all the industrial cities were entirely alike, however: Manchester and Birmingham, for example, diverged very strongly in their economic, social and political life. Birmingham was a city of small work-shops which produced a great variety of iron-ware goods and were often family businesses, or small enough to make it fairly easy for an energetic and intelligent workman to become an employer himself. It was therefore possible to develop a community consciousness and a broadly based reform movement which was later in the century to earn it the title of the best governed city in the country. The same was true, in a lesser degree, of Leeds, Sheffield, Newcastle and Glasgow. Manchester, on the other hand, was given over to a single product, cotton, and was also the business capital of a whole area comprising Salford, Wigan, Bolton, Bury, Rochdale, Oldham and Stockport, all of which were given over to the manufacture and sale of cotton. The essence of the cotton industry was mass-production and single firms employed hundreds, even thousands of workers. In the absence of course, of any idea of co-operation or planning – indeed 'free competition' was the battle-cry of the Manchester School of politico-economists – and also owing to foreign competition, it was an industry peculiarly liable to booms and slumps. The employers had, therefore, a strangle-hold on the working classes; slumps meant long periods of unemployment during which the employers accepted no responsibility for their employees; lack of social contact between employers and workers meant little mutual sympathy; unrestricted hours of work for low wages was almost universal; the only method of resolving grievances was the use of the strike, since it was the workers' only weapon.

Carlyle, had, in 1829, in his *Signs of the Times*, prophesied that the machines would take over men's minds, that there would be machines for education – by the Lancastrian and Bell systems one master could teach a class of a hundred children, public work would be done through the machinery of 'the public meeting, the committee, the prospectus, the public dinner', ideas communicated by 'the periodical, the monthly or the quarterly magazine [which would] grind meal for society.' In his *Chartism* in 1839, a year of great social violence, he attacked the new systems of production which would make the vast majority of workers 'skilless', 'menial' servants of the machines. And in 1843, his *Past and Present* opened with a phrase which was to echo and re-echo throughout the rest of the century, "The condition of England". Attacking the whole of what he called the 'cash-nexus', he expressed his contempt for the existing Political Economy and recommended a return to earlier ways of life. Of the poverty and masses of unemployed work-people, during what came to be known as the Hungry Forties, he thundered:

> England is full of wealth of multifarious produce, supply
> for human want in every kind; yet England is dying of
> inanition [and] two millions... sit in Workhouses...
> pleasantly so-named because work cannot be done in
> them.

It was during the strikes and periods of unemployment that Mrs Gaskell, her friends the Winkworth sisters (there were six in all), and their companions in the Manchester and Salford District Provident Society, trudged the noisome alleys of the city distributing what provisions they could muster; and, in better times, persuading the cotton-workers to join clothing clubs (2d a week) and savings banks in preparation for the next inevitable period of unemployment; and, at all times, trying to succour the vulnerable, the sick, the aged, and the under-nourished children.

The term middle class was not one which, as far as I am aware, Mrs Gaskell ever used, differentiating sharply as she did between the manufacturers, people in business, commerce and trade and what we would now call professional people. She expressed this quite clearly to Charles Eliot Norton regarding the marriage of a mutual friend, James Lowell the American writer whom she met in Rome:

> You don't understand what are our 'aristocratical feelings'
> when you make an apology about his marrying a
> governess. That does not hurt us in the least - it would if
> he married an uneducated girl, a daughter of a rich
> tradesperson. ... My dearest friends, all through my life
> have been governesses either past, present or future...[6]

In wealthy Manchester, therefore, where society largely consisted of rich tradespersons, she found entertaining dull and wearying even though she was extremely sociable by nature. Though she had announced that 'no congregation should expect to control the time of the minister's wife', much of her entertaining was actually 'duty'. William Gaskell, as minister of a congregation which was largely made up of the type of people his wife disliked, rapidly became an important figure in the city. What we today would call a 'committee man', he was, in addition to his ministerial duties, interested in social statistics, sanitation, the Portico Library (a subscription library for men only), and the Manchester Literary and Philosophical Society. Though much of it went against the grain, Mrs Gaskell could not avoid becoming involved in the social life which arose out of her husband's work and interests. But it was not without protests, which are a continuing theme in her letters, for example 'the Leislers to a sociable tea ... a sprinkling of Germans. It was very dull' - Leisler was a merchant whose wife had asked William Gaskell to accept their daughter as a private pupil. This private tutoring was a means of adding to the small stipends of ministers and the Germans were an important part of the Manchester industrial scene. Many of the latter were liberal Jews who had come from Germany to escape persecution or to set up subsidiaries of their own firms; they found the Unitarian chapels a congenial alternative to their synagogues. Amongst these were the Schwabes, who attended Cross Street Chapel:

> ... to the Schwabes last night [Mrs Gaskell groaned] a very dull evening. Not knowing or wanting to know anyone there ... the party consisted almost entirely of Germans... Tomorrow I go to a 'ladies party' at Mrs Sidney Potters...' [The Potters were Unitarian mill-owners.]

To the Manchester manufacturing and commercial class she was as merciless as she had it in her to be: '... a stupid dinner with the D's [Darbishires, Unitarian solicitors], Horners [factory inspector], Alcocks [Chairman of Cross Street Chapel] and Jas Turners [manufacturer].' Of the Gregs, Unitarian cotton manufacturers: 'I don't care an atom for them.' Of drinking tea with the Herfords, Unitarian wine-merchant: 'rather dull'. After a dance for three hundred people at The Park, a palatial residence of the Philips brothers, also Unitarian cotton merchants, she describes them, one a Member of Parliament for Manchester and the other for Bury, as 'not very gentlemanly' Sir James Watts, merchant and Mayor of Manchester in 1856, was 'a new man, and a Mayor unknown to most people here, as most of our Mayors are; they, being principally risen men, who are willing to give two or three thousand for the privilege of being Mayor, and the power which it gives them of getting into Society.' Of the Ewarts, Unitarian commercial agents, she fancied 'their dance last night was large, vulgar and overdressed.' Half-jokingly, of W.J. Fox, ex-Unitarian minister and co-Member of Parliament with William Cobbett for Rochdale, about his daughter's marriage in Rome, after a string of other enquiries about the bridegroom she asked, 'what has he (I live in Manchester [,] city sacred to Mammon)?' Only Sir William Fairbairn; the famous engineer, who was to become keenly and intelligently interested in her literary work; the Winkworth family; James Nasmyth, also a well-known engineer and partner of Holbrook Gaskell, a Liverpool relative; and the Satterfields, Unitarian drapers, with whom an evening was described as 'No ill-natured remarks but everything gentle and good', are seen with approval.[7]

This overall attitude to the Manchester manufacturing and commercial community is also evident in her published writing. In *Ruth*, (1853), Mr Bradshaw, the tradesman, is 'the patronizing pew-renter, the moralizing utilitarian, the self-righteous Non-conformist; the politician with a tender conscience who looked the other way when shady methods were mentioned.'[8] In chapel on Sundays when

> all the congregation stood up, and sang aloud, Mr Bradshaw's great bass voice was half a note in advance of the others in accordance with his place of precedence as principal member of the congregation. His powerful voice was like an organ very badly played and very much out of tune; but as he had no ear, and no diffidence, it pleased him very much to hear the fine loud sound.

At home

> There was tea, the equipage for which was as handsome and ugly as money could purchase. Then the ladies

produced their sewing, while Mr Bradshaw stood before the fire, and gave the assembled party the benefit of his opinions on many subjects. The opinions were as good and excellent as the opinions of any man can be who sees one side of a case very strongly, and almost ignores the other.

Finally

Stained by no vice himself, either in his own eyes or in that of any human being who cared to judge him, having nicely proportioned and adapted his means to his ends, he could afford to speak and act with a severity which was almost sanctimonious in its ostentation of thankfulness as to himself.[9]

How often must Mrs Gaskell, whose eldest girl, Marianne, had music lessons in London with Pergetti, the teacher of the Queen's children, have winced at that booming, out-of-tune voice, eyed that ugly tea-service, studied that pontificating figure warming his backside at the fire and keeping its warmth from the rest of the company while giving them the 'benefit' of his ignorant, bigoted, and sanctimonious opinions!

The novel in which these passages appear is said to have been burned by two male members of Cross Street Chapel congregation, on the grounds that its subject matter – the seduction of an innocent and orphaned working-girl by a rich youth – was not a fit one for a novel.[10] One cannot help but feel, however, that Mrs Gaskell's portrait of 'Mr Bradshaw' must have added fuel to the fire of their 'righteous indignation'.

In *North and South*, we have another picture of Manchester social life. The drawing-room of Mrs Thornton, the mother of a young self-made manufacturer, who had herself in her unmarried days been a mill worker

seemed as though no-one had been in it since the day when the furniture was bagged up with as much care as if the house was to be overwhelmed with lava, and discovered a thousand years hence...the carpet...covered up in the centre by a linen drugget, glazed and colourless... Great alabaster groups occupied every flat surface, safe from dust under their glass shades. In the middle of the room, right under the bagged up chandelier, was a circular table, with smartly bound books arranged at regular intervals round the circumference of its polished surface, like gaily coloured spokes of a wheel... [everywhere] there was evidence of care and labour, but not care and labour to procure ease, to help on habits of tranquil home employment; solely to ornament, and then to preserve from dirt or destruction...a room...to make people speak low, as if unwilling to awaken the unused echoes.

When Mrs Thornton enters to greet her visitors, she is 'rustling in handsome black silk as was her wont' and, before long, is saying to Mr Hale, an Oxford graduate and ex-Anglican clergyman who has given up his calling on grounds of conscience and become a tutor with whom her son is taking private lessons, that

Classics may do very well for men who loiter away their lives in the country or in colleges; but Milton-Northern [the industrial town in which the novel is set] men ought to have their thoughts and powers absorbed in the work of today.

When Mr Hale and his daughter Margaret are invited to dinner at the Thorntons', 'the sumptuousness of the dinner-table and its appointments' quite astonished Margaret: she 'felt the number of delicacies to be oppressive' and that the Thorntons 'had never known ... any kind of society but that which depended on an exchange of superb meals.'

During the dinner there was a very animated conversation going on among the gentlemen; the ladies, for the most part, were silent, employing themselves in taking notes of the dinner and criticizing each other's dresses (but) Margaret caught the clue to the general conversation, grew interested and listened attentively.

Though a newcomer to life in an industrial town, Margaret had already begun to interest herself, as she and her family had always done in their rural parish in the south, in the welfare of poor families and she notes that

38

> Mr Horsfall, the stranger, whose visit to the town was the
> original germ of the party, was asking questions relative to
> the trade and manufacture of the place; and the rest of the
> gentlemen – all Milton men – were giving him answers
> and explanations. Some dispute arose, which was warmly
> contested; it was referred to Mr Thornton ... who now
> gave an opinion ... they talked in desperate earnest... She
> wondered that, with all this dwelling on the manufactures
> and trade of the place, no allusion was made to the strike
> then pending. She did not know how coolly such things
> were taken by the masters...[11]

The young Margaret Hale, pious, cultured, romantic, over-emotional, at first alarmed and then attracted by the rough, frank pleasantries of the mill-workers with whom she rubbed shoulders in the streets, is generally recognised as a self-portrait of the young Mrs Gaskell and in it we see her, as in her letters, at the dinner-parties and teas which she found so dull, the only entertainment over-elaborate food, the only conversation matters of which 'the ladies knew little and on which they were not expected to have or at least to express any opinion ...' But the real Mrs Gaskell had ways of expressing her opinions that could not be denied her as long as she could find a publisher and *North and South* consists largely of conversational battles between Margaret and Thornton on the questions of 'trade and manufacture' and the 'coolness' with which such things as strikes and poverty were taken by the masters. One modern writer has identified Thornton with William Rathbone Greg,[12] a member of the family of Unitarian cotton manufacturers already mentioned. This may be the case but, though she almost certainly borrowed some of Thornton's arguments from Greg's *Essays an Political and Social Science* published a year before *North and South*, Thornton has, by the end of the novel, become a very different man from Greg, who remained a political and economic utilitarian all his life and died a bitter opponent of trade-unions and democracy.

Though Mrs Gaskell admits the energy both of workers and employers, she cannot like Manchester/Milton Northern but, like the workers in one of her earliest Manchester stories, *Libbie Marsh's Three Eras* (1847), it is in Manchester that 'their children had been born ... where their homes were, where God had cast their lives, and told them to work out their destiny.'

But the acceptance of this destiny laid a heavy burden on the young minister's wife and one which was to grow increasingly heavy as time passed. In her second letter to the Howitts in 1838, we read: 'I have had very delicate health since I married', and from that time similar references appear regularly in her correspondence. In 1848, she is convalescing at Southport, the winter of 1850 is spent mainly away from Manchester because of bronchitis and in 1851 she is 'very ill'. Often she has 'atrocious headaches'; 'I have not written one line of Margaret Hale for three weeks for headaches and dizziness'; 'I am so far from strong that my only piece of work yesterday (writing this letter) utterly knocked me up, and I have been unable to sleep'; 'I go on much as usual, swallowed up by small household cares, never feeling well in Manchester, and always longing for the country'; 'I should like to be ... out of this misty foggy Manchester, which gives me a perpetual head-ache very hard to bear'; 'Meta [her second daughter] has rather overworked herself [during the cotton depression in 1862] in this depressing Manchester climate which suits neither her nor me'. Her own bad headaches she was afraid were produced by the air of Manchester, '... as I hardly ever had them, certainly not anything like so violently anywhere else'. At the beginning of 1865:

> for three months in the autumn I was almost confined to the house: and I almost began to despair of getting out again, I was so very weak for so long. But now, thank God, I am a great deal better, nearly quite strong again, I shall be glad when the light comes back. I am always influenced so much by darkness and cloudy skies.

But in April came the tragic cry: 'I am not strong and not able to see anyone ... oh for a house in the country.' [13]

The bearing of six children, one a still-birth and one dying at ten months of scarlet-fever, at a time when obstetrics was still very primitive; the cold and damp which had actually given rise to the development of the cotton industry in the first place; bad sanitation; an industrially polluted atmosphere; professional writing combined with active social work; a heavy programme of 'duty' entertaining; and, finally, the emotional frustrations which undoubtedly produced psychosomatic symptoms (she had a severe nervous tic only relieved by a prescription which contained prussic acid), all these produced what was, for her, a deadly brew.

Not only did Mrs Gaskell not like Manchester, oral tradition[14] has it that Mrs Gaskell was not liked by the majority of Manchester Unitarians. One can well see the reason for the destruction and long suppression of her personal papers which may well have revealed even more embarrassing material.

CHAPTER 4
The influence of Carlyle and Wordsworth on *Mary Barton*

On the title-page of *Mary Barton* Mrs Gaskell put a quotation:

> "How knowest thou," may the distressed Novel-wright
> exclaim, "that I, here where I sit, am the Foolishest of
> existing mortals; that this my Long-ear of a fictitious
> Biography shall not find one and the other, into whose still
> longer ears it may be the means, under Providence, of
> instilling somewhat? We answer, "None knows, none can
> certainly know: therefore, write on Worthy Brother, even
> as thou canst, even as it is given thee."

The quotation is from an essay by Carlyle entitled 'Biography' and first published in *Fraser's Magazine* in 1832. Written in his distinctive style, dramatic, declamatory, scattered with capital letters, it puts forward the view that biography is a branch of history, and that the serious or 'earnest' novel can make a genuine contribution to an understanding of history, especially that of our own times. He sharply differentiated such works from the 'sensation' novels which merely sought to titillate the senses and pass an idle hour. In the *London and Westminster Review* in 1838, for example, he dismissed Scott's *Waverley Novels* as the work of a society entertainer, written to meet the worldly needs of a worldly man, the characters 'deceptively painted automatons' offering the reader no moral edification. All the novelists of the nineteenth century were influenced by the style and ideas of Carlyle; Dickens, for example, immediately springs to mind.

To the then anonymous writer of *Mary Barton* (though he had already guessed the author to be a woman), Carlyle wrote, by way of her publisher, a letter which she said gave her the only 'unmixed pleasure'[1] of all the letters she was to receive about the novel. He wrote of her 'social, clear and observant character', her use of 'new rich materials', of the book being worthy of a 'place far above the ordinary garbage of Novels', capable of giving 'Portraits of Manchester Existence still more strikingly real', and of her being 'already strong in 'veracity' or devout earnestness of mind.'[2] In short, Mrs Gaskell's 'unmixed pleasure' was due to the fact that Carlyle had recognised her purpose in *Mary Barton*, which was to write the 'fictitious Biography' of an intelligent working-man in such a way as to give her readers a deeper understanding of their own times and to give 'utterance to the agony which from time to time', as she said in her preface to the novel, 'convulsed' men like John Barton, whom she intended as the central character and whose name she intended to be the title of the novel. Mary Barton was the choice of Edward Chapman, the publisher. Among several references to this letter from Carlyle, it was to Chapman that she wrote: 'Mr Carlyle's letter remains my real true gain.'[3]

Carlyle had never considered the act of writing to be necessarily any more important than any other form of action, and, in his letter to Mrs Gaskell, he makes this clear to her personally. Twice within a matter of days, she refers to this letter with deep emotion. To Chapman again she says:

> I have not troubled myself about the reviews, except the one or two which I respect because I know something of the character of the writers; what I felt was the angry feelings induced towards me personally among some of those I live amongst; and the expressions of belief... that the book would do harm. I am sure in the long run it will not; I have faith that what I wrote so earnestly & from the fulness of my heart must be right... The best way is to put it on one side altogether, and to try & [quoting Carlyle's last sentence from memory] 'do silently good actions which is far more indispensible.'[4]

To a Miss Lamont, once her authorship was known, after expressing much satisfaction that her correspondent had seen John Barton as the 'central figure', her 'hero', and 'that the book shd have been called John B', she continued:

> Some people here are very angry and say the book will do harm, and for a time I have been shaken and sorry; but I have such firm faith that the earnest expression of anyone's feelings can only do good in the long run, – that God will cause the errors to be temporary [,] the truth to be eternal, that I try not to mind too much what people say in blame or praise. I had a letter from Carlyle, and when I am over-filled with thoughts arising from this book, I put it all aside, (or try to put it aside) and think of his last

sentence, 'May you live long to write good books, or do silently good actions which in my sight is far more indispensable.'[5]

It was a principle from which she was never to depart. Writing had, as we have already seen, from the beginning been carried on in the midst of the inevitable 'duties' at Cross Street Chapel, teaching classes of girls at the Lower Mosley Street School (even inviting them to her home on occasions), the visiting for the District Provident Society, and, above all, running a home on a small income and bearing and rearing children. The four-fold vocation was an ominous and exhausting one which took its inevitable toll as the years went by.

In her child-bearing years, life was necessarily too full to give much attention to writing. Her first child, still-born in 1833, was followed by Marianne in 1834, Meta (Margaret Emily) in 1837, Florence in 1842, 'Willie' in 1844, and Julia in 1846. Even so, writing was not entirely neglected. In 1836, she wrote a poem, 'On Visiting the Grave of My Stillborn Little Girl',[6] and in the following year there appeared in *Blackwood's Magazine* a poem, in collaboration with her husband, 'Sketches Among the Poor'.[7] Intended to be the first of a series of such poems to be written in the style of various poets, this first one was in the style of Crabbe, but the rest of the series never materialised. Presumably the collaboration was not a success. Gaskell has generally been referred to as a fine lecturer on English literature, but the hymns which he wrote, though they are still in use in Unitarian hymn books, show little of the quality of the Blackwood poem. Her Aunt Lumb had said on first meeting Gaskell: "Why, Elizabeth, how could this man ever take a fancy to such a little giddy thoughtless thing as you"[8] and it seems that the young husband soon took much the same view for, in 1838, after six years of marriage, she was writing to her sister-in-law and namesake at Warrington:

> When I had finished my last letter Willm looked at it and said it was 'slip-shod' – and seemed to wish me not to send it, but though I thought it was not a particularly nice letter I thought I would send it, or you would wonder why I did not write![9]

Another enlightening phrase occurs in an earlier letter to Warrington, one that also gives an idyllic picture of life at Sandlebridge in May 1836, and is an indication of her literary ambitions and abilities. Gaskell was present for part of the time since she writes that they had been riding together:

> We are up with the birds, and sitting out on the old flag steps in the very middle of fragrance – "far from the busy hum of men", but not far from the busy hum of bees. Here is a sort of little standard library kept – Spenser, Shakespeare, Wordsworth, & a few foreign books, & we sit & read & dream our time away – except at meals when we don't dream over cream that your spoon stands upright in, & such sweet (not sentimental but literal) oven-cakes and fresh butter (unobtainable in Manchester). Baby [Marianne] is at the very tip-top of bliss ... oh, you would laugh to see her going about, with a great big nosegay in each hand ... she is absolutely fatter since she came here, & I'm sure stronger ... I have brought Coleridge with me, & am doing him and Wordsworth (-) fit place for the latter! I sat in a shady corner of a field gay with bright spring flowers – daisies, primroses, wild anemonies, & the 'lesser celandine,' & with lambs all around me – and the air full of sweet sounds, I wrote my first chapter of W. yesterday in pencil – & today I'm going to finish him – and my heart feels so full of him I only don't know how to express my fullness without being too diffuse. If you were here, I think your advice, & listening, would do me so much good – but I have to do it all by myself alone, crunching up my paper, & all my composition of Ld B[yron], – & done Crabbe outright since you left & got up Dryden and Pope – so now I'm clear & straight before me ... If I don't get much writing done here, I get a great many thoughts on the subject, – for one can't think anything but poetry & happiness. Oh! that Life would make a standstill in this happy place![10]

The articles on the English poets were never published, perhaps not surprisingly so since she had to 'keep crunching up' her paper. But a story which she calls 'an old rubbishy one – begun when Marianne was a baby, – the only merit whereof is that it is founded on fact,'[11] was eventually published in 1857 in the American *Harper's*

New Monthly Magazine under the title *The Doom of the Griffiths*. A tragedy set in North Wales, the story is based on a local tradition of an attempt, in the fifteenth century, on the life of Owen Glendower, the last Welsh Prince. It is also the story of the unfortunate second marriage of a man whose son longs to 'find himself again the sole object and darling of his father', possibly an autobiographical touch. The only version of the story we have today is that of 1857, when it had presumably been improved but it is still somewhat melodramatic, mawkish, and representative of the short pieces which were written to make money.[12]

By 1857, Mrs Gaskell, as she herself said, knew 'what was what as well as anyone else' and she took trouble to see that both this story and another, 'Lois the Witch', should be published in America, wanting the latter to 'be kept out of England, – & the reach of reviews.'[13] (In the case of 'Lois the Witch', however, she was unsuccessful and it appeared in Dickens' *All the Year Round* in 1859).

But in the 1830s she was only beginning to learn her craft and the main interest in 'The Doom of the Griffiths' lies in its observation of the Welsh landscape, architecture, people, and a way of life which had, at the time of its composition, changed little over the centuries. The old hall is

> square and heavy-looking, with just that much pretension to ornament necessary to distinguish it from the mere farm-house; [a cottage is] built against one of the lower rocks of Moel Gest, which indeed formed a side to the low, lengthy house. The materials were the shingly stones which had fallen from above, plastered rudely together, with deep recesses for the small oblong windows.

The interior of the cottage is also described in great detail, and the cottagers' food is

> ewe-milk cheese, very hard and dry, oat-cakes, slips of the dried kids' flesh broiled after having been previously soaked in water for a few minutes, delicious butter and fresh butter-milk with a liquor called "diod griafol" made from the berries of the sorbus aucupania infused in water and then fermented.

Here we have the sort of close observation which was to play such a great part in *Mary Barton*.

But, in the meantime, it is not difficult to conjure up a picture of the young mother, sitting in the nursery when William was at his committee meetings, dreaming of summer days at Sandlebridge or in North Wales. In her first letter of May 1830 to the Howitts, she had thanked them for the great pleasure their works had given her by their charming descriptions of natural scenery and the thoughts and feelings arising from the circumstances of rural life, and she continues:

> I was brought up in a country town, and my lot is now to live in or rather on the borders of a great manufacturing town, but when spring days come... I feel a stirring instinct and long to be off into the deep grassy solitudes of the country...[but] I must stay at home and content myself with recalling the happy scenes which your books bring up before me...

It was during those solitary evenings in the nursery that she must have sat with a book on her knee and pencil and paper at hand. After the publication of *Mary Barton*, she wrote from her second home – necessitated by the growing family – in Upper Rumford Street – and after the death of her baby son, to one of her friends who had recently paid her a visit:

> I have just been up to our room. There is a fire in it... and oddly enough the feelings and recollections of 3 years ago come over me so strongly – when I used to sit up in the room so often in the evenings reading by the fire, and watching my darling, darling Willie, who now sleeps sounder still in the dull, dreary chapel-yard at Warrington. That wound will never really heal on earth, although hardly anyone knows how it has changed me.[14]

For two years, after the birth and death of her son in 1844, we know of no poems, romantic accounts of old houses and country customs nor even letters. If there were any, they have been destroyed. But they begin again in late September 1846 with one to the two eldest girls who were staying with their grandmother at Warrington on the occasion of the birth of her last child, Julia, and, in 1847, there follows a group of letters describing a round of visits that she was making to friends and which included one to the Howitts at Upper Clapton in the suburbs of London. She had first met the Howitts in 1841 and in 1847 they published two short stories of hers in *Howitt's Journal*, 'Libbie Marsh's Three Eras', a three-part story of the life of the Manchester workers and 'The Sexton's Hero', both of them based on fact, strongly didactic, and the latter set in the environs of Morecambe Bay, a favourite holiday place of the Gaskells.

Immensely popular and influential in the literary world, although they have been forgotten today, the Howitts also published at least a hundred and eighty books that had an extraordinary sale - popular history, literary miscellanies, children's books, works such as the *Visits to Remarkable Places* of 1840, in which Mrs Gaskell's piece on Clopton Hall appeared, and in 1846 *A History of the Aristocracy*. Yet they were also ardent supporters of reform, the full title of their journal being *Howitt's Journal of Literature and Popular Reform*, though their idea was not reform at the expense of the old rural values. Indeed, after the death of William Cobbett in 1835, they succeeded him as the foremost partisans of rural life, as well as paving the way for womens' rights and introducing to a wider audience poets such as Wordsworth, Keats, and the Rossettis. The Gaskell daughters claimed that it was their father who encouraged their mother to embark on a longer literary work when she found it difficult to recover her health after the death of her son. This may well be so and does not necessarily conflict with Mary Howitt's statement in her autobiography that it was she and her husband who first encouraged Mrs Gaskell to put her pen 'to some good purpose'. We know that it was to the Howitts that she took the completed manuscript of *Mary Barton* and it was they who, with the assistance of John Forster, an influential man of letters in London, found a publisher for the book.

Whoever was mainly responsible for Mrs Gaskell taking up her pen to write *Mary Barton*, the book had had a long preparation in her heart and mind. To the encouragement of the Howitts and William Gaskell, and the inspiration of Carlyle's writing, we have also to add that of Wordsworth. As early as 1836, she had said "... my heart is so full of him I only don't know how to express my fullness without being too diffuse." Brought up among the mountains and lakes of Cumberland, his life there had imbued Wordsworth not only with a love of nature in streams, mountains, rocks and such flowers as "the lesser celandine" mentioned by Mrs Gaskell, but also a deep affection, respect and compassion for the humble folk who peopled its landscape; its shepherds, 'statesman' farmers, pedlars, vagrants, the old and the young.

In his long poem, *The Prelude*, not published until 1850 after his death, a poem he called the story of the growth of a poet's mind and dedicated to his friend Coleridge, he wrote:

Thus my heart was early introduced
To an unconscious love and reverence of human nature,
Hence the human form became to me an index of delight,
Of grace and honour and worthiness (Book VIII, 277-281)

Lyrical Ballads, the collection of poems published by Wordsworth and Coleridge in 1798, had set the literary world by the ears. Castigated by most of the reviewers for the style and subjects of the poems, when the second edition (nearly twice the size of the first) came out in 1800, with a long preface by Wordsworth, John Wilson, who was to become Professor of Moral Philosophy at Edinburgh (where he became a friend of the young Elizabeth Stevenson), wrote, what was for a boy of seventeen, a remarkable letter to Wordsworth, from which it is only possible to quote a few phrases.

> You have ... explained the wonderful effect which the appearances of external nature have upon the mind [and in] forming the human mind; ... your poems ... present us with a body of morality of the purest kind... They represent the enjoyment resulting from a cultivation of the social affections of our nature; they inculcate a conscientious regard to the rights of our fellow-men; they show that every creature on the face of the earth is entitled in some measure to our kindness.[15]

A few weeks later, Henry Crabb Robinson, a non-practising barrister of independent means then studying in Germany, wrote to his brother:

> I would rather have written 'The Thorn' [in Lyrical Ballads] than all the tinsel, gaudy lines of Darwin's 'Botanic Garden'. The one is an artificial Versifier, the other is a feeler and a painter of feelings.[16]

Both Robinson and Erasmus Darwin were Unitarians, and were to become life-long friends of Wordsworth. Erasmus Darwin was a doctor and scientist who put forward a theory of evolution long before his famous grandson, Charles, and who put his botanical ideas into verse. Coleridge also, at the time of the publication of *Lyrical Ballads*, called himself a Unitarian and had even taken practical steps to enter the Unitarian ministry which were only abandoned by the offer of an allowance by Josiah and Tom Wedgwood which allowed him to give all his time to his poetry and other writing. Catherine Byerley, as a child, claimed to have heard Coleridge read his poetry at the home of the first Josiah Wedgwood at Etruria in Staffordshire. Both Wordsworth and Coleridge had absorbed Unitarian ideas during their student days at Cambridge. Both of them had been intended by their families for the Anglican priesthood but both had turned away from this since they were unable to accept the Anglican creeds and articles of belief; and, though it was not long before they returned to the Church, their beliefs were always both deeper and wider than the narrow orthodoxy of their day.

The end of the eighteenth and the beginning of the nineteenth century was a great stirring-up time, a time of revolution and, before long, of War. Like all liberal thinkers, Wordsworth and Coleridge had been, at first, deeply sympathetic to the French Revolution as a release from corruption and the oppression of the masses. But, as it turned into a reign of terror, both became horrified at the excesses, especially at the French wars in Europe, in which, as Wordsworth wrote in *The Prelude*, the revolutionaries... "had become oppressors in their turn ... losing sight of all which they had struggled for..." (Book XI, 206 - 8).

Eventually, the French Revolution merely resulted in replacing oppression of the people by the aristocracy with that of the bourgeoisie, and in England, though by less violent methods, their counterpart, the manufacturers, also fought for political power for their own class, resulting in the first Reform Act of 1832, thus bringing about the same transference of political power (economic power they had already) from the aristocratic Tories, 'the country gentlemen' as they had been called, to the Whigs or, as they later liked to call themselves, the Liberals. These latter naturally included a large number of Unitarians since they made up a considerable section of the manufacturing class. Desire for greater representation in Parliament and a larger number of Members of Parliament for the industrial towns was what chiefly bound Unitarians together, and, suffering as they did from both religious and political disabilities, their battle-cry became 'Civil and Religious Liberty'. Championing several other oppressed minority groups such as Jews, Catholics, slaves, and women who wanted higher education, they achieved much genuine reform. But, like the majority of Liberals, they opposed any further extension of the franchise to the working classes. Since most Liberals were also utilitarian in their social and economic philosophy (according to which even a child of seven was considered capable of 'standing on his own feet' in the hurly-burly of the industrial world) every Unitarian Liberal Member of Parliament, with the exception of the single Unitarian manufacturer, John Fielden of Todmorden, fought to the bitter end against any control by Parliament of working hours in factories. They were not few who considered that the masses of the people were worse off after the political landslide of 1832 than they had been before.

In his old age, Wordsworth is reported as saying: "I have a great deal of the Chartist in me"[17], a reference to the great campaign for working-class political representation which plays so large and tragic a part in *Mary Barton*, while Coleridge, after his first three great poems, 'The Ancient Mariner', 'Kubla Khan' and 'Christabel', became, through his prose writings, the arch-enemy of utilitarianism and the father of the Christian Socialism in which Mrs Gaskell herself was to play a not insignificant part. She was, in fact, one of the minority of Unitarians who could not identify themselves with rationalism and utilitarianism but, after the Bible, found their greatest inspiration in the writings of Carlyle, Wordsworth and Coleridge. Coleridge's influence increased considerably after his death in 1834 through the editing of his important works on church and state by his daughter and nephew, Sara and Nelson Coleridge. In one of Mrs Gaskell's earliest letters to Mary Howitt, she had reported that her husband had

> lately been giving four lectures to the very poorest of the weavers in the very poorest district of Manchester, Miles Platting, on 'The Poets and Poetry of Humble Life' [which] even in a town, is met with on every hand. We

have such a district and we constantly meet with examples of the beautiful truth in the passage of 'The Cumberland Beggar':

'Man is dear to man: the poorest poor
Long for some moments in a weary life
When they can know and feel that they have been,
Themselves the fathers and the dealers out
Of some small blessings; have been kind to such
As needed kindness, for the simple cause
That we have all of us a human heart.'[18]

'The Cumberland Beggar', one of Wordsworth's contributions to *Lyrical Ballads*, seems to have touched a deep chord in Mrs Gaskell's heart and mind. The phrase appears in *North and South*[19] and, writing of the Crimean war, she said

Babies ad libitum are being christened Florence here; poor little factory babies, whose grimed stunted parents brighten up at the name [of Florence Nightingale], but it's the old story, 'for we have all of us one human heart' ... for they feel her as theirs, their brother's nurse, their dead friend's friend, – in a way they don't know how to express; [20]

in 1857 she concluded her preface to an American novel with the words:

... however different may be national manifestations of this fact, still, below accents, manners, dress, and language, we have "All of us one human heart."[21]

In Wordsworth's preface to the 1802 edition of *Lyrical Ballads*, discussing the true nature of poetry, he had said that he saw little essential difference between poetry and prose at their highest level and Mrs Gaskell herself called *Mary Barton* "a tragic poem". For Wordsworth, "the two cardinal points of poetry [were] the power of exciting the sympathy of the reader by a faithful adherence to the truth of nature, and the power of giving the interest of novelty by the modifying colours of imagination." No better description can be given of *Mary Barton*. With her family background, her education, her powers of observation, her reading, her sympathy, her independence of mind, her personal knowledge of her subject, at thirty-six it seems as though all her life had been a preparation for this work. Only one catalyst was wanting. We already know that the precipitating factor in the writing of *Mary Barton* was her grief after the death of her baby son from scarlet-fever, that scourge of Victorian childhood.

In 1910 Mrs Chadwick wrote:

> Mrs Gaskell once told Travers Madge, a Unitarian minister in Manchester ... that the wish to write such a book as *Mary Barton* came to her when she was visiting a labourer's cottage in one of the poverty-stricken districts of Manchester. She was trying to sympathize with, and at the same time allay the bitterness towards the rich, which was a constant feeling of the poor, when the father of the family gripped her arm, saying: "Ay, ma'am; but have you ever seen a child clemmed [starved] to death?"[22]

It is this man who is enshrined in *Mary Barton* and which, in spite of its title, Mrs Gaskell intended both as a 'fictitious Biography' and a 'Lyrical Ballad'. When she met Wordsworth, by an arrangement of Crabb Robinson, in the Lake District in the summer of 1849, a matter of months after the publication of *Mary Barton* and a few months before the poet's death, in her autograph album he wrote:

> He who feels contempt
> For any living thing, hath faculties
> Which he has never used...[23]

At the end of his life he had chosen these lines from one of his poems written in youth and when he was having to make a choice as to the mode and purpose of his own life. The words are taken from 'Lines left upon a Seat in a Yew-tree which stands near the Lake of Esthwaite, on a desolate part of the Shore, commanding a beautiful Prospect.' It was finished in 1795, after he had seen, in the French Revolution, the full horrors of "man's inhumanity to man". The hero of Wordsworth's poem is a man who returns to nature as a result of bitter experiences in the world. In 1794, he himself had been on the point of joining the Girondins, the more moderate party of the French revolutionaries, but had returned to England. In 1814, in his preface to The Excursion, he had promised to "make authentic comment" on "sorrow barricaded evermore within the Walls of Cities."

But, though Carlyle had thundered, though Wordsworth had meditated unendingly on the nature of man, and though Coleridge had talked unceasingly in his 'evenings' at Highgate in London on 'the condition of England', it was in the end left to Elizabeth Gaskell – a woman and a mother – to bring home in *Mary Barton*, the full agony of the labouring masses to the British public.

CHAPTER 5
Puritanism in South Lancashire

At the height of the controversy about *Mary Barton*, Mrs Gaskell wrote:

> I have such firm faith that the earnest expression of anyone's feelings can only do good in the long run, – that God will cause the errors to be temporary [,] the truth to be eternal ...'[1]

Though she was the daughter of one Unitarian minister and the wife of another, there is no evidence that her religion was merely formal. There were many Unitarians she disliked and much about the dominant traits in Unitarianism which she also disliked, but she had a deeply personal faith and never repudiated or became indifferent to that particular form of religion to which she had been reared. It was one which had had an unusually long and complicated history and, to come to an understanding of it and of Elizabeth Gaskell, we must retrace our steps and reconsider the history of the Holland family.

We have seen that they had been called, in the reign of Richard II, 'friends of the Lollards' and 'deriders of images.' The Lollards preached a 'New Learning' which had begun a generation earlier with the translation of the Bible by Wycliffe. They did not believe in Transubstantiation nor the literal truth of the Bible. In the reign of Henry VIII a priest, John Asheton, a member of an important Lancashire family, was brought before Cranmer for preaching against the orthodox doctrine of the Trinity, and Francis Kett, a Fellow of Cambridge, was burned for similar ideas. Little more was heard of these again until the accession of Elizabeth when Protestant divines returned from exile on the continent whither they had fled during the reign of the Catholic Mary. Many of them had spent their exile in Geneva and returned full of enthusiasm for the kind of church and government established there by John Calvin, a virtual theocracy in which theology and church discipline intruded into every aspect of life. It was characterised by a view of men as essentially depraved creatures, some of whom would attain salvation purely by the will and foreknowledge of God while others were foredoomed to everlasting punishment in the after-life. Those who were to be 'saved' would have been purchased from God's wrath by 'the blood of Christ' and salvation could only be attained, not by anything the individual could do in any active way but by finding out what the will of God was and following that will as revealed in the Scriptures, as closely as possible. Those who took this way came to be known as Puritans because they wished to 'purify' both church and government and society in general. Richard Holland (1546-1619), Sheriff of Lancashire four times during the reign of Elizabeth, was very active in 'purifying' the Church. Much honoured by the Queen for his zeal against recusants, mainly Roman Catholics who refused to attend their parish church, he was described by Edmund Campion, the priest executed at Tyburn in 1581, as "Holland of Denton" and "a rigid Puritan."[2]

However, Puritanism was never an entirely cohesive movement. At the beginning of the seventeenth century, a group of Anglicans came to be known as Arminians, since they took their inspiration from James Arminius (1560-1609), a distinguished Dutch theologian who taught a more tolerant and progressive Protestantism that gave to man a greater part in the working out of his own salvation. Arminius disliked intensely the type of Calvinism which forced the Church 'to drag into open contentions those who [were] meditating no evil.' Some followed his teaching in England, notably the 'Great Tew group', so-called because they gathered round the aristocratic Royalist and Anglican Lord Falkland, whose home was at Great Tew, near Oxford, and who was killed at the battle of Newbury in 1643.[3] On the whole, however, great bitterness arose between the established Church and those who wished to 'purify' and reform both church and state. All these feelings and conflicting demands centred about the person of the King, Charles I. In 1642 this state of affairs culminated in the outbreak of civil war.

Though there was great variety of theological belief among those opposed to the King, the main parties were the Independents and the Presbyterians and the difference between these is crucial for an understanding of the Holland family and of Mrs Gaskell.

The Independents, mainly represented by the army and the 'lower orders', wanted to break away from the established Church altogether, in fact to abolish it on the Scriptural grounds that 'wherever two or three' were gathered together there was a Church. They also encouraged lay preachers, i.e. those who had not been ordained in the Church of England, and who were thereby responsible for the proliferation of the innumerable sects which arose, including, for example, the Quakers. The Presbyterians, on the other hand, were civilian gentlemen and merchants who wanted to retain a national church in the Anglican tradition but with the hierarchy of Bishops abolished and the Trinitarian creed not to be legally enforced. At first the Presbyterians were in power in Parliament and in 1648 what is known as the Westminster Confession of Belief was drawn up. It was not legally enforceable and was comprehensive enough to satisfy even the most recalcitrant nonconformist and included words that are worth recording:

> The Spirit of Christ is in himself too free, great, and generous a spirit to be used by any human arm to whip men into belief; he drives not, but gently leads into all truth ... which would lose of its preciousness and value if that sparkle of freeness shone not in it.[4]

This, together with the substitution of church government by bishops by one of presbyters or ministers, as being more Scriptural, was the Presbyterian ideal. (It is important to note that English Presbyterians had no connection theologically with their Scottish counterparts). It was not the basic doctrines of the Church that the English Presbyterians attacked but its organisation and what they considered its papal and superstitious accretions.

Because of the predominance of Presbyterians among the 'Original' Puritans as they came to be called, an attempt was made in 1641 to set up a national Presbyterian Church with a system of ministers who would be responsible only to their own congregations and who would be 'assisted' by lay elders elected by the congregation. In matters of religion the ministers were to 'rule' in their own congregations and there was to be a network of regional assemblies culminating in a National Assembly which would include five learned and godly persons from each of the Universities. There was, therefore, to be greater liberty of conscience to the ministers in their services and more power to the laity. The new congregations were to be based on the old parishes and Roger Thomas in *The English Presbyterians* (1968) points out:

> It would be quite improper to distinguish between Presbyterians and Anglicans at this period, for Presbyterians were

57

> Anglicans ... They might be vocal critics within the
> Church but they hated separatism and sectarianism, . . .

and he suggests that a better name for the Presbyterians would
have been 'Church Puritans'.[5] However, they had to contend on the
one hand with a large body of Anglicans who were devoted to the old
system and its liturgy and on the other with the Independents who, as
we have seen, were opposed to any idea of a National Church. The
result was that, within seven years, the Presbyterians, 'the sounder
and more enlightened of the Puritan body', found itself reduced to
political insignificance. The King, to their horror – for though they
had fought him in the first Civil War they always opposed his
execution and in the second war were Royalist – was put to death,
some of the most eminent among them were driven from their places
in Parliament and the power of the state passed into the possession of
a party whose leading principle was as opposite to theirs as was the
principle of Episcopacy itself. The National Church, therefore,
remained only a parliamentary project which never materialised on a
national scale but so strong was Presbyterianism in Lancashire and
Cheshire that the full system was set up, apart from a National
Assembly. In all this the Hollands played their part. Richard Holland
of Denton, called by the Jesuit Edmund Campion 'a rigid Puritan',
was succeeded by his nephew Richard Holland who took part in the
opening skirmish of the Civil War at Manchester in 1642 and became
head of the Manchester Defence Committee, Commonwealth
Governor of Manchester and Colonel of the Salford Hundred. Though
there were many Catholics among the gentry in Lancashire and
Cheshire who were Royalists, others, among them the Egerton and the
Shuttleworth families, eventually well known to Mrs Gaskell, were on
the Parliamentary side and Bernard Holland writes of his ancestor,
Colonel Holland: 'He was a moderate man of the Presbyterian Party
opposed to the Independents', and described as 'a very prudent, able,
Commonwealth man'. It was he who signed a petition in the reign of
Charles II protesting against the proposed ejection from their livings
of local Puritan clergy which claimed that many of them had been
'diligent and painful preachers among them for nearly forty years',
'men of great years, some gentlemen by birth', all of them 'peaceable
among their neighbours.'[6] Ironically, it had been the Presbyterians
who had, on his promise of toleration, negotiated Charles' return to

England after the Commonwealth period, thereby contributing to their own downfall.

Of the clergy who were ejected in 1662 because of their unwillingness to subscribe to the 39 Articles of Religion in the Prayer Book, Mrs Gaskell made her own commemoration in *North and South*. Mr Hale, the clergyman who had decided that he could no longer accept the theology of the Anglican Church, shows a book to Margaret and says:

> I have been reading today of the two thousand who were ejected from their churches ... this is the soliloquy of one who was once a clergyman in a country parish, like me: it was written by Mr Oldfield, minister of Carsington, in Derbyshire, a hundred and sixty years ago, or more ...

He then goes on to read the 'soliloquy' taken from the *Account of the Ministers and Others Ejected and Silenced* (1660-62) by Edmund Calamy (1600-1666), a leading Puritan divine. The soliloquy includes the words

> When thou canst no longer continue in thy work without dishonour to God, discredit to religion, foregoing thy integrity, wounding conscience, spoiling thy peace, and hazarding the loss of thy salvation ... thou mayest, yea, thou must believe that God will turn thy very silence, suspension, deprivation and laying aside, to His glory, and the advancement of the Gospel's interest. When God will not use thee in one kind, yet he will in another.[7]

The last sentence finds an echo in Carlyle's letter to Mrs Gaskell about her writing.

John Oldfield was ejected from his parish in 1662 and afterwards preached in 'conventicles' but often attended the established church. This was typical of Puritans of the Presbyterian sort and earned them the title of 'reluctant dissenters'. Mrs Gaskell's choice of Oldfield's statement also points to her belief in religion not as theological wrangling, but as spirituality and a duty to follow the promptings of conscience, whatever sacrifice that may entail and however it may contradict one's own ideas of personal usefulness and the apparent 'fulfilment' of one's life.

The declaration of faith in the old Westminster Confession of 1648, (see p48) however, also includes the words:

> I will maintain nothing in point of doctrine but what I believe to be most agreeable to the word of God [i.e. the Bible]; nor in point of discipline, but what may make the most for God's glory and the peace and good of His church...

which although comprehensive within themselves also carry the seeds of dissension. Putting the Bible in the place of ecclesiastical authority had the result of opening the door to endless diversity of opinion, strife, and the perpetual struggle of party. Joseph Hunter, a Unitarian historian writing in 1842, contrasted the Original Puritans, who, at the Reformation, had only wanted to replace what they felt to be indifference and superstition in the Church with spiritual freedom, a greater purity and a more practical expression of faith and worship, with those Dissenters of the later period who became corrupted by 'entering the contentions of political life and becoming candidates for political power.' He deplored, too, some aspects of the 'severity of life' which the Puritans had adopted, their 'contempt of the elegant ornaments and refreshments of life ... a certain lack of charity towards those who differed from them' and 'the superstition that there may be in rejecting as in adopting a ceremony.' He lamented that the peace and unity of the church should ever have been disturbed about

> the shape or colour of a robe, the ring in marriage ... the sponsors and ... cross in baptism, the turning to the east, the bowing at the name of Jesus, the kneeling at the Eucharist, which are innocent, respectful and picturesque customs, and are moreover descended to us from primitive antiquity. The observance of ecclesiastical times and commemorations keeps alive attention to spiritual affairs, and the memory of the just who are gone ...; little is to be gained by disconnecting the exercises of religion from all that is most pleasing to the eye and most agreeable to the ear ... it does not follow that everything in popery is evil; and there are many things in every mode of Christian profession ... for which Scripture warrant cannot be produced.[8]

Twelve years after Hunter expressed these opinions, Mrs Gaskell wrote to her daughter Marianne, then at school in London:

> I quite agree with you in feeling more devotional in church than in Chapel; and I wish our Puritan ancestors had not left out so much that they might have kept in of the beautiful and impressive Church service.[9]

We also know from other letters of hers that she was a great lover of sacred music, art, and architecture. Nevertheless, in this same letter, she asserts her loyalty to her own tradition:

> . . .the one thing I am clear and sure about is this, that Jesus Christ is not equal to His Father; that however divine a being he was not God; and that worship as God addressed to Him is therefore wrong in me, and that it is my duty to deny myself the gratification of constantly attending a service, (like the morning service) in a part of which I thoroughly disagree. I like exceedingly going to afternoon service.

After the ejections of 1662, Presbyterians had been distinguished by their readiness to take Communion in the parish church when permitted to do so, while the practice of attending their own service in the morning and the afternoon or evening service in the local parish church persisted for a considerable time. If absent from home where there was no church of their own persuasion, the Gaskells always attended the local parish church and Mrs Gaskell died shortly after returning from the afternoon service at a nearby Anglican church. Revd Henry Green, minister at Knutsford, records several cases in Cheshire where there was a good relationship between the ejected ministers, their former parishioners, and the new incumbents.[10]

Little by little after 1662, however, a whole tangle of restrictive and repressive acts were passed by an increasingly Royalist parliament, reversing almost everything the Puritans had fought for over the past twenty years. A fifth of the parish clergy had been forced out of the Church, often with great injustice, to live a life of poverty and insecurity, even when fortunate enough to have the patronage of the Puritan gentry who were themselves also harried by laws restricting the practice of their faith. Gradually, the Act of

Uniformity, intended to establish religious unity in the country, had the opposite effect, since the Puritan clergy and their lay-followers refused to compromise with conscience. So there came about the establishment of Non-conformity and the beginning of a dissenting ministry whose members, in addition to ministering to their own flocks, became private tutors, schoolmasters, and lecturers in dissenting academies in order to earn an adequate living and provide an education for those young men who were shut out from other establishments by their religion (and indeed many of those who were not, for they generally provided a better education than was available at most of the Grammar Schools).

In his unpublished thesis, *Reflections of Unitarianism in Mrs Gaskell's Novels*, Professor W.A. Boggs sees a general deprecation of Calvinism.[11] This is supported by her letters, in one of which, to Charles Eliot Norton in 1861, she wrote that she had only one antipathy and that was to the Calvinistic or Low Church creed.[12] The Presbyterians had, by the nineteenth century, come to reject all that Calvinism stood for theologically, but their religious attitude remained formed in the Calvinistic mould; 'intellectual, moral, and political, but not particularly spiritual.'[13] In Mrs Gaskell's letters, however, we read such expressions as:

> Oh for some really spiritual devotional preaching, instead
> of controversy about doctrines – about which I am more
> and more certain we can never be certain in this world.[14]

This must also have applied to her own husband's sermons, since these were described in 1850 in the following terms:

> His sermon was written but he scarcely looked at it. He
> used few or no gestures, his sermon was intellectual rather
> than spiritual, logical, penetrating, polished but scarcely
> original, and lacking in warmth and anything that could be
> called emotional.[15]

The severity of life complained of by Hunter also continued to show itself not only in religious attitudes but also in the buildings which dissenters were permitted to erect for worship in 1689, after the 'Glorious Revolution' by which Protestantism was finally established as the state religion. Brook Street Chapel, Knutsford, built in or soon after 1689 with William Holland of Mobberley as one of its trustees, appears in both *Mary Barton* and *Ruth* and it is in the latter that Mrs Gaskell describes the chapel as it was in the 1850s, plain and unassuming but with an austere beauty greatly magnified by its surroundings and Mrs Gaskell's observation and imagination:

> It stood on the outskirts of the town, almost in fields. It was built ... when the Dissenters were afraid of attracting attention or observation, and hid their places of worship in obscure and out-of-the-way parts of the town in which they were built ... The chapel had a picturesque and old world look, for luckily the congregation had been too poor to re-build it, or new face it in George the Third's time. The staircases which led to the galleries were outside at each end of the building, and the irregular roof and worn stone steps looked grey and stained by time and weather. The grassy hillocks, each with a little upright headstone, were shaded by a grand old wych-elm. A lilac bush or two, a white rose tree, a few laburnums, all old and gnarled enough, were planted round the chapel yard; and the casement windows of the chapel were made of heavy-leaded, diamond-shaped panes, almost covered with ivy, producing a green gloom, not without its solemnity within. This ivy was the home of an infinite number of little birds, which twittered and warbled, till it might have been thought that they were envious of the power of praise possessed by the human creatures within ... The interior of the building was plain and simple ... When it was fitted up, oak timber was much cheaper than it is now, so the woodwork was all of that description; but roughly hewed, for the early builders had not much wealth to spare. The walls were whitewashed, and were recipients of the shadows of the beauty without; on their 'white plains' the tracery of the ivy might be seen, now still, now stirred by the sudden flight of some little bird. [16]

The members of the original congregation of Brook Street Chapel were Calvinists of the Presbyterian persuasion and definite anti-Trinitarian doctrines were not introduced until 1740 when a new minister was appointed. This chapel, symbolising the importance given to preaching, is an example of the oldest Puritan chapels; the pulpit is on the long side – there is no altar of course – with what may seem to visitors a curious space in front of it so that, apart from the gallery, most of the seats are on the left and right of the preacher. It is in this space that there was originally a large table where members came to sit in order to take Communion.

After the ejections of 1662, in spite of Hunter's lamentations about the corrupting influence of politics in the real world, the Presbyterians depended for their survival on gaining political power and in the eighteenth century they became, with other Protestant nonconformists, an important section of the Whig party in opposition to the Tories, 'the country gentlemen'. For nearly two hundred years, the Whigs tried to wrest political power from the Tories, or rather to gain the power which would enable them to do so. Theologically, the Independents, an umbrella term which included Congregationalists and Baptists, remained faithful to orthodoxy while the Presbyterians were more adventurous in their thinking. The combination of the Calvinist emphasis on the use of the mind in seeking out God's will as seen in the Bible, their great interest in education and science, the increasing material prosperity of many of its adherents gave them the means of living very comfortably in this world and discouraged the continual preoccupation of Calvinists with their fate in the next.

Lucy Aikin (1781-1864), niece of the eighteenth century poet and educator, Mrs Barbauld, and herself the author of historical works praised by Macaulay wrote to Dr W.E. Channing, an American Unitarian

> Long before my time, my kindred ... had begun to break
> forth out of the chains and darkness of Calvinism, and their
> manners softened with their system ...; [they] came nearer
> to the church than to their own stricter brethren, yet in
> doctrine no sect departed so far from the Establishment.[17]

As time passed, they were joined by Congregationalists, Baptists, Anglicans, Universalists and Methodists, either individually or in whole congregations. It is not surprising then that there came to be a great variety of theological opinion both within and amongst congregations. The first chapel to be known explicitly as Unitarian was opened in Essex Street, off the Strand in London, in 1774 by Theophilus Lindsey, ex-vicar of Catterick in Yorkshire, thus representing the anti-Trinitarian tradition long present in the Church itself. The term Unitarian, however, had been first defined in 1673 as 'those men's opinions concerning Christ, who ... call themselves Unitarians because they own but one Person and one substance or Essence of the Most High and Independent God.'[18]

But the Unitarians, as they were now openly called, had travelled on the wings of the so-called 'Open Trusts' of chapels originally licensed merely for 'the Worship of Almighty God by their Majesties' Protestant subjects dissenting from the Church of England', so far along the road of rationalism and political radicalism that, during the French and American revolutions, they gained for themselves the reputation of atheists, revolutionaries, and traitors. A considerable number were thrown into prison. Among others, an effigy of John Holland, minister of Bank Street Chapel, Bolton, (he also conducted a well-known boarding-school to which Josiah Wedgwood sent his sons) was burned in the streets.[19] The odium attached to the name Unitarian was to linger on.

In 1858, for instance, Mrs Gaskell and her three eldest daughters were staying in Heidelberg where they met Charles Bosanquet, a young Englishman of Huguenot descent who, hoping to become a lawyer, was studying German and 'the Anglo-Saxon basis of our language and laws there.' One Sunday, he and the Gaskell ladies had attended the English Church (Anglican of course) and Bosanquet afterwards talked to Meta a great deal about the sermon. Mrs Gaskell writes: 'Meta asked me to tell him we were Unitarians, - which I accordingly did, and found it did not shock him so much as we expected; though he and I had a long talk, about the Three Witnesses[20] which he gave up as spurious, & the non-mention of the Trinity in the Bible & ... in short we had a long theological talk ...'[21] And, in 1861, she was to write to Charles Eliot Norton about the same incident: 'I told him what I did believe – (more I suppose what would be called Arian than Humanitarian) ...; he all the time getting over the 'shock' of coming in contact for the first time with Unitarians.'[22] Mrs Gaskell obviously hoped that Bosanquet would marry Meta, but the hope came to nothing. Bosanquet's father, a Low Church Anglican clergyman, put pressure on his son not to have any 'doctrinal' talk with the Gaskells, proposed mutual visits of the parents were cancelled and Mrs Gaskell told Bosanquet: 'we should never ask him again, but if he felt it right to come he would be sure of a welcome.' She had come to realise that her husband's eminence, her own literary reputation, the excellent education her daughters had received, all made little impact on the continuing social and religious prejudice against dissenters, particularly against Unitarians for their denial of the divinity of Christ which set them apart from other dissenters.

It is, therefore, not surprising that Mrs Gaskell played down the subject in her novels, not because she was ashamed in any way of her religious heritage but because then, as now, very few of her readers understood the history of it, the great amount of variety brought about both in congregations and between one congregation and another by that history and the fact that no creed was imposed on its adherents. The very closeness of the old Presbyterian tradition, for example, in which Mrs Gaskell herself had been raised at Knutsford, to the Church of England, made it quite natural for her to alternate between the two in her writing as she did in life. In an undated letter, possibly to John Bright, a Quaker, she wrote: 'I am not (Unitarianly) orthodox',[23] while to Bosanquet, the young Evangelical lawyer, she had called herself an Arian rather than a Humanitarian, terms which today require some explanation.

Arianism, deriving from the name of Arius, an Alexandrine priest of the fourth century, taught that Christ, though a divine being, was not co-equal with God the Father and Supreme Being. For a time, this doctrine was the official theology of the eastern Roman Empire and was only crushed in A.D. 325 at the Council of Nicea by Athanasius, who established the theological supremacy of the equal deity of Christ as the third member of the Trinity, the originator of the creed which bears his name and has been such a bone of contention in the Christian Church ever since. In the nineteenth century, there was a revival on the part of a minority of Unitarians of this Arian idea of Christ as a divine being, even coexistant with the Father before his birth, differing strongly from the majority who held what had come to be called the Humanitarian idea that Christ was born an ordinary human being, a 'mere' man, who only became the Messiah when he was baptised and accepted his mission, his miracles being the essential proof of this. Joseph Priestley, both scientist and a Unitarian minister, was, somewhat surprisingly, a Humanitarian who believed in Christ's miracles as proof of his Messianic mission.

By 1808, however, both Priestley and Lindsey, the first openly Unitarian ministers, were dead, thus bringing to an end an era which was, nevertheless, to leave indelible marks on the Unitarian movement. Over-emphasis on the place of reason in religion, no central organisation or hierarchy, power in the hands of wealthy and scientifically-minded merchants and manufacturers with strong political ambitions, virtual identification with the middle-classes, and the dominance of Humanitarian ideas on the nature of Christ, all made the Unitarians powerful but theologically and socially unpopular. Nevertheless, Mrs Gaskell herself strove always for religious toleration and viewed with humour the general attitude to and misunderstandings about dissent. In *Cranford*, (1853) for example, Miss Matty's runaway brother returns from India where "he had been living for a long time among savages – all of whom were heathen – some of them he was afraid were downright Dissenters!"

During the nineteenth century, Unitarianism became increasingly identified with the utilitarian philosophy of 'enlightened' self-interest and a Political Economy with which the Manchester cotton trade became closely associated. It was Thomas Belsham, tutor at the Daventry and Hackney academies, who attacked both Arianism on the one hand and, on the other, any idea that Christianity could be founded on a 'natural religion' such as that expounded by Wordsworth and the Romantics. He founded the Unitarian Society which published controversial theological pamphlets defending Unitarian beliefs against orthodox attacks and membership of which was restricted to those who accepted the Humanitarian idea of Christ. He called Arians 'utterly unworthy of the name Unitarian' and, in 1818, with reference to the proposed Bill to limit the working hours of children in cotton mills, had written:

> I think that a morbid spirit of philanthropy is abroad ... hundreds and thousands of children who maintained themselves very comfortably ... will now be turned adrift to live in rags and idleness. The good people, however, have been disappointed with regard to climbing boys about which much nonsense has been prated ... if climbing boys were put down the rate of insurance would immediately be raised.[24]

Though Dr Travers Herford, in some unpublished reminiscences, claimed that William Gaskell, as a student, accompanied Belsham on preaching expeditions and was his favourite pupil – Belsham died in the year Gaskell came to Cross Street Chapel – it would be unfair to say that Gaskell was another Belsham. Whereas Belsham revelled in controversy, Gaskell was reserved, avoided political involvement, was at the centre of private philanthropy in Manchester and sat on committees to promote sanitation, temperance, and working-class literacy. It would, however, be fair to say that he had received the imprint of Belsham's theology, and his sermons, written over a period of forty years, show a remarkable unity of opinion. As Professor Boggs puts it: 'Apparently as a young man he had made up his mind, and he did not find it necessary to change his religious ideas.'[25] Gaskell's Unitarianism was closely allied to that expressed by most of his fellow-ministers who were, from 1825, promoting the Belsham doctrine of positive denominationalism and Humanitarian theology.

There was, however, still the minority who either adhered to or returned to the older spirituality of Arianism, which, though based on reason, did not take the extreme views expounded by Priestley which, taken in their entirety, were in fact a form of materialism. James Martineau, a man of high spirituality and, by the end of the century, the best known and most respected of all Unitarian ministers, wrote, in 1840, that, while acknowledging his debt to Priestley:

> . . . his metaphysical system is incompatible with any true and operative sentiments of religion, it is at variance with the characteristic idea of Christianity, and will spontaneously vanish whenever our churches become really worshipping assemblies, instead of simply moral, polemical, or dissenting societies.[26]

In spite of theoretical toleration within the Unitarian movement, there was great antagonism between Arians and Humanitarians as evidenced in Belsham's remarks in 1818. Indeed, Henry Solly, a ministerial friend of Mrs Gaskell's, was asked to give up his pulpit at Carter Lane Chapel in London because he was 'too Arian'.[27] The majority of ministers, however, trained in the rationalism of Priestley and Belsham fell an easy prey to the Utilitarian theories of Bentham and Mill when faced with the problems of the Industrial Revolution. Jeremy Bentham (1748-1832), on whose ideas Utilitarianism was based, was Unitarian in theology, as was John Bowring (1792-1872), his secretary and editor of his works. Bentham himself claimed that his theory of 'the greatest happiness of the greatest number' as the sole ethical criterion of right and wrong had been inspired by Joseph Priestley.[28]

Utilitarianism was developed into a coherent social and economic philosophy by James Mill (1773-1836), who was educated partly at a dissenting academy for the ministry but held a high post in the East India Company; Ricardo (1772-1823), an economist who attended the Unitarian chapel in Essex Street; Malthus (1766-1834), a writer on population who, though a clergyman of the Church of England, had also received part of his education at a dissenting academy (his views were satirised by Dickens in Scrooge's comment on the poor, "let them die and decrease the surplus population"); and, finally, John Stuart Mill (1806-1873), James Mill's son, who received an extraordinary education based on his father's ideas and who was to modify his Utilitarian theories so far as eventually to destroy them.

Though they criticised one another on certain points, it was this group which developed the system of Political Economy which came to be looked on, particularly by the manufacturers as an unalterable law of the universe and a justification for the miserable conditions of the workers and the social alienation depicted in *Mary Barton* and *North and South*, a 'law' which, in the end, meant nothing more than 'each for himself and the devil take the hindmost'. It is not surprising, therefore, that Mrs Gaskell should describe herself as not '(Unitarianly) orthodox', not only in theology but in social theory for, when looking for a suitable school for Marianne, her eldest daughter, she called one of them 'so common – the very worst style of dogmatic hard Unitarianism, utilitarian to the backbone.'[29]

Though in the vanguard of many kinds of social and political reform, (far beyond the Church of England, for example) owing to the origin of the movement in scientific enquiry and a legal struggle for individual freedom, Unitarians had little idea of the importance of community values or how best to use the freedom they had achieved for the benefit of all. Those Unitarians who, like Mrs Gaskell, could not accept the harsh crudities of Utilitarianism had to look for inspiration beyond their own movement and, indeed, beyond the shores of England. It was in Heidelberg, far away from the stifling (in several senses of the word) atmosphere of Manchester that the young Mrs Gaskell was to be in her true element.

CHAPTER 6
From Manchester utilitarianism to German romanticism

In 1841, Elizabeth and William Gaskell visited Germany, sailed
down the Rhine, and stayed at, among other places, Heidelberg. To
her sister-in-law at Warrington, Mrs Gaskell wrote of how, on 'a
splendid day', she and her husband had climbed 'the Drackenfels
(sic), breakfasting among the vineyards at the top, with a party
including some relations of Coleridge – one a son of Judge Coleridge,
[the Judge was a great-nephew of the poet and had recorded some of
his famous Table Talk], and all remembering and speaking with
affection of "the old man eloquent." I should like to tell you of our
conversation it was so high toned and so superior, – not that we spoke
much, we only listened and admired.'[1]

In this extremely long letter, Mrs Gaskell describes 'the sublime
beauty of the cathedrals in the grand old cities in Flanders ... such
practical poetry ... Bruges, Ghent and Antwerp ... so solemn and
sublime, appearing so deserted and lonely, as if the world had stood
still with them since the 14th century.' Heidelberg she had found
beautiful almost beyond description:

> You must fancy 'an union of all beauties' – splendid
> scenery, dark pine woods, rocks and the picturesque town,
> and noble castle to complete it... The waters of the Neckar
> as like sea-water exactly – gushing and foaming over red
> sand-stone rocks, which make the most beautiful colouring
> imaginable. All this is to relieve my own mind from the
> oppressive recollection of so much beauty – just the sort of
> scene of loveliness which made one sigh to look at it ... As
> for legends ... the place is haunted. There is an Ondine
> (the name of a genus as well as an individual), who dwells
> in the secret spring of the sea-green Neckar.

It was at Heidelberg that Mrs Gaskell also met the Howitts for the
first time[2] and recounts how, in the same party, they sallied forth one
evening

> with very dancing spirits along the picturesque road
> overhung with walnut trees and winding by the side of the
> Neckar, the moon rising over the hill-tops – Presently we

left the road and began to follow a rougher path through a pine wood, – very mysterious dark looking. We began to hear music – the most lively Waltzes and presently came to a splashing fountain, set round with coloured lamps – 20 yards, and another turn and we were in an open space in the dark wood – boarded over, the grass, & about 20 people whirling to the most spirited band I ever heard – About 200 stood by ready to spin off when anyone gave up. Most of the men were Heidelberg students, with their pointed beards, mustachios, caps and blouses – the girls were peasant girls, in their picturesque dresses – the dark trees round were hung with lamps ... The peasants don't learn dancing [,] it comes by instinct. A very fashionable waltz step came up while we were at Heidelberg, the ecossaise, – and the little girls with their empty milk-pails were dancing it along the road. To go back to our merry night scene, Mrs P[3] was afraid the students, a most riotous race, might get too boisterous so we did not stay half so long as I should have liked but came home and a merry supper ended our first evening ... We never drank tea alone I think. Sometimes some of the students [came], when we had music, dancing and all manner of games – we all told the most frightening & wild stories we had ever heard – some such fearful ones – all true – then we drank tea at the Howitts, – looking over all the portfolios of splendid engravings, casts etc., they have collected ... [we were also at] the Webers – he a Dr of Philosophie – grave, German & philosophical, to say nothing of politico-aeconomical evenings at the Schlossers ... Mme Schlosser ... lives in a house 450 years old, which till lately was a convent, has a picture-gallery filled with the oldest productions of art Van Eycks, Albert Durers, &c... – She is a highly accomplished woman – has made some very fine published translations from the Spanish dramatists and is in correspondence with many foreign literati (sic). Wordsworth has lately been staying there – James the novelist, Mrs Jameson ... She (Mme Schlosser) is a cousin of Göethe ... We first went to call & present our letters [of introduction] and were taken over the old conventual house & grounds – terrace below terrace – walks trellised with vines – and farther away, a wilderness of wood, rock & waterfall – the house with noble oak furniture, polished floors, a library with 40,000 vols – room within room &

recess beyond recess, with the fine painted glass arch windows throwing 'a dim religious light' over all.

The chapel is magnificent though small, and in every nook – on the wide stair-case, along the galleries were orange trees & oleanders in tubs – in full flower ...; a gay party were assembled on the terraces where footmen were handing them coffee in a very alfresco style.

[On another] lovely evening about 7 we found ourselves in the middle of 180 gay people who were promenading about on the terraces. Fancy the picturesqueness of this, with the setting sun lighting up the noble views in the background. No one had hat, bonnet or shawl on ... No one under 40 in summer wears anything but muslin, white of course in general – Artificial flowers too are quite out of the question, yet if you mean to dance, flowers in your hair is the signal, so every German girl knows how to weave the prettiest natural garlands – Mine was geranium but the prevalent fashionable flower was the intensely scarlet pomegranate blossom with its deep green leaves ... when the end of the evening came I had danced every dance but one, the great mistake of the eveng. William said I was sadly tired and very dizzy, when a very ugly man asked me to dance – I told him I was too much tired when lo & behold he turned out to be Wolfgang von Göethe, grandson to the illustrious Wolfgang – and Wm said I should have danced with the name – numbers of illustrious names were in the room. The von Berlichingens, descendants of the good bright & true Gotz von Berlichingen, Luther's friend and Göethe's hero ... the von Herders, grand-daughters of the illustrious von Herder, the great German writer of the last century...[4]

It would be difficult to find another passage in Victorian literature expressing in so spontaneous and yet succinct a fashion the attractions which German culture had for certain intellectual elements in English society at that time as well as its origins and the means by which it was transmitted to England. Göethe, for example, with whose 'name' Mrs Gaskell should have 'danced', and in not doing so made 'the great mistake of the evening', during his long life (1749-1832) dominated the whole period of what came to be known as European Romanticism. Educated at the University of Leipzig, he came under the influence of Lessing, a dramatist-philosopher and a key figure in a new culture. After a year of retreat, due to ill-health, Göethe passed on to the University of Strasbourg where he met Herder, already a professional writer and engaged in the study of old folk ballads. Göethe himself had been writing poetry for several years and, while editing a collection of folk-songs in co-operation with Herder, secretly introduced into it one of his own lyrics. It was 'Heidenroslein'. Translated into English as 'Hedgeroses', and set to music by Schubert, it was to be part of the German poetry and music which was to sweep through the English drawing-rooms and concert-halls of the nineteenth century: Bach ('that mediator among nations'), Mozart, Beethoven, Schubert, Schumann, Brahms, Handel, and Mendelsohn. Such music as this played an important part in the Gaskell family life. It was at this time that Mr Hallé, a German immigrant, (1819-1895) was getting together the 'band' which became the world-famous Hallé Orchestra, and the Gaskells subscribed to his concerts. He gave piano lessons to Marianne, the eldest daughter. When she spent a year in London she had singing lessons from Signor Pergetti, who gave lessons to the Quenn's children, and also lessons in harmony at Queen's college, a newly founded college for girls, also in London. Meta, the second daughter, had lessons in German and her music at her boarding school in Liverpool and, on one occasion, Mrs Gaskell writes to Geoffrey Lushington, a social reformer, 'I can not write sensibly for I am listening with both my ears, & half my heart to something that you must hear sometime ... oh it is so exquisite now - like the music of heaven - I keep forgetting what I wanted to say. Marianne is charmed with the Abend Lied which she has been singing to me, & bids me tell you it is the most beautiful thing ... Meta is very much obliged to you for the minuet which she hopes to have the oppy (sic) soon of playing to you ...'[5] It was Herder also who introduced Göethe to the Bible, Greek literature, and the works of the great Dutch philosopher, Spinoza, who rejected the dualistic division between God and nature.

It was 'the good bright and true Gotz von Berlichingen, Luther's friend and Göethe's hero' of Mrs Gaskell's letter who was the subject of Göethe's first great dramatic success, one which stimulated a new interest in nationalism and in mediaeval values in a Germany which was, at that time, merely a collection of small states under the domination of France. Frustrated and stifled by the rigidities of social conventions and outworn nationalistic thought and discontented with their isolation at their provincial universities, students and professors initiated a second Renaissance. Amongst the names not mentioned in Mrs Gaskell's letter, but closely associated with them, were Schelling, professor of philosophy; August and Friedrich Schlegel, translators of Shakespeare and lecturers in literary history, philosophy, and Oriental studies; the great Idealist philosopher, Hegel, who saw philosophy as a legitimate development of Christianity, sought to unite all opposites in a single unity, and is said to have kept a figure of the Buddha in his study; Eichhorn, professor of Oriental languages and, though no theologian, the foremost originator of the radical criticism of the Bible which was, in time, to shake the foundations of the English Church. All these were, at one time or another, students and lecturers at the universities of Leipzig, Strasburg, Tübingen, Jena, Berlin, Vienna, Göttingen, – and Heidelberg.

Göethe himself, however, spent most of his long life as resident poet and dramatist at the small arch-ducal court of Weimar but was in constant contact with all the intellectual elements in Europe – indeed it became the fashion for anyone of note travelling in Germany to pay him a visit and so popular did his poetry become that he was known as 'the prince of poets', a fact noted by a reviewer in 1851 in the English Unitarian paper *The Inquirer*, founded in 1842. The writer added, rather sardonically, that an English lady was known to have written to Göethe addressing him as 'Prince Göethe' years after the great man had been in his grave!

The literature produced by these young German intellectuals, at first called the Sturm und Drang (Storm and Stress) movement, after a sensational play by a young dramatist named Klinger, for, amidst the pre-occupation with the life of the feelings and of immediate experience – Göethe was to write in his autobiography, *Poetry and Truth:* "I shaped only what I felt, what burned in my heart" – there were also elements of violence and horror.

This element of Sturm und Drang seems to have remained as a tradition among German students, but the greater figures in the movement soon left it behind. It was they who were to change the face of European literature, philosophy, religion, and social thought. The Bible, for instance, every word of which was the infallible word of God to Calvinists, was, well before the end of the eighteenth century, being seen by German intellectuals as one Oriental scripture among others and, in the light of the new sciences such as archaeology, not strictly 'true' in the usual meaning of the word. To them, the Bible was an epic, a great poetic drama portraying, to borrow Lessing's phrase, "the education of the human race." What mattered to them, and to those who found new inspiration in their ideas, was not 'is it true?' but 'what does it mean?'

Summed up in brief – and this has incalculable significance for an understanding of Mrs Gaskell's social and religious thinking as portrayed in her writings and demonstrated in her life – the thesis of the German Romantics in general was that nature is mind made visible. Nature and mind, however, both suffer periods of regression, after which they are reconciled and brought together on a higher level, particularly through art in its widest sense. Nature is no longer alien and hostile to man but a friendly collaborator, contributing to man's creative process and the functions of society and the world in general, while God is no longer merely a 'First Cause', a watch-maker who made the watch and then left it to tick away, each piece fulfilling its function in isolation, but a living power working within the whole. As Coleridge, a devotee of the Germans, said in 1802: "Everything has a Life of its own & we are all one Life."[6]

Coleridge and Wordsworth, both named in Mrs Gaskell's letter quoted above, were in Germany at the end of the eighteenth century, the poems *Lyrical Ballads* having been published to provide funds for the expedition. Coleridge's purpose was ostensibly to write a life of Lessing. Like so many of his projects, it was never written but he stayed in Germany for a year, learned the language and in 1817 in his *Biographia Literaria*, his literary autobiography, introduced the British public to this 'Idealist' philosophy as it became known. Wordsworth, however, who was accompanied by his sister Dorothy, stayed, on this occasion, for only a few months, adversely affected by winter weather and social isolation. But in the preface to the second edition of *Lyrical Ballads*, though criticising the more sensational features of the Sturm und Drang movement, what he called 'frantic novels, sickly and stupid German Tragedies and deluges of idle and extravagant stories in verse … this degrading thirst after outrageous stimulation', he nevertheless asserted that the feelings are 'undoubtedly (connected) with our moral sentiments and animal sensations … with the operations of the elements and the appearance of the visible universe; with storm and sunshine, and the revolutions of the seasons, with cold and heat, with loss of friends and kindred, with injuries and resentments, gratitude and hope, with fear and sorrow ... Poetry is the spontaneous overflow of powerful feelings; it takes its origin from emotion recollected in tranquillity.'

In Mrs Gaskell's letter, Heidelberg – that 'union of all beauties', its dark pine woods, rocks, and picturesque town crowned by its castle, the 'sea-green' Neckar 'gushing and foaming over red sandstone rocks' like the sea itself, and haunted by an Ondine who dwelt in its 'secret spring', the girls in peasant dress, the 'riotous' students, the telling of 'frightening and wild stories', tea-drinking at the Webers, 'he a Dr of Philosophie', 'politico-aeconomical' evenings at the residence of the Schlossers, which had once been an old convent and had a chapel, terraced gardens leading to a wilderness of wood, rock and waterfall, dancing – the introduction of the waltz, – flower garlanded women with their escorts promenading on the terraces before the ball, 'with the setting sun lighting up the noble views in the background' – all these provide both a concrete and a symbolic background to the 'illustrious' figures who inhabit it. Even the humbler English names in the letter, after Coleridge and Wordsworth, make their contribution to the scene. George Payne Rainsford James was the author of many popular historical novels and poems, and had, in 1836, published a *Life of the Black Prince*. He and Anna Jameson, a critic of art and literature who published her well-known *Shakespeare's Heroines* in 1832, represent the popular revival of interest in history, folk-ballads, and Shakespeare which had taken place in England over the past half century.

Though this letter of Mrs Gaskell's is a splendid example (there is a great deal more than I have been able to quote) of her 'spontaneous' literature, the final impression is one of a mind which had already had some preparation and of a letter written to someone who would understand something of its implications. Unitarians had, in fact, been visiting Germany and learning German for the past half century. German had been taught in the dissenting academies when this was unheard of at Oxford and Cambridge; the original attraction to the language being the new Biblical criticism initiated by Eichhorn at Göttingen. Though Coleridge and Carlyle – the latter translating so many German works that Göethe said of him in 1828: "He is almost more at home in our literature than we are" – are generally given the credit, it was Unitarians who, within the limits of their disadvantageous position in English society, were earliest in absorbing and disseminating the new German culture.

Translations from Eichhorn's work on the Bible had appeared in 1805 in the first volume of the Unitarian journal, *The Monthly Repository*, and in 1821-2 there appeared further portions of his works. Belsham and other Priestleyans, rationalist and utilitarian, knew Eichhorn's work and studied it in order to draw from it the ammunition with which to destroy the theological doctrines of the Protestant Christians who had replaced an infallible Church with an infallible Bible. In 1821, Belsham preached a sermon in which he praised Eichhorn and said "If the history of the creation of Genesis be inspired [i.e. uniquely true], then all the discoveries of Kepler and Galileo, of Copernicus and Newton, are false, and all their demonstrations must be erroneous, which is impossible."[7]

But other Unitarians of a different sort were interested in the new German literature and in the new Biblical criticism (Higher Criticism as it came to be called) for different reasons, translating and writing long review-articles in Unitarian periodicals from as early as 1796 when William Taylor of the Octagon Chapel in Norwich published a translation of Bürger's 'Lenore' which inspired a later version by Sir Walter Scott. Crabb Robinson, who spent five years in Germany and studied at the University of Jena, contributed, in 1806, to *The Monthly Repository*, the first translation of Lessing's 'Education of the Human Race' and thirty years later (1832-3) nine articles on Göethe which are considered to be "memorable as the first systematic introduction of Göethe into England."[8] But it was after Göethe's death in 1832, that English and also American journals began to be inundated with review-articles on his works and *Table-talk* which reached their height in the 1840s and 1850s. *The Inquirer*, the Unitarian weekly paper twice mentioned by Mrs Gaskell in her letters as being passed on by her to friends and relatives, had from its first appearance in 1842 given a large place in its pages to German literature, and in 1851 not long before she began to write her controversial novel, *Ruth*, it included, in one edition, long articles on Eckermann's *Conversations with Göethe* and the *Dramatic Works of Göethe*, both of which had recently been translated, the latter by Anna Swanwick, a Liverpool Unitarian.

During the 1840s, William Gaskell had been giving private lessons in German to Catherine and Susanna Winkworth, in the first instance in order to improve their qualifications as possible teachers, for at that time their father was in financial difficulties. But the difficulties were overcome and in the 1850s these two close friends of Mrs Gaskell produced two Victorian best-sellers, both of which are still to be found in many second-hand bookshops. In 1854, Susanna published a translation of one of the fourteenth century, near-heretical, mystics of the Rhine Valley, anonymously entitled *Theologia Germanica* and in the following year Catherine produced a translation of a collection of German hymns of a deep spirituality to which she gave the title *Lyra Germanica*. Also in the 1850s, Susanna translated works on Barthold Niebuhr (1776-1831), a German who can be termed the first social historian, as well as on Luther, Tauler, and a work on liberal religion by Baron Bunsen, German ambassador to England and a man of high culture and spirituality.

Memorials of Two Sisters, the reminiscences of Susanna and Catherine, and edited by their niece Margaret Shaen in 1908, presents a vivid picture of the influence of Bunsen on them and on Mrs Gaskell in the 1850s. It was Mrs Gaskell who first met him at the Lake District home of Mrs Arnold, the widow of Thomas Arnold (one of Bunsen's sons had married an Arnold daughter), and it was through her that the Winkworth women both met him and were encouraged by him in their German translating. But the matter did not end there. All three became part of the group which met regularly at Bunsen's London home in Carlton Terrace. This included Kingsley, Maurice, Ruskin, Max Müller, German born Orientalist and a protégé of Bunsen; A.J. Scott, first principal of University College, London, the first English University without doctrinal tests, J.H. Green, Coleridge's literary executor, and Arthur Stanley, chief Anglican protagonist after Arnold (whose chief disciple and biographer he was) of a broader church. These were the men who publicly praised both *Mary Barton* and *Ruth*. In 1851, Bunsen gave Mrs Gaskell his 'book of devotions', inscribed to his 'beloved friend',[9] and in 1854 he wrote a preface to *Theologia Germanica* which included the words 'we must ... contemplate [God's] eternal nature as the real substance of our own soul.' In 1856, George Smith, her publisher, sent her Susanna's translation of Bunsen's *Signs of the Times*, a work on religious liberty, and in her letter of thanks she said that Bunsen had previously sent her the book 'in the original language which unfortunately I can not read.'[10]

Mrs Gaskell's inability to master German sufficiently to read such works as these is not, perhaps, surprising since she did not learn it at school along with the Latin, French, and Italian which, in her youth had been considered sufficient educational equipment for even a Unitarian young lady. She seems to have made sporadic attempts at German from time to time but her impatient temperament (which she admitted as her chief fault), her child-rearing and other commitments, as well as her attraction to the writing of fiction, were presumably too distracting for her to achieve proficiency, though verses of German poetry and German expressions such as 'Heimweh' (homesickness) frequently appear in her works in the original German. Hints of her attempts to master German are to be found in her Sandlebridge letter of 1838 in which she wrote: "Bessie and I have our German novel here", but at the same time she was trying to write about the English poets, as well as looking after her first baby. In 1848, after the birth of four more children and the death of one, she ended a letter to Catherine Winkworth, who was convalescing at Southport where Mrs Gaskell had been visiting her: '...believe me, dearest Kate-Bettina (for somehow you two are inextricably blended)...' and in a second letter: 'the very name of Bettina [reminds] me of you and Southport.'[11] Susanna Winkworth later added a note to the latter that Bettina referred to Bettina von Arnim who had known Göethe when she was a child in Frankfurt, which was also Göethe's birthplace. She had published a rather romanticised version of letters, which Göethe had written to her, under the title *Correspondence with a Child* and it seems certain that this was the sort of simple German book that Mrs Gaskell might have taken the opportunity of reading with Catherine during a period of rest and quiet at the sea-side.

Other evidence of Mrs Gaskell's knowledge of German literature and philosophy, particularly that of Göethe, though slight, is by no means insignificant. In May 1854, when she was working on what was to become *North and South*, she wrote to John Forster that Mrs Shaen liked the story as far as she had got, which had put her 'into spirits' since Mrs Shaen was 'trained in German criticism.' The following October she wrote to Mrs Shaen herself, in answer to a letter received, and said that she had read Carlyle's translation of *Wilhelm Meister* – 'once or twice.'[12] Mrs Shaen was the former Emily Winkworth, sister of Susanna and Catherine and by then living in London after her marriage to William Shaen, lawyer and Unitarian.

Emily was Mrs Gaskell's closest friend among the Winkworths and several of her letters are written from the Shaens' London home, which appears in *Memorials of Two Sisters* as another regular meeting-place of religious and political reformers. We know that Emily was concerned with F.D. Maurice and his friends in the founding of a Working Women's College in London in the early 1850s but she appears to have written nothing and, soon after her marriage, became an invalid. Nevertheless, in a letter to John Forster, Mrs Gaskell claimed that Mrs Shaen was 'a far severer judge' on the subject of German criticism than Forster himself, a professional writer on historical and biographical subjects and editor, at that time, of the *Examiner*. Finally, in 1859, in a letter to Charles Eliot Norton, she refers to George Henry-Lewes as the 'author of Life of Göethe' and in 1860, again to Norton, of 'Goethian theories of self-development', saying of these: 'I believe it to be right in all things to aim at the highest standard; but I can't quite work it out with my conscience.'[13] The problem to which she is referring is one regarding the painting techniques of Meta, who had studied in the Paris ateliers and also under Ruskin, – should she paint to please herself or other people who did not understand the aims of her work? The subject is slight but serves to illustrate Mrs Gaskell's familiarity with the terms of Göethe's philosophy. As to her works, Göethe's poem 'Herman and Dorothea' is, for example, referred to in *North and South* (ch 46) and the man himself in *Cranford* (ch 4).

Mrs Gaskell retained a particular love of Heidelberg, where, by 1858, Bunsen had returned to live permanently, it being his family home. In 1860, she wrote, in two letters, one to Marianne and the other to Norton, of the social life in Heidelberg, of a sunset and a rainbow on the river Neckar, a student torch-light procession, the small industries of the Black Forest and good working-class German housing. But it was in 1858, when she made a nine week stay in Heidelberg accompanied on this occasion by Meta, Florence, and a young orphan girl, 'a friend of Meta's', that again to Norton, she wrote of

> the most poetical wintry November; clear deep blue sky, –
> white snow not very deep, except where it had drifted into
> glittering icicles a foot long, hanging on fountain and well,
> – trees encased in glittering ice, – weighed down with their
> own beauty, – streets – walks – clear & clean – and the

high peaked house-tops so beautiful ... we went to see
Spire & Worms & Strasburg Cathedral, – & the girls
worked away at German; ... I hired a piano & music, and
laughed harder than I ever laughed before or ever shall
again, the air, clear, delicious dry Air, put one in such
health and spirits. And we knew nearly everybody in
Heidelberg, – from the man milliner, who offered to drive
us in his 'Chasse' in the Black Forest, to Bunsen –[14]

CHAPTER 7
Göethe and German romanticism as seen in
Ruth and *North And South*

In *Sylvia's Lovers* (1863), Philip Hepburn, eventually Sylvia's husband, is, at the beginning of the novel, an ambitious young shop-assistant. A worthy, though unimaginative young man, he tries to teach Sylvia, a farmer's daughter, to read. Philip's lack of imagination is shown in his choice of reading material:

> he could have taken her many a pretty ballad, a story book, such as were then in vogue. He did try her with the translation of *The Sorrows of Werther*, so popular at the time that it had a place in all pedlars' baskets, with *Law's Serious Call*, the *Pilgrims' Progress*, *Klopstock's Messiah*, and *Paradise Lost*. But she could not read it herself, and after turning the leaves languidly over, and smiling a little at the picture of Charlotte cutting bread and butter in a left-handed manner put it aside on the shelf...[1]

Klopstock's Messiah, a great dramatic epic arising out of the German Higher Criticism of the Bible, and *The Sorrows of Werther*, a work of fiction, were indeed extremely popular. That Sylvia would not attempt to read the latter is an indication of the girl's childishness, as well as Philip's lack of imagination in failing to provide her with reading matter that would have been more suitable. For all its popularity, *The Sorrows of Werther* was a ridiculous choice for a girl such as Sylvia, both in subject and in style. The important thing, however, at the moment, is that Mrs Gaskell knew of an illustrated version of the book which contained 'a picture of Charlotte cutting bread and butter in a left-handed manner.'

The Sorrows of Werther, or to give it its more common English title *The Sorrows of Young Werther*, is a novella, or short novel, a form in which German writers have excelled, but one almost completely neglected by English writers, apart from Mrs Gaskell, many of whose minor works are in this form.[2] Written in 1774 by Göethe and believed to be a vindication of the suicide of a former fellow-student at Leipzig, it was published in England in 1779 from a

French version. No less than twenty-six different editions in English had appeared by 1800 and it was the most widely read European novel for thirty years. Written in the form of letters to a friend, it was also the first German psychological novel with very little in the way of plot, the drama played out in the mind and heart of its hero. A more accurate rendering of its title in English is *The Sufferings of Young Werther*, but this title was only given to the novel as translated in 1957 by Bayard Quincy Morgan. My quotations are from his 1977 edition published by John Calder.

Werther, a young minor aristocrat, sensitive and a lover of nature, falls in love with Charlotte, the good and beautiful daughter of the steward of an estate. She is already happily affianced and is soon married to Albert, a steady young man of business, but Werther cannot overcome his passion for her and continually seeks her company. Like Werther, she also is sensitive, visits the sick and dying, cares for a large family of brothers and sisters as she had promised her dead mother, with great affection and sense of responsibility. She also plays the piano 'with the touch of an angel so simple and so full of meaning', her singing always curing Werther of any 'grief, bewilderment and care' from which he might be suffering, and her dancing of the waltz with him plays an important part in his first falling in love with her. It is at this first dancing together that he wears the famous blue coat and yellow waistcoat which he was to wear for the rest of his short life and in which, at his request, after his suicide, he was buried. So great was the impact of this novel that many young European men were to follow his example, some even to the point of suicide.

Both Werther and Charlotte love the beautiful countryside in which the small provincial town of the story is set. They prefer the life of simple people to the pedantry, snobbery and narrow-mindedness of the court where Werther, for a short time, takes up a minor secretarial post and dislikes intensely the arrogance of 'people of rank' towards those of the lower classes and the poor. After a reference to the joys of nature, Werther describes himself in one of his letters to his friend, as lying on the floor surrounded by Charlotte's young brothers and sisters, 'some of them scrambling over [him]', playing with them as an animal plays with its young and he calls the children 'little creatures.' The story also includes innumerable descriptions of nature in all its aspects and moods, from the great mountains and the sky to one which perhaps sums up, in one passage, Werther's deepest feelings about nature:

> ... millions of swarming mites danced bravely in the last red rays of the sun, whose last quivering glance freed the buzzing beetle from its grass, and the humming and stirring about me drew my attention to the earth, and the moss, which wrests its nourishment from the resistant rocks, and the underbrush that creeps down the sandy slope would reveal to me the glowing inner holy life of nature – how I would take all that into my warm heart, feeling as if it were deified in the overflowing abundance... I saw all the unfathomable forces in the depths of the earth working and creating within each other; and now above the ground and under the sky swarm the living creatures in their untold diversity. Everything... peopled with myriads of forms; and then the people seeking joint security in their little houses ... breathes the spirit of the eternally creating One, rejoicing in every speck of dust that hears him and is alive.

All this is personified in the girl Charlotte, whom Werther idealises to the point of saying: "She is sacred to me." Since he can neither possess nor abandon her, his suffering continues to intensify and he contemplates suicide. Discussing the subject with Albert, whom he calls a rationalist, he says: "It is not a matter of whether a man is weak or strong, but whether he can outlast the measure of his suffering – be it spiritual or physical..." and he asks: "What is human destiny other than to endure his measure of suffering, drink his cup to the dregs!?..."

The Sorrows of Young Werther is, therefore, a philosophical treatise as well as a tragic love story. Posing the question, what is the meaning of life, the purpose of existence, it is easy to see why it was a key-work in the development of Romanticism, the term first used in this special sense by Mme de Staël, whose book *On Germany*, published in France between 1810 and 1813 and in England in 1813, opened the windows of Europe to the German literary and philosophical movement in which God is 'the eternally creating One'. The life of feeling, and especially of romantic love, Werther exalts so far above that of cold reason and moral censoriousness that he even asks: "Who will cast the first stone ... against, the girl who in an hour of rapture loses self control in the irresistible joys of love?"

Ultimately, Werther realises, however, that perfect happiness is not to be found in the finite world. "What is man, the eulogized demi-god? Does he not lack force at the very point where he needs it most? And when he soars upward in joy, or sinks down in suffering, is he not checked in both, is he not returned again to the dull cold sphere of awareness, just when he was longing to lose himself in the fullness of the infinite?". The 'Storm and Stress' of Werther's sufferings increase as he moves towards his self-destruction and nature also moves from a summer to a winter landscape but in the end there is no despair, only a certainty that his sufferings are complete. In a last letter to Charlotte he writes that he would have died joyously if he could have offered himself up for her in order to restore to her the peace and rapture of her soul which he had so disturbed: "But, alas to few noble souls is it given to shed their blood for their dear ones, and by their death to enkindle a new, hundredfold life for their friends!"

At his request, Werther is buried beside two lindens in the church-yard but it is at night and no clergyman escorts him. Workmen carry him, and only Charlotte's father and older brothers, who had all loved Werther, follow him to his grave. Albert had found it impossible to be present and there were fears for Charlotte's life. The husband and wife had drifted apart during Werther's pursuit of Charlotte but one is left with the final impression that, in his death, they are reconciled for already they have come to a greater sensitivity and understanding of each other and of Werther himself.

When they have recovered from their grief at his death, their marriage will have been enriched by his life and his sacrifice. This theme of reconciliation and the achievement of personal maturity through a sacrifice of some kind was to be carried on in Göethe's *Wilhelm Meister* novels (1777-1829) and was to be the dominant theme of his life and works.

The *Wilhelm Meister* novels (which are really one novel written in many episodes over several years) are the first example of the 'bildungsroman', the novel of character, which, as H.M. Waidson writes in the introduction to his translation of the works,

> includes the idea of the formation of the individual
> personality, both through inner effort and outward

85

influence, and that of the unfolding of natural potentialities. Progress is from error and confusion to truth and clarity and as the novel proceeds it makes or implies judgements on what may be right or wrong from the point of view of the hero's development in life. Such a novel is ultimately optimistic; the central figure will keep on striving, and others will help him in a variety of ways, in his quest for fulfillment. Constructive lessons will be taught [and the] outcome is utopian, as there is the hope that the ideal of a higher form of humanity can be realized in earthly society.[3]

Göethe, who was 'a man of two worlds', interested both in literature and science and troubled about the possible consequences of the development of the industrial society which he could already envisage, casts his hero in the Wilhelm Meister novels as the son of a family of prosperous merchants who, at the very beginning of the novel, asks his mother: "is everything useless which does not put more in our pockets and which does not procure us possessions?" He leaves his urban home and joins a troupe of travelling players. Soon he becomes the leader of a group that he sees as the beginning of a National theatre, one which will educate the people, and they perform Shakespeare and plays about the mediaeval life of Germany.

During this time, Wilhelm rescues from ill-treatment a young girl, hardly more than a child, of unknown origin. She is strong, robust, an acrobat, and an exquisite dancer. Becoming devoted to Wilhelm, she makes herself his servant and, completely innocent, she often embarrasses him with her enthusiastic embraces. She is also very religious, attending daily Mass, where Wilhelm sees her "praying devoutly." It is through her that he learns that he can help people on a personal level as well as through his theatrical activities. But Mignon, as she is called, is a strange little figure. She sometimes passes into a kind of trance and she can only express her longings in music, both in her dancing and in songs which she both composes and sings. Though happy with Wilhelm, she can only find, or rather yearn for a happiness which lies, as it had done for Werther, in something 'beyond'. Her first song begins (in Morgan's translation):

Know you the land where lemons are in flower ...
Oh there, yes there
Beloved, goes the way that you and I should share ...

words that were to be exquisitely translated by the young Coleridge. In her second song, she sings:

> He alone who knows yearning
> Knows what I suffer
> Wholly undiscerning
> Of all kinds of joy
> I look to the sky above -

And in her third song appear the words:

> Each one seeks peace and calm in his friend's arms
> And yet my lips ...
> Can only be unsealed at a god's behest

Also in *Wilhelm Meister* there appears a strange lady on a white horse when Wilhelm and his party, while travelling, are attacked by robbers and he is wounded. The lady is very lovely, a 'noble creature', an 'Amazon.' Dismounting, she removes her coat, revealing her beautiful figure, places it gently over him and, when he intends to stammer a few words of thanks, the vivid impression of her presence has such a strange effect on his already strained senses that it appears to him as if her head were encircled by rays and a gleaming light gradually suffuses her whole person. He loses consciousness, and when he recovers, though she has disappeared, he feels 'an electric warmth' and a feeling of quiet and gentleness, which, in spite of his wound, seems to flow from the coat. He can still visualise the coat falling from her shoulders and the noble figure surrounded by rays of light. Later, he is happy to know that the robber-attack had been intended for her and her entourage and he is happy that he has been wounded, for his sacrifice has saved 'a perfect mortal woman.'[4]

Let us now turn to the text of Mrs Gaskell's first three novels. It has been said with monotonous regularity by modern critics that *Mary Barton* is an application of simple Biblical Christianity to the problems of the emerging industrial society. *Ruth* has been criticised for a lack of consistency in the character of Ruth herself and *North and South* for its lack of plot in a novel of such length. But we can now see that Mary Barton is not only "a tragic poem" in the Wordsworthian sense, showing forth the inherent dignity, nobility and worth of "humble folk", it is also the first English novel to show the Bible as a great poetic and psychological drama set in the modern world and presented in the light of the German Biblical critics of the past half century. It is not merely that *Mary Barton* is well-sprinkled with didactic quotations from the Bible; the imagery and symbolism of the Bible continually 'comes through' in the various situations in the story, often very poignantly as, for example, when Esther, the prostitute, visits her young niece, Mary, in an attempt to help her. After the interview, full of longing to give up her way of life but knowing that this is now impossible, Esther[5], like Peter, after his betrayal of Christ, 'rushed into the outer darkness of the street; and then wept long and bitterly.' George Eliot's *Daniel Deronda* (1876) has been put forward as the last English novel to show the influence of the mythical and psychological view of the Bible initiated by Eichhorn[6], *Mary Barton* can claim to be the first, while *Ruth* and *North and South* show the same influence but with a difference, the added influence of Göethe and Baron Bunsen.

Ruth is never thought of as an 'industrial' novel, though Ruth, like Mary Barton, is an apprenticed dress-maker in a sweat-shop, working till the early hours of the morning and sleeping in a dormitory in an area where houses of an earlier period, with good carving and stained-glass windows, have been turned into workshops of various kinds as had happened in Manchester. The girls are turned out on Sundays to fend for themselves without food or money to buy it, and, as a result, this orphan child of fifteen years is seduced by a wealthy, educated young man, of which there were also a great many in Manchester, the centre of prostitution in the north of England, especially in periods of economic depression. When Ruth's employer fails in business the young apprentice is consequently turned out of her employment without money or friends. We know from Mrs Gaskell's letters that Ruth's story is partly based on that of a girl whom she found in the new prison for women in Manchester.[7]

We also know that Bradshaw, who later employs Ruth as a governess and dismisses her when he knows the truth about her and her child, is a 'tradesman'. There is no doubt that this novel was written with the object of practical reform – that of changing the attitude of society towards the girl who has an illegitimate child and wishes to make a decent life for herself and her child. But there is an added dimension to this novel, as there is to *North and South*, which was also written with a view to practical reform. Let us turn again to Young Werther and Wilhelm Meister.

Ruth, like Werther, is a young and sensitive lover of nature and, like him also, of an old family, for Ruth's home, before the death of her parents, had been an ancient farm-house, "a grange." Like him too, she has an unhappy love affair and both Ruth and Werther die because of this, a death that is sacrificial, Werther's by intention, Ruth's of typhus caught from her former lover when, at the end of the novel, she is working as a nurse and insists on nursing him. The apparent contradiction in Ruth's character between her "living with her lover in North Wales and positively enjoying it" compared with the nobility and spiritual maturity she later shows, without there having been any process of 're-adjustment', still puzzles modern critics,[8] as it enraged Mrs Gaskell's contemporary critics. Ronald Grey, in his Göethe, a critical introduction (1976) describes Mignon, the girl-child in *Wilhelm Meister* as a symbol of "the all-embracing divine life." There is no need for 're-adjustment' in Ruth. Both she and Mignon have been sinned against but retain their original innocence and remain pure to the end.

Asked by many, including Charlotte Brontë, why Ruth had to die, giving the impression still current among critics that she, in the end, accepted the conventional view that the 'fallen girl' must be punished, Mrs Gaskell made no reply, but again, like Mignon, Ruth can only find ultimate happiness in the 'beyond'. Catherine Winkworth wrote to a sister-in-law:

> Lily [Mrs Gaskell] has been rather ailing and low-spirited lately; she has taken to heart very much all the evil that is said of Ruth... (Bunsen, by the way, does not agree with you, for he says that anyone with real insight will see that Ruth's death was absolutely necessary:) 'sie musste untergehen' [she must perish] and thereby conquer.[9]

One of the early chapters of *Ruth* has the title 'Storm-Spirit Subdued' and in Göethe's philosophical 'Divan' poems (1819) appear the words: "Die, and become", meaning the 'self' must die in order to become at one with the world-soul. Bunsen had written in his introduction to Susanna Winkworth's translation of *Theologia Germanica:*

A godly life is the steadfast working
out of inward freeness from self;
to become thus Godlike is the bringing
back of man's first nature.

Finally, in 1906, Sir Adolphus Ward, in his introduction to the Knutsford Edition of *Ruth*, wrote: "The last chapters of Ruth cannot very easily be treated from a purely literary point of view..." and he likens them to "The long and enigmatic part of Göethe's "Faust," [which] is designed to symbolize the love that rises above self." Göethe himself had said of the end of Faust: "In Faust himself there is an activity that becomes higher and purer to the end, and from above there is eternal love coming to his aid."

Ruth has, by the end of the novel, become completely purged of whatever of 'self' there might have been in her and, through her sacrificial death, she attains not only eternal life but is the means of changing Bradshaw, the puritanical hypocritical tradesman and shady politician, who had persecuted her and her benefactor, Mr Benson, and of reconciling the two men. Little wonder that Mrs Gaskell wept bitter tears at the reviews of *Ruth* which had completely missed the novel's philosophical and spiritual meaning and on hearing that it had been burned by two male members of her husband's congregation, as an immoral book.

Let us now turn, briefly, to *North and South*. Again, Margaret is very much a child of nature, her origin a country vicarage. On the heath near the village in Hampshire where she had lived before coming to Milton-Northern, she had walked with her father, as a child, and had felt herself a part of nature, "wafted along by the autumnal breeze", by "the soft violence of the west wind", "crushing down the fern with cruel glee" as she felt it "yield under her foot", and send up "the fragrance peculiar to it...[seeing] multitudes of wild, free living creatures, revelling in the sunshine and the herbs and flowers it called forth."[10] This is very similar to my quotation above from *Young Werther* and, in another passage, Werther writes to his friend: "The most innocent walk costs the life of a thousand poor insects ... and stamps down a little cosmos." The Sturm und Drang element of *Young Werther* is also evident in Mrs Gaskell's novel, the word "violence" appearing in hers a surprising number of times, from the "soft violence" of the wind near its beginning, to the end, when Thornton shows Margaret some dead roses, the remains of those he had gathered when on a pilgrimage to her old home and "with gentle violence" she tries to take the flowers from him.

There is, indeed, extreme violence in the strike scene in which Thornton is pelted with stones by his employees while standing on the steps of his house. The violent scene is described in an extremely vivid fashion, consciously or unconsciously, almost as sexually explicit as the earlier novels of D.H. Lawrence. Margaret happens to be in Thornton's house, and, in a part-reversal of the Wilhelm Meister situation, saves him from actual injury by shielding him with her own body. She is herself wounded by a stone intended for Thornton and afterwards, to him, everything seemed "dim and vague ... besides the touch of her arms ... the soft clinging."[11] This is the beginning of a change for the better in this arrogant young industrialist.

Mrs Gaskell had been frequently asked, after *Mary Barton*, to write another novel that would 'put the employers' point of view.' She had always refused to do so on the grounds that she did not feel so strongly about this and claimed to lack sufficient knowledge of the technical and trade problems involved. In *North and South* it is generally supposed that she changed her mind and that the novel does put the employers' point of view. Actually, this is not the case; it only transfers the main plot to a middle class setting against a background of industrial strife. It explores once again the same problems that had already appeared in *Mary Barton*, this time through a stormy love-affair conducted by means of arguments on social and economic questions between Thornton and Margaret. Again, many critics have seen Mrs Gaskell's solution as the application of 'simple' Christianity. This is only partly true and, as in *Ruth*, the Christianity proposed is not so simple as it appears. Both Göethe and Hegel thought of Christ as a 'divine being' and Christianity as contributing to their philosophy. But Göethe is also reported by Eckerman, in his Conversation with Göethe, as having said: "One must become something before one can do something." By the end of *North and South* both Margaret and Thornton have, by means of their mutual, often violent explorations and also by each having sacrificed something of their own ego, reached a personal maturity and, once again, a reconciliation on a higher level which leads Thornton and his employee, the intelligent working-man, Higgins, to see one another as human-beings rather than mere 'master' and 'hand.' This fictional 'reconciliation on a higher level after a period of regression' was to find its factual counterpart in what came to be called Christian Socialism.

CHAPTER 8
Christian socialism

Writing to Charles Eliot Norton in 1861 about young Bosanquet, the Anglican whom she says she had met 'constantly' at the Bunsens' home in Heidelberg and who was then about to visit America, Mrs Gaskell remarked that he was somewhat like Dr Arnold and had also been a pupil of Jowett's at Oxford. Though Dr Arnold's name appears several times in Mrs Gaskell's letters and she was on intimate visiting terms with his widow from the late 1840s, Arnold himself had died in 1842 shortly after being appointed Regius Professor of Modern History at Oxford and it is not possible to say for certain whether Mrs Gaskell actually met him. She may have heard him preach at Rugby, where Unitarian boys were admitted, or only have read his sermons since many of these were published. Writing to Lord Hatherton from Oxford, she says: "We heard Mr Temple, the newly elected Master of Rugby, in St Mary's. He is a very striking preacher; I kept thinking of Dr Arnold and his school sermons ..."[1]

Arnold had been at the centre in the 1830s of the movement to revive the idea of a reformed National Church, much on the lines of that put forward by the Presbyterians in the seventeenth century. He had 'experienced misgivings regarding the doctrine of the Trinity'[2] during his youth and in his *Principles of Church Reform* (1833) showed a knowledge of and a friendly attitude towards Unitarianism, while Arthur Stanley, Professor of Ecclesiastical History at Oxford, when Mrs Gaskell met him there on her first visit in 1857, was, as we have noted earlier, Arnold's disciple and biographer and a member of the Stanley family of Alderley in Cheshire, one well-known to Mrs Gaskell and one which had always shown favour towards dissenters. Stanley was also an intimate friend of Jowett who, in 1838 became a Fellow of Balliol, in 1855 Regius Professor of Greek, and in 1870 Master of Balliol. A considerable Oxford personality, drawing to himself groups of brilliant students at informal social gatherings, Jowett's influence on Balliol was immense and the college continued to produce men celebrated in the fields of literature, art, science, and social and religious ideas.

From 1855 until the end of his life, however, Jowett was under a cloud, theologically, because of his 'heretical' views on New

Testament criticism i.e. the Higher Criticism of the Bible, the cause of endless controversies for years to come. Mrs Gaskell wrote after meeting him on one occasion: 'I do like Mr Jowett and I am so glad to feel we are getting really intimate.'[3] This remark, made to Charles Eliot Norton, was followed by several pages about the persecution of Jowett by members of the university who were deeply antagonistic to his determination 'not to submit to this abominable system of terrorism which prevents the statement of the plainest facts and makes true theology or theological education impossible.'[4] The deciding vote against Jowett had been cast by a Dr Jelf, whom Mrs Gaskell describes as 'principal of King's Coll[ege], London and who turned out Mr Fred Maurice from his professorship there on acc[oun]t of his heresy about the eternal duration of punishment.'[5] Stanley, two of whose Oxford sermons to undergraduates she sent to Norton, had done all he could to support both Jowett and Maurice and three years later, in 1860, Higher Criticism and thus German theological and philosophical ideas reached the very centre of English thought in *Essays and Reviews*. This was a publication which included essays by Temple, Jowett and Rowland Williams, the latter on Baron Bunsen's Biblical Studies. The book convulsed England with indignation and panic. The main article by Jowett,' On the Interpretation of Scripture', was largely inspired by his study of Lessing, Hegel and the other Germans whose works, as we have seen, Unitarians had already been translating and studying for half a century. It was enough to deprive Jowett of any hope of advancement in the Church of England even though the avowed aim of *Essays and Reviews* as a whole was to reconcile Christianity with 'the intellectual tendencies of the age and the discoveries of science.'

Mr Fred Maurice, as Mrs Gaskell called him in her letter to Norton, she was meeting at Bunsen's London home in the 1850s. Frederick Denison Maurice was chaplain of Lincoln's Inn from 1846 to 1860 and from 1846 professor of Theology at King's College from which post he was dismissed in 1853 because of his theological views. He was, from 1860 to 1869, incumbent of St Peter's, Vere Street, London, and from 1866 professor of moral philosophy at Cambridge. The son of a Unitarian minister, he became a follower of Coleridge, yet even in 1860 he wrote:

> I now deliberately regard it as one of the greatest mercies
> of my life that I had this birth and the education that
> belonged to it ... My ends have been shaped for me, rough
> hew them how I would, and shape has been given to them
> by my father's function and this name 'Unitarian' more
> than any other influences, though I have been exposed to
> many of the most different kind which have strongly
> affected and may appear to some to have entirely disturbed
> that primary one.[6]

Though Maurice claimed that he was not a founder or even a member of the Broad Church movement, as the movement for a National Church was now termed, it was in him that one of the principles associated with it came to its greatest fruition, that of Christian Socialism, deeply rooted as it was in Maurice's idea of God as the 'ground' of society, the 'natural' laws of which were also the laws of the Gospel. While the title of 'father' of the Broad Church movement has generally been given to Arnold, the real father of the movement was Coleridge with his statements on the nature of Biblical inspiration, the necessity for a national church, the importance of science and tolerance, statements such as: 'If Reason justly contradicts an article it is not of the household of faith'; and 'I do not so much care for men's religious opinions – they vary, and are dependent on that which usually surrounds them – but I regard with more attention what men are.' There can be little doubt that Coleridge, like Maurice, took with him into the Church of England a form of Unitarianism not far removed from that of the comprehensive Presbyterianism of Mrs Gaskell's ancestors.

By the 1850s, then, there was a distinguished and influential group on the Anglican-Unitarian border, to which were attracted people such as Dickens (who for several years attended Unitarian chapels in London), Hallam, Tennyson, Monckton Milnes, Browning, Froude, Florence Nightingale, John Forster and those already mentioned in connection with *Ruth*. In 1853, for example, Catherine Winkworth wrote:

> Lily [Mrs Gaskell] ... gets the very highest praise from Mr
> Scott, Bunsen, and from Mr Maurice and Archdeacon
> Hare, from Hallam and Monckton Milnes, besides many
> other less celebrated names ... all the ... younger men ...

say that [*Ruth*] is one of the most virtue-stirring works they have ever read.[7]

To this list we must also add the author of *Tom Brown's Schooldays*, Thomas Hughes, and the lesser-known Unitarians, Henry Solly and William Shaen, both 'moral-force,' i.e. non-violent, Chartists.[8] Most of these 'younger men' had been pupils of Arnold at Rugby, of Jowett at Oxford, at the newly established non-sectarian University College, London, or at Cambridge where there was a more liberal tradition of religious thought and a greater interest in science than at Oxford. Most of them were Christian Socialists and one, Charles Crompton, member of an old Lancashire Unitarian family, was to marry Florence, Mrs Gaskell's third daughter, in 1863. Mrs Gaskell first described him as:

> I should have said not clever; but he was 4th Wrangler at Cambridge and is a Fellow of Trinity, and is getting on in his profession (barrister) ... his eldest sister ... is married to Mr Llewellyn Davies, a clergyman ... of Mr Maurice's school [who] has ... published sermons on the Atonement – true meaning of sacrifice etc. Mr Crompton is not exactly a Unitarian, nor exactly Broad Church – but perhaps more of the latter than the former.[9]

Llewellyn Davies who contributed to the last joint effort of the Christian Socialists, *Tracts for Priests and People* (1861 and 1862), described Maurice

> as putting to the England of the day the point-blank question 'Is human life, as it is now and as it has been in the past, founded by the Maker's design upon selfish and competitive instincts or upon the law of mutual help and fellow-work?' He would not endure that the question should be put in this form – 'ought not human life to be founded on the principle of mutual help?' The distinction between the two forms was a vital one. The notion that wise and good men were set to work to make an improved society out of their own ideas was one which he repudiated with all his energy and he did not care what bewilderment the repudiation might cause.[10]

Coleridge, to whom Maurice said he owed 'his whole self', had been not only concerned with the theology and philosophy of Christianity but with its practical application to society. His view was that the clergy did not discharge their full duty unless they educated men to be good citizens in the widest sense. He had denounced the factory system because it treated working class people as 'things', the rural rich who joined 'house to house' and 'field to field' in order that they might be alone in the land (a quotation from Isaiah Ch 5 v 8) and the industrialists who employed the time between their morning and evening prayers 'in the pursuit of ... a temptation so perilous that ... no power short of Omnipotence could make their deliverance from it credible or conceivable.'[11] In his *Table Talk* (1819-23) he is recorded as having said:

> It is not uncommon for 100,000 operatives (mark this word, for words in this sense are things) to be out of employment at once in the cotton districts and, thrown upon parochial relief, to be dependent upon hard-hearted taskmasters for food. The Malthusian doctrine would indeed afford a certain means of relief if this were not a two fold question. If, when you say to a man, – "You have no claim upon me: you have your allotted part to perform in the world, so have I. In a state of nature, indeed, had I food, I should offer you a share from sympathy, from humanity, but in this advanced and artificial state of society, I cannot afford you relief: you must starve. You came into the world when it could not sustain you." What would be this man's answer? He would say, "You disclaim all connection with me: I have no claims upon you? I can then have no duties towards you, and this pistol shall put me in possession of your wealth. You may leave a law behind you which shall hang me, but what man who saw assured starvation before him ever feared hanging?" It is this accursed practice of ever considering only what seems expedient for the occasion, disjoined from all principle or enlarged systems of action, of never listening to the true and unerring impulses of our better nature, which has led the colder hearted men to the study of political economy, which has turned our Parliament into a real committee of public safety. In it is all power vested; and in a few years we shall either be governed by an aristocracy, or what is still more likely, by a contemptible democratical oligarchy

of glib economists compared to which the worst form of aristocracy would be a blessing.[12]

This would have made an admirable preface to *Mary Barton* and it is striking that the situation posed in the above passage is the nub of its plot. Thomas Ashton, a Unitarian mill-owner of Hyde, near Manchester, whose factory-school had been praised by government inspectors, was killed in a dispute with trade-unionists, who were outlawed in his factory. The family, related to Sir John Potter, a member of the Cross Street congregation, felt Mrs Gaskell had deliberately pilloried them in this incident in the novel, but in a letter to Potter Mrs Gaskell disclaimed this (the murder had occurred seventeen years previously).[13]

On the other hand, she had expressed admiration and affection for Coleridge, "the old man eloquent" of her German letter of 1841, when distress among the cotton-workers had been particularly severe. She was also on friendly terms with Lord Coleridge, custodian of the Coleridge Notebooks. She and her daughters visited him on several occasions. In 1859 she wrote to him, 'I have copied S.T. Coleridge's letter'[14] and in the same year informed Marianne that Mrs Nicholls, who had been post-mistress at Ambleside when Wordsworth was a young man there at Dove Cottage and Coleridge a frequent visitor, had sent her "an oval-framed likeness of poor Sam."[15] Two portraits of Coleridge by Hazlitt, executed when Coleridge was living at Greta Hall, Keswick, have disappeared and 'poor Sam' was an expression used in affection by those who admired him (as well as by others in contempt), who knew of his long fight against opium addiction. She may even have heard her father speak of Coleridge with admiration. We know that the latter visited the Manchester dissenting academy in the 1790s, quite possibly during the time when Stevenson was minister at Dobb Lane Chapel, Failsworth, and classics tutor at the academy. Coleridge met, in a discussion group associated with the academy, Robert Owen, industrialist, philanthropist, and founder of English (secular) Socialism.[16] Both Stevenson and Coleridge considered the Unitarian ministry but both rejected it, disliking, as did many young men at that time, being 'hired' by the congregations of the day. Coleridge took up Pantisocracy, the idea of an educating, agriculturally-based community and Stevenson for a time took up experimental agriculture in Scotland.

In *Mary Barton*, the Church is conspicuous by its absence; in *North and South*, a conscientious clergyman leaves the Church and becomes a tutor in the industrial north where he and his daughter attempt to bring to the manufacturers a wider culture, a deeper insight into the meaning of life and friendship and support to working-class people. We find representations of the Christian Socialist type of clergyman in Mr Benson of *Ruth* and Mr Gray of *My Lady Ludlow*. In *North and South*, we hear echoes of Arnold and Coleridge. On the neglect by the rich of their duty to the poor, Arnold says that they 'measure their wants by far too low a standard, content by doing too little for them' and he deplores:

> the ignorance of the poor and ... their feeling of the suffering and degradation of their present condition...; many persons confound reading and writing with education ... I never knew any poor man who could properly be said to be educated; except in some rare instances where men, breaking through all difficulties, have by their own power of mind and indefatigable industry, succeeded in educating themselves. If we call our own children educated at the age when we commonly send them to school for the first time – if their education is completed at 8 or 9 years old, then we may call educated those who have been taught to read or write at our parish schools. But if reading and writing are not education but the mere preparatory steps to it, then to talk of education of the poor is to talk of a thing that does not exist.[17]

In *North and South*, Margaret says to Thornton:

> I heard ... that it was considered to the advantage of the masters to have ignorant workers ... the ignorance and the knowledge of which I was speaking did not relate to reading and writing – the teaching or information one can give a child. I am sure that what was meant was ignorance of the wisdom that shall guide men and women. I hardly know what that is. But he, that is my informant – spoke as if the masters would like their hands to be merely tall, large children – living in the present moment – with a blind, unreasoning kind of obedience;[18]

and it is Higgins, the intelligent working-man, who says:

99

If I'm going wrong when I think I'm going right it's their sin, who ha' left me where I am, in my ignorance.[19]

As Arnold set out at Rugby to educate a generation of gentlemen who would know their Christian duties, so Maurice and his friends started workers' co-operatives and the working-class 'education of the whole man' in the first Working Men's College in London in 1855 and in this Mrs Gaskell was intensely interested. She had heard Maurice preach on her visit to London in 1849, from where she wrote: 'On Sunday ... to church to hear Mr Maurice whom I like very much indeed.'[20] The roots of her dislike of sermons in general would seem to have been that the majority of those she heard in the Unitarian chapels were either the arid 'moral discourses' referred to by Henry Solly in his autobiography[21] or the theological controversy that was incomprehensible and unhelpful to the young, to the working class attenders, and to those who were seriously trying to live a spiritual life and apply their religion to the problems of their day. She wrote in 1859, on the departure of Mr Ham, assistant minister at Cross Street:

> we Gaskell women are none of us sorry – oh for some really spiritual devotional preaching instead of controversy about doctrines – about whh I am more and more certain we never can be certain in this world[22]

and of Dr Stanley's farewell sermon at "Ch[rist] Ch[urch]", to Charles Bosanquet: 'Do read it if it comes your way. It is published by Parker of the Strand the Oxford publishers.'[23]

Mrs Gaskell's feelings for the vulnerability of the uneducated poor persisted. In *Sylvia's Lovers* (1864), overtly an historical drama set during the French Revolutionary wars, there is a good deal of criticism of both the Church and State authorities. All the main characters are drawn from the working classes, except for two saintly old Quaker bankers, the Fosters, who lent money without interest (as did many of the middle-class Christian Socialists), while Kester, the old farm-servant, is one of Mrs Gaskell's noblest creations. At the beginning of the novel, at the funeral of a young whaler killed by the press-gang, though he had been legally exempt from naval service;

the vicar mumbled hastily over a sermon on the text, "In
the middle of life we are in death" which might have done
as well for a baby cut off in a convulsion fit ... the hearers
went away as full of anger as they had entered the church
and some with a dull feeling of disappointment as to what
they had got there ...

It is only in the ancient liturgy of the Church, at the grave-side,
that the dead man's old parents find comfort. Sylvia's father is
eventually hanged because of his ignorance of the law and Sylvia
herself, towards the end of the novel, in grief and perplexity comes to
ask the help and advice of a wise and pious old Quaker woman who
tells her to read the Bible. Sylvia says: "I'd fain read ... if anybody
would learn me." The next day the old woman bade Sylvia come to
her, and then and there she began to teach Sylvia to read the first
chapter of Genesis.

Fourteen years earlier, in 1850, Mrs Gaskell wrote to William
Robson, her husband's brother-in-law at Warrington:

I hope you will not think that I have taken too great a
liberty in having requested a pamphlet and two papers ... to
be forwarded to you. The pamphlet is the first of a series
on Christian Socialism proposed to be issued by the writers
of 'Politics for the People'; those writers were as you
probably know, the Revd Frederick Maurice, the author of
No 1 of the Present tracts; the Revd Charles Kingsley (who
will soon publish No 2 of tracts on Christian Socialism),
Mr Ludlow, a barrister writing under the pseudonym of
'John Townsend', Mr Scott the Prof. of English literature
at University College etc. They are anxious to obtain a
circulation among the working-classes for these tracts, and
it is they who have instituted the Co-operative Tailors
Society; and who hope to form a similar Society for
Needlewomen. Even if you differ considerably from them,
by helping them to circulate their views, and have their
plans discussed, you will be helping them in their earnest
loving search after the Kingdom of God, which they hold
far above any plans of their own. (If you will allow me I
will just copy a sentence out of a note of Mr Kingsley's)
'But, like Dicken's (sic) barber, 'most folks draw the line
somewhere, we does at coal-heavers' – and we at
'household suffrage and free-trade'; and we at 'the triumph

101

of the intellect', and we, going further, at barricades, – but all stop somewhere, and begin to curse the poor enthusiast, who runs right ahead into the infinite unknown possible, and will stop at nothing short of – 'God's Kingdom come.' Now, my dear Mr Robson, I have written thus far, for you to read aloud (save me the trouble of writing) to Philip Carpenter; to whom I am also sending tracts &c & what I want you both to do is to get them circulated among working-men, – they, (the editors) want their advice & thoughts & practical sense. Can you help in circulating them by getting some sellers of working-men's papers to put them in their shops? Mr Solly of Cheltenham, – Oh, I don't know what I was going to say I have been interrupted – and now I must end.[24]

In *Sylvia's Lovers* Mrs Gaskell gave the name Robson as surname to Sylvia and her parents. Philip Carpenter was the Unitarian minister at Warrington who, at an anti-slavery meeting in the 1840s, had refused to sign a censure of the American Unitarians, on their lack of urgency in this matter, on the grounds that 'Unitarians as a body had not taken such a stand in the unpopular reforms of the day as to give them the right to lecture other people.'[25]

Though the Church of England and other religious bodies, particularly Unitarians, were engaged in much educational and philanthropic activity, it was only within the existing capitalist economic system, one which they unquestioningly accepted. The Christian Socialists, however, set out to change the system and the philosophical and religious ideas which supported it. In 1851, Maurice, whose 'tracts' Mrs Gaskell had been distributing, published Reasons for Co-operation, and in a sermon about the same time, said:

Either the Gospel declares what society is and what it is not, what binds men together, what separates them, or it has no significance at all. Either it shows how a uniting principle may be an effectual, living principle – how those tendencies which lead to separation may be overcome – or it fails to do what it professes ... if [the law of bearing one another's burdens] is not the law by which all things and all men are governed now, it never will be ... We see society dragged along by that mighty power of competition which wise men commend and declare to be the sovereign principle in the universe ... Oh! that we may come [to believe that he who] bore all our burdens ... can quicken us with His Spirit to bear each other's burdens.[26]

These ideas on the essential and natural unity of humanity and therefore of society and the necessity for thought and feeling to be followed promptly by social action would seem to be what had first drawn Mrs Gaskell to Maurice. Here was a kind of preaching that was not mere theological wrangling, but a high spirituality combined with the fearless exposition of a social Gospel without any accommodation to the rich and powerful. *Memorials of Two Sisters* throws considerable light on the subject. In 1849, Emily Winkworth to her sister Catherine:

> Ask Lily [Mrs Gaskell] about the breakfast at Monckton Milnes, and Professor Whewell and Guizot and Archdeacon Hare, and Maurice and Ludlow ... She had good long talks with them, and all about the right things and nothing else. They are now going to all the lowest 'People's Meetings', political, religious or otherwise; looking at all their publications in order to find out all they can of their real character and wants. They say that hitherto they have met with the highest principles, especially upon moral subjects, among the Socialists. This agrees with Will's [William Shaen's] account of the very few Socialists who belong to the Whittington Club.[27]

In 1853, Catherine to Emily: 'Have you begun [Mr Maurice's Theological Essays] yet? I have read a little and of course I like it. It puts me in mind of Bunsen in his way of looking at some things...' The following year, Maurice sent Mrs Gaskell a copy of his *Lectures on the Unity of the New Testament*, in the second chapter of which he had referred to 'the beautiful tale of Ruth ... which is, I think, as true to human experience as it is to the divinest morality.' In 1855, Emily to Susanna Winkworth regarding the opening of "Mr Maurice's College": 'How he does bring things to pass! When he spoke to Lily that Sunday – two months since perhaps – he was only beginning the plan; it has all grown up since then.'[28]

On the question of anti-slavery meetings in England, Mrs Gaskell had said: 'I don't call the use of words action; unless there is some definite, distinct, practical course of action logically proposed by those words ...'[29] And, from London in June 1853, she wrote of:

> two Mr Spottiswoodes ... young men much distinguished at
> Cambridge. .. printers (blue books, acts of Parlt. etc) ...
> [who] live in a large house in Farringdon St. and here they
> have all the 'printers devils' and apprentices etc to live with
> them. They have a room fitted up as a chapel at the top of
> the house, in which prayers are read and hymns sung to an
> organ played by one of the Mr Spottiswoodes every
> morning and night. They take their meals, their work, and
> pleasures all under the guidance of this Mr S. as if he were
> their elder brother. They have good engravings from all
> the great religious pictures (Christus Consolator, Christus
> Remunerator) etc etc, hung round their clean and cheerful
> eating room; they have a Christmas tree at Christmas – in
> short they are like a large and happy family – it seems such
> a beautiful life...[30]

Here, indeed, is a picture of an industrial community that could
hardly be in greater contrast to that described in *Mary Barton* and
North and South. In the latter, conditions had really improved very
little, especially for women, and the novel ends with the setting up of
a small co-operative venture, a factory canteen, very obviously based
on Christian Socialist ideas. In the same year that *North and South*
was published, Mrs Gaskell wrote to John Furnivall, another Christian
Socialist, a Cambridge graduate and founder of the Chaucer, Shelley
and Browning societies:

> I do talk and send my pamphlets to everybody I meet and I
> am constantly hearing and consequently often repeating
> instances of people who have owed more than they can
> speak to Mr Maurice's writing or Mr Maurice's self ...
> There is no doubt whatever, it seems to me of the fact –
> that Mr Maurice has more influence over the thoughtful
> portion of the English people than anyone else I know of...

This is in reply to a suggestion that she might send, contribute to,
or sign, a letter to the press protesting at Maurice's dismissal on
theological grounds from King's College though she had said in a
previous letter to Furnivall: 'I wish so, I might do something for Mr
Maurice', she was unable to face the publicity of writing to the press
in her own name. In a third letter on the subject she makes the

statement which is of the utmost importance to a full appreciation of Mrs Gaskell's fictional work:

> It is different when speaking as the character in a story or even as the author of a book. Do you think I cd say or write in any letter (except one that I was sure wd be regarded as private by some dear friend), what I have said both in M.B. & Ruth? It may seem strange and I can't account for it, – but it is so.[31]

Actually, it is not at all strange that Mrs Gaskell could "say" things in her stories that she could say in no other way. Her situation as wife of the minister of Cross Street Chapel, Manchester, was reason enough for the greater part of even her fiction being first published anonymously. But almost as soon as *Mary Barton* had made its impact, she had written, in November 1849, to Eliza Fox.

> I mean to copy you out some lines of my hero, Mr Kingsley; and I want to ask you and Mr Fox if you know anything of a co-operative tailors' shop established by Prof Maurice, Archdeacon Hare, Mr Ludlow, Kingsley (many clergymen) on Louis Blanc's principles, Jules Chevalier for a guide, in the New Rd or Tottenham Court Rd.[32]

and a few months later, again to Eliza Fox: 'One of my 'Me's' is, I do believe a true Christian (– only people call her a Socialist and communist) ...'[33] Two of her short stories, 'Christmas Storms' and 'Sunshine and The Sexton's Hero', appeared anonymously in the periodical, *The Christian Socialist*, in March and April, 1851.

Regarding the college for working-men in London, she wrote in 1858, again to Furnivall, who was responsible for the literature classes, giving the impression that it was she, assiduously working behind the scenes, who was the real driving force behind the founding of a similar college in Manchester later that year:

> I feel quite ashamed when I think that Mr Gaskell has left your letter about the London W.M.C. class so long unanswered ... from his having his time so completely occupied ... he is going to London next week Saturday, and if you will let him know at what hour your class is, I feel sure he will, if possible attend.[34]

In a further letter, she asks for the correct number of the house in Ormond Street where the college was conducted – it had formerly belonged to an aunt of Henry Solly. She had also again written to Furnivall, in a letter which Chapple and Pollard tentatively date June 1853, but which is almost certainly 1856 since this was the year when the women's classes were started in Red Lion Square and Mrs Gaskell was always careful to attend only lectures where other women were present:

> IF I do go to Mr Ruskin's class, I shan't have a minute to spare for anything else I'm afraid – I EXTREMELY want to go. But this week is in a mist. I fear I shan't be near Carlton Gardens [Baron Bunsen's residence].[35]

Not only Ruskin but Dante Gabriel Rossetti, as well as other members and associates of the Pre-Raphaelite Brotherhood, taught at the working-class college in London and Mrs Gaskell knew most of them and admired their work, frequently visiting Rossetti in his studio. On the other hand, A.L. Grieve, in *The Art of Dante Gabriel Rossetti* (1976) suggests that their work in the late 1840s and early 1850s may well have been influenced by the subject-matter and pictorial qualities of *Mary Barton*. She and Rossetti also shared a common friendship with the Howitts. In 1858, she again wrote to Furnivall, apologising for the fact that she could not return to him the four copies of *The Germ* which he had lent her, since she had put them away so carefully that she could not find them. *The Germ* was published by the Pre-Raphaelites and these are the only four issues that appeared.[36]

In a letter to Maurice, Henry Solly wrote at this period:

> I had been in the habit of regarding Working Men's Colleges as institutions simply for promoting the education of the more intelligent, skilled and steady artisans, whereas, deeply as I felt interest in these colleges, I doubted whether they were fitted for meeting the great Wants of the industrial classes as I have just described them (long hours of work, want of early education, miserably limited space and the incessant temptation of the public house and beer shop) but you have invariably based it [the London College] upon the idea of Brotherhood, and

106

> maintained that we must revert to the original fundamental
> conception of the College as a Society for mutual help in
> the great purpose of life – viz.: education – education of the
> whole man, physical, intellectual, moral and spiritual ...
> the permanent organisation of learners and teachers in a
> brotherly Fellowship for education and recreation,
> attracting the humblest working man by rational amusement
> and instruction in a form he can enjoy and inviting the
> more educated artisan by affording the higher culture which
> he requires; while at the same time all are expected to give
> as well as receive.

He also quotes a working-man as having said to him: "You must remember, we have masters all day and don't want them at night", and he comments: "a hint which reminds us not only that if we offer education, it must be given as by a friend, in an easy, pleasant, perhaps conversational way, but also that the management of the club must be left in the hands of the committee."[37]

As we have seen earlier, Mrs Gaskell took her own teaching at the Lower Mosley Street School in Manchester just as seriously, recounting in her letters exhausting schedules fitted in with her other duties and inviting the older girls regularly to her home. She also encouraged the twenty-two year old Meta not only to teach one of their own domestic servants every evening and French to 'a little orphan lad', but even to learn how 'to whip-a-top in order to show some boys at the Ragged School.' But, above all, she saw, with the rapid increase in the reading of novels and periodicals then taking place, that, in spite of statistics, reports, and even tracts, what was needed was information in a form that would touch the heart of the reading public as well as its head. And this was what she proceeded to do with her talent as a born story-teller and her unique personal experience, to write not only 'how it was' but also how it might be.

S.C. Carpenter, in his *Church and People 1789 to 1889* (1933), claimed that Christian Socialism was 'helped by the novels of Mrs Gaskell, in whom the group saw an ally.' With the advantage of *The Letters of Mrs Gaskell*, we can now see that the connection was much stronger than that. It is a pity that her letter to William Robson in 1850, entirely devoted to the matter of distributing Christian Socialist literature, should be broken off abruptly with: 'Mr Solly of Cheltenham, – Oh I don't know what I was going to say I have been so interrupted.' It was Solly who said that his ministry at Yeovil, in 1849, was 'knocked on the head' by his Chartist sympathies, the tradesman who was the financial mainstay of the congregation, having withdrawn the half of Solly's stipend for which he had made himself responsible. There is a similar case of Mr Benson's stipend in *Ruth*, published four years afterwards, though it is Benson himself who refuses Bradshaw's contribution because of Ruth.

Finally, it is perhaps worth noting that, in the second phase of Christian Socialism in the 1880s, the name of Henry Scott Holland is prominent. In 1861, Mrs Gaskell had, at the request of her cousin, Edward Holland, and because of her friendship with Canon Richson, an Anglican clergyman and educationalist in Manchester, found a curacy there, in Ancoats, one of the worst slum areas, for Frederick Holland, younger brother of her future son-in-law, Thurstan. In the following summer, she wrote from London:

> Fred Holland was in town for a week, staying at a Colonel Knox's in Belgrave Square, (curious contrast to his life in Ancoats) ... Thurstan [called] and left a request for us to go to Eton the next day, it being the annual day for boat races, fireworks ... we set out the next day with Thurstan [,] Fred & Scott Holland, – a young cousin still at Eton, for our squires...[38]

Henry Scott Holland was that 'young cousin'. It is pleasant to think that he may well have imbibed some of his Christian Socialist ideas from Mrs Gaskell.[39]

Brookfield Unitarian chapel, Knutsford.

Heathside, Gaskell Avenue, Elizabeth Gaskell's childhood home

Tabley house in the 1840s from an aquatint (photograph by F H Done)

Rev. William Turner, tutor to Elizabeth Gaskell, 1830-31

William Gaskell

Industrial Manchester in the first half of the 19th century.
Picture courtesy of Manchester Central Library (Local Studies Unit)

Elizabeth Gaskell, pastel by Richmond, 1851

Reproduction of one of the original watercolours of Brock for the novel
Cranford, *1853 — scene from chapter thirteen, 'Stopped Payment'*

Thornton and Margaret, illustration from North and South, *1855*

Knutsford in 1863 (the Misses Holland at the window)

CHAPTER 9
Ruskin and *Cousin Phillis*

Four articles on political economy by John Ruskin appeared in *The Cornhill* in 1860, articles so critical of the prevailing utilitarian theories of political economy that they caused a furore and had to be withdrawn by Thackeray, the editor and this series was completed in *Fraser's*. In 1862, they were published in a little book with the title *Unto This Last*, the title, of course, taken from the New Testament parable of the vineyard in which those workers who came last were paid the same as the rest by the master of the vineyard. The message of the book was summed up by Ruskin as follows:

> There is no wealth but life. Life including all its powers of love, of joy, and of admiration. That country is the richest which nourishes the greatest number of noble and happy human beings; that man is richest who, having perfected the functions of his own life to the utmost, has also the widest helpful influence, both personal and by means of his possessions, over the lives of others. (Essay IV, *Ad Valorem*, Penguin p.222)

The "Last" of the title are, of course, the working classes of England, the least fortunate members of society. In 1860 the fifth and last volume of Ruskin's *Modern Painters* had also appeared, a work that had taken him seventeen years to complete and turned him from an artist into a prophet and a sociologist. Many of the ideas in this last volume are also to be found in *Unto This Last*.

The name of Ruskin and his works, as well as those of the Pre-Raphaelite group of painters whose paintings he made acceptable to the British public, appear almost every year in Mrs Gaskell's letters after the publication of *Mary Barton*. In 1849, it is Ruskin's *Seven Lamps of Architecture* which she longs to read. In the next year both she and Charlotte Brontë like *Modern Painters* and again *The Seven Lamps* is mentioned. The same year she is 'very happy ... making flannel petticoats and reading *Modern painters*.' In 1851, on a London visit, she met Ruskin and his wife and, later in the same year, she again mentions *The Seven Lamps of Architecture* as an example of Meta, at the age of fourteen, being able to appreciate 'any book I am reading.' In 1854, regarding the mass of rumours surrounding Ruskin's separation from his wife, she writes a long letter on the former Effie Grey's background, for they had been at the same school, had many friends in common, and though she knows Mrs Ruskin's faults she also 'remember[s] her unusually trying position.' Of Ruskin himself she says: 'I can not bear to think of the dreadful hypocrisy if the man who wrote those books is a bad man.' A few weeks later she is planning to go 'out to Denmark Hill to call on Mrs Ruskin', Ruskin's mother. In 1855, to Furnivall, she is sorry that 'Mr Ruskin is not well', while to Eliot Norton, who was a close friend of Ruskin's, she writes in 1857: 'we were inspired by Lady H[atherton] (and partly you, and partly Mr Ruskin in the background) with a great desire to see Oxford.' Earlier that year she had also said to Norton, when they were both in Italy, that if she were confined on a desert island and had to choose one book by a living author she would have *Modern Painters*. In 1859, Ruskin called at Plymouth Grove when lecturing in Manchester and she writes, again to Norton: 'He was so "nice," simple and noble.'[1]

In 1860, she enquired of the publishers of *The Cornhill* if the author of one of the articles signed J.R. was John Ruskin.[2] The articles which became *Unto This Last* are signed J.R. and this article may well be the first of the series which was withdrawn from *The Cornhill*. In a brief undated note of hers, among others to Furnivall which are now in the British Museum and were almost certainly written in 1862, she writes cryptically:

> Thank you very much. I know well what to do with them, both according to the author's and the giver's wish. This is about as disagreeably short a note as I ever wrote; but I am 'dazed' with business of all kinds.[3]

Over the word "them" someone has written[12] "copies of Ruskin's tract." It may well be that the extremely cautious wording of the note – the fact that it was in 1862 that she was "dazed" with the work she undertook to alleviate the distress of the Lancashire cotton-workers – plus the controversial nature of Ruskin's essays, add up to a reasonable assumption that the tract was *Unto This Last*. The extreme smallness of the book and the fact that Ruskin frequently referred to it as his *'Political Economy'*, would make its description as a tract appropriate. To Mrs Gaskell's caution in her note and her continuing interest in and concern for Ruskin right up to the year of her death must be added a significant silence on the subject of *Unto This Last* in her letters as distinct from all his previous works. In a second similar note to Furnivall in the same collection she asks him for information about 'co-operative Stores' for George Melly of Liverpool "post-haste".[4]

In *Cousin Phillis*, written after Ruskin's articles and in the same periodical, it would seem that we have an example of her 'saying' things 'as the author of a book' which she claimed she could say in no other way but not as she had done in the controversial *Mary Barton* and *Ruth*. The social issue is now so deeply buried in the story as to give the impression that it was written to fulfil only a deep need in herself, or as in the sense of a parable – 'he that hath ears to hear, let him hear'. If we abstract the purely rural element from the story, we are left with a blue-print of Ruskin's ideal society as put forward in *Unto This Last*, the principles of which are just as valid in an industrial setting, and had indeed been set out in Mrs Gaskell's letter about the Spottiswoode's printing venture in 1853.

Mrs Gaskell had, to the seventeen year old Marianne at school in London, expressed her own doubts as to the limitations of Adam Smith's definition of wealth[5] and in the preface to *Unto This Last*, as we have seen already, Ruskin gives a very different interpretation. His aim was also to 'show that the acquisition of wealth [is] finally possible only under certain moral conditions of society'; to re-establish the principle of honesty among the 'captains' of industry, 'to ensure that every child is taught a trade' and 'habits of gentleness and justice' in Government schools, workshops established 'under Government regulation for the production and sale of every necessary of life, and for the exercise of every useful art. And that interfering no whit with private enterprise ... leaving both to do their best ...', that every man, woman, boy or girl should have security of employment, if out of work received at once into a Government establishment and paid 'a fixed rate of wages determinable every year' for 'such work as it appeared, on trial, they were fit for, [those] being found incapable of work through ignorance ... should be taught ... [or] through sickness, should be tended', while those 'objecting to work' should be given the less pleasant occupations; and, finally, 'for the old and destitute, comfort and home should be provided ... and it ought to be quite as natural and straight-forward a matter for a labourer to take his pension from his parish, as for a man in higher rank to take his pension from his country, because he has deserved well of his country.' Thus Ruskin, in this slim volume, little more than a pamphlet, anticipated all the principles of State intervention in industry, State education, the Welfare State, and the kind of mixed economy accepted by most Socialists of today.

Most Christian Socialists, however, were not democrats in the sense that we use the word today. Like Mrs Gaskell, Arnold had had a great respect for the aristocracy, though he chastised it when it failed in its responsibilities to the poor; and had seen the remedy for social ills in "those great means of blessing whose inefficiency had been the cause of so much evil, but whose destruction would render the matter utterly hopeless, the Aristocracy and the Christian Church."[6] The Socialist co-operatives were mainly initiated and funded by the enlightened aristocracy, the clergy, and professional men and women who, like Maurice, had been influenced by Arnold and Coleridge. 1848, however, 'the year of revolution', which was also a year of great ideological confusion, found Mrs Gaskell writing to Eliza Fox:

> I never can ascertain what I am in politics and veer about
> from the extreme Right, – no I don't think I ever go as
> far as the extreme Left ...[7]

She was familiar in 1849 with the names of Jules Chevalier, Louis Blanc, and Jean-Paul Richter, all left-wing European Socialists. When, eventually, she read Ruskin's *Unto This Last* she must have felt a lift of the heart, for what he wrote chimed in so well with her own long-held convictions:

> Among the delusions which at different times have
> possessed themselves of the minds of large masses of the
> human race, perhaps the most curious – certainly the least
> creditable – is the modern soi-disant science of political
> economy, based on the idea that an advantageous code of
> social action may be determined irrespectively of the
> influence of social affection. Of course, as in the instances
> of alchemy, astrology, witchcraft and other such popular
> creeds, political economy has a plausible idea at the root of
> it.   "The social affections", says the economist, "are
> accidental and disturbing elements in human nature; but

> avarice and the desire of progress are constant elements.
> Let us eliminate the inconstants, and, considering the
> human being merely as a covetous machine, examine by
> what laws of labour, purchase, and sale, the greatest
> accumulative result in wealth is obtainable." (Preface
> passim)

Ruskin then proceeded to demolish this argument by claiming that society despises any soldier, physician, lawyer, or clergyman who works only from the motive of avarice rather than honour, service, justice, and unselfishness and only secondly for an income and asks why then it should be considered acceptable, even normal and praiseworthy, for the merchants, i.e. all those concerned in the provision of the necessities of life, to work only for profit and not for any of the other qualities mentioned above.

The merchant's function in society, says Ruskin, is to provide for the nation, as the soldier's is to defend it, the pastor's to teach it, the physician's to keep it in health, and the lawyer's to enforce justice in it. He continues:

> because the production or obtaining of any commodity
> involves necessarily the agency of many lives and hands,
> the merchant becomes in the course of his business the
> master and governor of large masses of men in a more
> direct, though less confessed way than a military officer or
> pastor; so that on him falls in great part, the responsibility
> for the kind of life they lead; and it becomes his duty, not
> only to be always considering how to produce what he
> sells, in the purest and cheapest forms, but how to make the
> various employments involved in the production, or
> transference of it, most beneficial to the men employed in
> his office as governor of the men employed by him, the
> merchant or manufacturer is invested with a distinctly
> paternal authority and responsibility; ... as he would then
> treat his son, he is bound always to treat every one of the
> men under him. (Preface passim)

We have here a beam of light which illumines *Cousin Phillis*, for no more paternal a figure in English literature is to be found than in its farmer-parson, Mr Holman, his name presumably taken from that of Holman Hunt of the Pre-Raphaelite brotherhood whose religious

113

paintings Mrs Gaskell several times mentions in her letters.[7] Mr Holman's work as both farmer and dissenting minister is indivisible and it is around his double role of father of his family and of his employees that the story revolves. In the opening paragraph, the young narrator, Paul, an apprentice railway engineer, at once introducing a non-rural element into the story, refers to his father as 'a mechanic by trade [who] had some inventive genius ... and had devised several valuable improvements in railway machinery. He did not do this for profit, though, as was reasonable, what came in the natural course of things was acceptable.' But the tale is set in the country and Ebenezer Holman is the owner of Hope Farm which had come to him through his wife, Phillis Green, daughter of Thomas Green, and it is 'an estate of near upon fifty acres.' Mrs Gaskell's use of proper names is always transparent. Ebenezer Elliot, the anti-Corn Law Poet, had provided several of the quotations in *Mary Barton* and *North and South*, including, in the former, the very dramatic song, 'God Save the People'. Thomas was one of the early family names of the Hollands, Henry Green was the minister of Brook Street Chapel, Knutsford, and he and his daughters were her close and sympathetic friends. One of her Holland ancestors had, like Holman, acquired Sandlebridge Farm, her mother's home, by marriage.

Of Holman, the local inn-keeper says to Paul:

> Minister Holman knows what he's about as well as e'er a farmer in the neighbourhood. He gives up five days a week to his own work, and two to the Lord's; and it's difficult to say which he works hardest at. He spends Saturday and Sunday a-writing sermons and a-visiting his flock at Hornby; and at five o'clock on Monday morning he'll be guiding his plough on the Hope Farm yonder just as well as if he could neither read nor write.[8]

Even the name Hope Farm would seem to be symbolic. Though the character of Mr Holman has been accepted by some critics as a tribute to Mrs Gaskell's father, there is no record of the latter having continued to preach after his short and unsuccessful career in farming. Holman plainly owes much in character to Mrs Gaskell's grandfather, Samuel Holland of Sandlebridge, but again there is no evidence that he ever acted as a dissenting minister.

114

Paul's immediate superior, Holdsworth, the engineer who has been engaged to build a new railway nearby, asks his apprentice, after the youth has visited the Holmans, his relatives, "How do preaching and farming seem to get on together? If the minister turns out to be practical as well as reverend, I shall begin to respect him." And certainly Holman is worthy of respect. When Phillis says to Paul, on his first visit to the farm, that her father rises at three in the morning and Paul asks what he has to do at that hour, she replies:

> What has he not to do? He has his private exercise [spiritual devotions] in his room (which usually last an hour); he always rings the great bell which calls the men to milking; he rouses up Betty, our maid; as often as not he gives the horses their feed before the man is up – for Jem, who takes care of the horses, is an old man; and father is loath to disturb him; he looks at the calves, and the shoulders, heels, traces, chaff, and corn before the horses go afield; he has often to whip-cord the plough whips; he sees the hogs fed; he looks into the swill-tubs, and writes his orders for what is wanted for food for man and beast; yes, and for fuel too. And then, if he has a bit of time to spare, he comes and reads with me – but only English; we keep Latin for the evenings (mainly Virgil and Horace), that we may have time to enjoy it; and then he calls in the men to breakfast, and cuts the boys' bread and cheese; and sees their wooden bottles filled and sends them off to their work; and by this time it is half past six, and we have our breakfast.[9]

When Paul and Phillis cross the fields to find Mr Holman,

> "There is father," she exclaimed, pointing out ... a man in his shirt sleeves, taller by the head than the other two with whom he was working ... [He] looked, thought Paul, like a very powerful labourer, and had none of the precise demureness of appearance... characteristic of a minister... He, like his daughter, was largely made, and of a fair, ruddy complexion ... His hair... grizzled. Yet his grey hairs betokened no failure in strength. I never saw a more powerful man – deep chest, lean flanks, well-planted head.[10]

Holman had been working with his men in one of the fields but they were finished for the day and, as Phillis and her cousin entered the field, he briefly welcomed them and then gave his fellow-labourers some last-minute instructions:

> "Ned Hall, there ought to be a water-furrow across this land ... and thou and I must fall to, come next Monday... and there's old Jem's cottage wants a bit of thatch; you can do that job tomorrow while I am busy." Then, suddenly changing the tone of his deep voice to an odd suggestion of chapels and preachers, he added, "Now, I will give out the psalm, 'Come all harmonious tongues,' to be sung to 'Mount Ephraim' tune." He lifted his spade in his hand and began to beat time with it; the two labourers seemed to know both words and music... and so did Phillis: her rich voice followed her father's as he set the tune; and the men came in with more uncertainty, but still harmoniously ... There we five stood bare-headed, excepting Phillis, in the tawny stubble-field ... Somehow, I think that if I had known the words [recalls the story-teller, Paul] and could have sung, my throat would have been choked by the feeling of the unaccustomed scene. The hymn was ended, and the men had drawn off before I could stir. I saw the minister beginning to put on his coat, and looking at me with friendly inspection in his gaze, before I could rouse myself. "I dare say you railway gentlemen don't wind up the day with singing a psalm together" said he, "but it is not a bad practice ..."[11]

After a while, Paul noticed that the minister had taken his daughter's hand as they went along towards their home. Crossing a lane, they came upon a couple of children crying over a broken pitcher of milk, for they feared a whipping from their mother. The minister at once promised them a can with a lid, a further supply of milk, and sent Phillis home with them to tell their mother what had happened and to give her the information that he had 'the best birch-rod in the parish', so that if she ever thought her children wanted a 'flogging' she must bring them to him and, if he thought they deserved it, he would 'give it them better than she could.' To Paul, he added as they entered the farm-yard, "Their mother ... is a bit of a vixen and apt to punish her children without rhyme or reason, and I try to keep the parish rod as well as the parish bull."[12]

In the evening at the farm-house, Holman makes himself 'reverend' by putting on a voluminous white muslin neckcloth. There are volumes of Matthew Henry's Bible (a Calvinistic commentary) on a table in the parlour, but a "beaupot of flowers" has been placed upon them, while in the 'house-place' on a small shelf, obviously for regular reading, are Virgil, Caesar, and a Greek grammar. In the minister's own small room, "part study, part counting-house", there are other old divinity books as well as books on farriery and farming, a box of carpenter's tools on the floor, and some manuscripts in short hand on the desk. Paul had been invited into this sanctum and the minister says: "It's not many a one I would bring in here. But I was reading a book ... that was left here by mistake one day; I had subscribed to Brother Robinson's sermons [one of the other ministers in the district]; and I was glad to see this instead of them, for sermons, though they're ... well, never mind." The book he sought was one on advanced mechanics of which he understood the mathematics but not some of the technical terms and he had expressed the hope that Paul could help him with these. While in this little room, Paul's eye catches sight of some papers 'stuck against the white-washed walls with wafers, nails, pins, anything that came readiest to hand.' He reads one of them. 'At first it seemed a kind of weekly diary; but then he saw that the seven days were portioned out for special prayers and intercessions; Monday for his family, Tuesday for enemies, Wednesday for the Independent Churches.' Though Mrs Gaskell makes Mr Holman an Independent minister, perhaps again in the interests of anonymity, Holman is far more characteristic of Unitarianism in his intellectualism and dislike of Calvinism and he is strongly, throughout the story, contrasted with the other ministers. The 'diary' continues. 'Thursday for all other churches, Friday for persons afflicted, Saturday for his own soul, Sunday for all wanderers and sinners that they might be brought home to the fold.'

At supper, which the family has in the 'house-place', the door to the kitchen, where the farm-workers and servants had their meals, is open and all stand up in both rooms while the minister says grace. After Paul and the family have helped themselves, the dish is taken to the kitchen where the servants are waiting for their share and though the door is then shut the minister's wife remarks that this is only because they have a guest and that normally the minister keeps the door open and talks to the 'men and maids' as much as to his daughter and herself. Holman explains: "it brings us all together like a household just before we meet as a household in prayer." Again this household is strongly contrasted with the family prayer-meeting of another Independent minister described at the beginning of the story. Here, at Hope Farm, all kneel with the minister in 'a long impromptu evening prayer' in which were long pauses for thought, waiting to see if there was anything else Mr Holman wished to lay before the Lord, to use his expression, before he concluded with the blessing. But he also prayed for the cattle and "live creatures". At the conclusion of the prayer:

> the minister, still kneeling in their midst, but with his eyes wide open, spoke to the elder man, "John, didst thou see that Daisy had her warm mash tonight; for we must not neglect the means, John – two quarts of gruel, a spoonful of ginger, and a gill of beer – the poor beast needs it, and I fear it slipped out of my mind to tell thee; and here was I asking a blessing and neglecting the means, which is a mockery ..."[13]

One day, however, the minister asks his wife if they cannot change their bedroom for another, since he has cut himself so often shaving lately through irritation at seeing one of his workers in the yard, Timothy Cooper, whom his wife calls 'a downright lazy tyke' though Holman says he is but a 'half-wit', with a wife and children dependent on him. "More shame for him" retorts the minister's wife. Holman replies:

> "But that is past change. And if I turn him off, no one else will take him on. Yet I cannot help watching him of a morning as he goes sauntering about his work in the yard; and I watch, and I watch, till the old Adam rises strong within me at his lazy ways, and some day, I am afraid, I shall go down and send him about his business ... and then his wife and children will starve. I wish we could move to the grey room."[14]

Sadness and trial come to this gentle little community in the shape of Holdsworth, the intruder from the larger world of railroads and overseas business. At the end of an idyllic summer, having disturbed Phillis's peace of mind by his obvious but undeclared love, he suddenly departs, without warning, to build a railway in Canada, saying to Paul: "You see the salary they offer me is large; and beside that, this experience will give me a name which will entitle me to expect a still larger in any future undertaking." Though the 'harvest of the first fruits' comes that year 'more bounteous than usual, and there was plenty all round in which the humblest labourer was made to share', Phillis fades and sickens. In his anxiety about her, the minister falls into the temptation he had feared, that of sacking Timothy Cooper after seeing him kill, by a stupid mistake, a tree loaded with apples and though Timothy was but a 'half-wit' and had a wife and child, and though Holman had 'laid it before the Lord and striven to bear with him...,' he could stand it no longer; Cooper had 'notice to find another place', while Phillis collapses with a brain-fever brought on by grief at Holdsworth's departure, and for a long time she hovers on the edge of death. Paul, though only a visitor, stays on because he feels he is needed in the house:

> Every person (I had almost said every creature, for all the dumb beasts seemed to know and love Phillis) about the place went grieving and sad. They did their work ... in fulfilment of the trust reposed in them by the minister. For the day Phillis had been taken ill, he had called all the men employed on the farm into the empty barn; and there he had entreated their prayers for his only child; and then and there he had told them of his present incapacity for thought about anything in this world but his little daughter, lying nigh unto death, and he had asked them to go on with their daily labours as best they could, without his direction. So, as I say, these honest men did their work to the best of their ability, but they slouched along with sad and careful faces, coming one by one in the dim mornings to ask news of the sorrow that over-shadowed the house ... But, poor fellows, they were hardly fit to be trusted with hasty messages, and here my [Paul's] poor services came in.[15]

During this long weary time, 'all the neighbours hung about the place daily till they could learn from some out-comer how Phillis Holman was. But they knew better than to come up to the house, for the August weather was so hot that every door and window was kept open and the least sound penetrated all through.' Even the cocks and hens were driven into the barn by Betty, the old servant, in an effort to silence their 'crowing and clacking'. At last Phillis takes a turn for the better and is sleeping. Paul walks down that same evening to the bridge 'where the lane to Hope Farm joined another road to Hornby.' Here he finds Timothy Cooper, the 'half-wit,' sitting on the edge of the bridge. Cooper makes no sign of recognition and Paul thinks him 'sullen at being dismissed'. However, he feels 'it would be a relief to talk a little with someone' and sits down beside the man, who was yawning wearily. With patient questioning, Paul finds that Cooper has been sitting on the bridge all day and is now about to go home after having turned all the carts away from the lane that passed the farm on their way to Hornby market, which everyone else had forgotten was on that particular day, such carts 'as might ha' wakened yon wench.'

Paul returns to the house to find that Phillis had now awakened naturally and spoken a few words. 'The rest of the household were summoned to evening prayer for the first time for many days. It was a return to the habits of health and happiness.' Paul tells the minister as soon as he can about Cooper's unsolicited watch on the bridge during that long summer day. "God forgive me" said Holman, "I have been too proud in my own conceit. The first steps I take out of this house shall be to Cooper's cottage." Paul comments: "I need hardly say that Timothy was reinstated in his place on the farm; and I have often since admired the patience with which his master tried to teach him how to do the easy work which was henceforward carefully adjusted to his capacity."[16]

Again we hear distinct echoes of *Unto This Last*. But it would be crass indeed to trace in every detail the ways in which this literary masterpiece echoes, illustrates, and extends the ideas of *Unto This Last* and of Christian Socialism, from the Mr Spottiswoodes' printing community, so like a 'large and happy family', Solly's education of 'the whole man', Ruskin's concern for the vulnerable, the aged, the right of the less able members of society to make what contribution they can, and all of these under the paternal care of an employer who does not work for money alone but shares what wealth he has, in the widest sense of the word, with those for whom he considers himself morally responsible. Marx and Engels had written contemptuously of what they called 'feudal socialism' in their *Communist Manifesto* in

1848, but one feels that Coleridge, who had himself hoped to form an ideal community in America, would have approved of Hope Farm and Ruskin have felt that 'the social affections' had indeed been fully realised there.

There is little doubt that Mrs Gaskell's heart was not in large scale capitalism even when it was beginning to prosper, as it was in the 1860s, but at Hope Farm, where spiritual values formed the basis of both social and economic relationships and the work-unit was small enough for individual needs to be recognised and provided for. No one could ever accuse Mrs Gaskell of 'asking a blessing and neglecting the means which is a mockery', or, in more prosaic terms, claiming to accept the principles of Christianity but ignoring its social demands. *Cousin Phillis* stands, of course, in its own right as a literary masterpiece, an English classic, and there are also other aspects of it to which I shall return. Here, I have been concerned to demonstrate Mrs Gaskell's continuing loyalty to the cause of Christian Socialism at a time when it was flagging. Mrs Gaskell was fond of her parables, of 'speaking as the character'; "what I have said in MB & Ruth."

I cannot close this chapter without repeating what I have quoted earlier, the passage in *Unto This Last* so vividly exemplified in *Cousin Phillis:*

> There is no wealth but life. Life including all its powers of love, of joy and of admiration. That country is the richest which nourishes the greatest number of noble and happy human beings; that man is richest who, having perfected the functions of his own life to the utmost, has also the widest helpful influence, with personal and by means of his possessions, over the lives of others.

CHAPTER 10
Cranford and the weapon of laughter

Cranford first appeared as a series of 'papers' in *Household Words* from 1851 until 1853 when these episodes in the life of a small country town were gathered together in a volume, with some minor changes to give the work a greater unity and chronological consistency. It sold in huge numbers and in 1864 there appeared an illustrated edition, the first of many such which have continued almost up to the present, as well as dramatised versions both for stage and television, an indication of its appeal to continuing generations.

The 1864 edition coincided with the revival of the ancient May Day celebrations in Knutsford[1] and these may well have been inspired by the great popularity of *Cranford*. In 1859, Rev Henry Green, in his *Knutsford, Its Traditions and History*, had stated categorically that Cranford was Knutsford. Many curious visitors must have been attracted to the town and this may well have increased the pride of the local inhabitants and resulted in a desire to give some visible embodiment to its history and traditions. Whether the 1864 procession included them we do not know, but within living memory it has included them and they are so listed in the official programme for 1975: 'Victorian Lady in Sedan Chair,' 'Cranford Ladies in Phaeton' and 'Cranford Ladies and Gentlemen'. The sedan chair is the same one which played a prominent part in the story of *Cranford*. In 1891, half a century after the first publication of *Cranford*, Lady Ritchie, daughter of Thackeray, wrote in her preface to a new edition that she did not think of *Cranford* as a story at all but as 'a visionary country home' which she had visited at intervals in spirit all her life for 'refreshment and change of scene.' Mrs Gaskell herself wrote to John Ruskin about *Cranford*: 'I am so much pleased you like it. It is the only one of my books that I can read again; ... And it is true too...'[2] Comparing the book with Jane Austen's works, Lady Ritchie thought that, though the latter's heroines might be younger in age there was more "real feeling" in the "few signs of what once was, than all the Misses Bennetts' youthful romances put together" and that *Cranford* itself, though further removed from the world, was more attuned to its interests than any of the similar small rural communities of Jane Austen. Describing a conducted tour of Knutsford in her introduction to the 1891 edition with a "kind Interpreter", probably Meta Gaskell since she and her sister had long been friends of the Gaskell daughters, she writes of Knutford's oak beams and solid brick walls, the slanting gables and lattices which gave the High Street 'the look of a mediaeval street', the narrow courts and passages, 'the aristocratic quarter' where were the old houses with their walled gardens, one of these passages running, as it still does, right through the Royal George Hotel. In this 'old ancient place', as a shop-woman calls it, all the houses had gardens with flowers in abundance where, even though it was autumn, everything was swept and tidy. In the Royal George, Lady Ritchie describes a beautiful oak stair-case, panelling and banisters, old oak settles and cupboards, Chippendale cabinets and old china. But the modest little houses were also full of 'worthy things', and the old Unitarian chapel is described as beautiful with its 'ivy-clad walls and latticed windows'.

Nearly twenty years earlier, Mary Sybilla Holland, the mother of Bernard Holland, the historian of the family, was regularly visiting Mrs Gaskell's cousins, Mary and Lucy Holland, who were still living in extreme old age at the house Mrs Gaskell made famous in *Wives and Daughters* as the home of Molly Gibson. In May 1876, Mrs Holland described Knutsford in one of her letters, the cobbled lanes edged with banks of primroses, the broad and beautifully kept roads bordered with great beeches.

> The cottages look like small home-steads, and many of the labourers keep a cow in the little croft which is nearly always added to the cottage. The hedges of the crofts and gardens are full of plum and damson trees in full bloom. The older women wear short petticoats, wooden soles or clogs, a little plaid shawl pinned across, and a large white frilled cap They stand knitting at their garden gates, and laugh pleasantly when you speak to them, answering with a loud voice and with the strong clipped accent of the country. I do so love this loud voice which gives one the feeling of independence ...[3]

Of Mrs Gaskell herself, Lady Ritchie wrote that, though she 'loved country things and farming things' and had 'a special gift' for training domestic servants, she also 'read Adam Smith and studied Social Politics', and it was 'because she had written *Mary Barton* [that] some deeper echoes reach us in Cranford than are to be found in any of Jane Austen's books.' In our own time, when *Cranford* is often dismissed for its superficial qualities of quaintness and sentimentality, Barbara Hardy, too, has called it 'a story of unguessed at integrity [in which] what looks like insipidity, or mere charm turns out to rebuke us and teaches us not to be too easily charmed by quaintness, not to pity precipitately what we may eventually have to admire ... the kind of delicacy which reveals strength ... its apparent charm and sweetness are as profound and as deceptive as Miss Matty's...'[4] and, finally, to return once more to Lady Ritchie, *Cranford* 'is everywhere, where people have individuality and kindliness and where oddities are tolerated, nay, greatly loved for the sake of individuals.'

If *Cranford* is primarily a loving and penetrating evocation of Knutsford both as fact and as a symbol of a rural community, so Drumble, the 'great noisy manufacturing town' linked to it by the new railway, is also as certainly Manchester, as both fact and symbol of the industrial city, where individualism of a very different kind was practised but the benefits of which were felt only by the fortunate few. Here, 'the Mechanical age', so graphically described by Carlyle in 1829, had taken over: 'men are grown mechanical in head and in heart, as well as in hand.' Crabb Robinson, too, on a visit to Manchester about 1821 had seen, in "The Old Church", the baptism of fifty-five children about which he had written in his diary with his usual dry humour:

> I heard a strange noise which I should elsewhere have mistaken for the bleating of lambs. Going to the spot, a distant aisle, I found two rows of women in files, each with a babe in her arms. The Minister went down the line sprinkling each infant as he went. I suppose the efficiency of the sprinkling – I mean the fact that water did touch – was evidenced by a distinct squeal from each. Words were muttered by the priest in his course but one prayer served for all. This I thought to be christening by wholesale and I could not repress the irreverent thought that, being in the metropolis of manufactures, the aid of steam or machinery might be called in.

In *Cranford*, however, it is not men and machines but the ladies who are in charge and in its very first words we are told that 'all the holders of houses above a certain rent are women.' Men, in this little circle, are rare and where they do exist their prolonged absence is accounted for as being with their ships, regiments or 'closely engaged in business all the week in the great neighbouring commercial town of Drumble.' In *Cranford*, in a very skilful way, Mrs Gaskell, as so often elsewhere in her work, merges the past with the present and, though writing of her youth (the narrator of the story, Mary Smith, is, like Margaret Hale, generally agreed to be the young Mrs Gaskell herself), we have all the appurtenances of pre-Victorian England, pattens, gigots (a type of petticoat) and the sedan chair, all co-existing with the railway which did not come to Knutsford till 1862. John McVeagh in his *Elizabeth Gaskell* (1970) has called Cranford "the last outpost of a departed civilisation ... under the pressure of a new age."

The women appear to run the place quite satisfactorily for themselves with minimal help from the men, who are 'so in the way in the house'. With the help of their neat maidservants they keep house and garden admirably, even against invasion by small boys and geese, decide 'questions of literature and politics [without] unnecessary reasons or arguments', are full of 'kindness (somewhat dictatorial) to the poor, and real tender good offices to each other whenever they are in distress', each with 'her own individuality, not to say eccentricity, pretty strongly developed [yet] good will reigns among them to a considerable degree', with 'only an occasional little quarrel [of] a few peppery words and angry jerks of the head; just enough to prevent the even tenor of their lives from becoming too flat.' Very independent in dress, they are no slaves to fashion, but 'the material of their clothes is, in general, good and plain.'

Though the touch is very light, and this has consequently led to a lack of appreciation of the qualities referred to by Professor Hardy, the story paints the picture of a society which is diametrically opposed to that depicted in *Mary Barton, North and South*, and *Ruth*. It is rural rather than industrial; small rather than large; one in which women are independent, each of them her 'own woman' as Charlotte Brontë put this matter in a letter to Mrs Gaskell. They dress to please themselves and practise an 'elegant economy', independent of men who tend to look on the dress of their women folk, the furnishing of their homes, and their entertaining as opportunities for what we call today conspicuous consumption. *Cranford* is a place "where everybody knows us" rather than one where people could rub shoulders in the streets all day with strangers as in Manchester. *Cranford* is also a place where the aristocrats have a "kindness" to the poor and "tender good offices" to one another rather than one where the rich are indifferent to or ignorant of the distress of the poor and in fierce competition with one another. It is, of course, 'elegant economy', not 'Political Economy', which dominates *Cranford* and with which it has become indelibly associated. Though the economies, as well as the foibles and small snobberies of the group of elderly ladies who make up the cast of this delicate comedy, are described with wit, humour, and even a certain irony, there are serious undercurrents. Though in *Cranford* 'we none of us spoke of money, because the subject savoured of commerce and trade', in fact, incomes were very small indeed when compared with those of people of similar social standing in Drumble and, says Mrs Gaskell rather tartly,

> There were one or two consequences arising from this general but unacknowledged poverty and this very much acknowledged gentility ... which might be introduced into many circles of society to their great improvement ... it was considered vulgar [for example] to give anything expensive, in the way of eatables or drinkables, at the evening entertainments.

In 'Company Manners', an article on the art of entertaining, written for *Household Words* in May 1854, after the completion of *Cranford*, she describes a visit 'at a very respectable tradesman's house' which lasted from half-past four until after supper at which no entertainment at all was offered except food and drink and which consisted of wine, cake, oranges, almonds, raisins, tea, coffee, bread of all kinds, cold fowl, tongue, ham, potted meats, more cake and wine, hot jugged hare, hot roast turkey, hot boiled ham, hot apple tart and hot toasted cheese. "No wonder I am old before my time", was her conclusion.[5]

Such a meal would indeed have been considered unspeakably vulgar in *Cranford*, where 'fragments and small opportunities' for kindness were to be seen in rose-leaves gathered for a pot-pourri to give to someone without a garden and lavender 'to strew the drawers of some town dweller, or to burn in the chamber of some invalid. Things that many would despise and actions which it seemed scarcely

126

worth while to perform were all attended to in *Cranford*.' Even Captain Brown, the 'vulgar' newcomer in this community of 'Amazons', 'was not above saving the little maid-servant's labours in every way – knowing, most likely, that his [invalid] daughter's illness made the place a hard one.' And, though the formidable Miss Deborah Jenkyns, elder daughter of the deceased rector, deemed Captain Brown's loud voice and preference for Dickens rather than Dr Johnson, vulgar, she yet 'stuck an apple full of cloves to be heated and smell pleasantly' in his sick daughter's room and when he is killed on the railway line, when reading *Pickwick Papers*, and Miss Brown is dying, Miss Jenkyns is the first to visit her and support the nurse, the younger and prettier Miss Jessie Brown.

It is in chapter three of *Cranford* that we visit Woodley, one of the recognisable pictures of Sandlebridge Farm and Thomas Holbrook, its owner, another portrait of Samuel Holland, Mrs Gaskell's grandfather. The old yeoman farmer, built up from her own childish recollections – those of her "old aunts and uncles", her elderly cousins Mary and Lucy Holland, her uncle, Dr Peter Holland, and his son and her cousin, Sir Henry Holland, who recorded his memories of Samuel in his *Recollections of Past Life* (1872), presents an attractive and significant figure. We must remember, yet again, that there was a Thomas Holland, Earl of Kent in Plantagenet times, while Holbrook was a Gaskell name.[6] Thomas Holbrook had been a suitor of Miss Matilda Jenkins, Miss Debórah's younger sister, in their youth, but the match had been prevented by the rector under pressure from Miss Debórah on the grounds of his 'social inferiority.' In his old age he still lived on his small estate four or five miles from Cranford but was very much part of the Cranford community, being the cousin of Miss Pole, one of the Cranford ladies, a prosperous retired dress-maker:

> his property was not large enough to entitle him to rank higher than a yeoman, or rather with something of the 'pride that apes humility' he had refused to push himself on, as so many of his class had done, into the ranks of squires. He would not allow himself to be called Thomas Holbrook Esq; he even sent back letters with this address, telling the postmistress at Cranford that his name was Mr Thomas Holbrook, yeoman... He despised every refinement which had not its root deep down in humanity... He spoke the dialect of the country in perfection and

constantly used it in conversation, though Miss Pole said
that he read aloud 'more beautifully and with more feeling
than anyone she had ever heard, except the rector.'

Mary Smith, the story-teller, and Miss Matty, with Miss Pole,
visit Woodley:

> The house stood among fields; and there was an old
> fashioned garden where roses and currant bushes touched
> each other, and where the feathery asparagus formed a
> pretty back-ground to the pinks and gilly-flowers; there was
> no drive up to the door. We got out at a little gate, and
> walked up a straight box-edged path.

Showing Mary round his garden and farm, Mr Holbrook surprised
her

> by repeating apt and beautiful quotations from the poets,
> ranging easily from Shakespeare and George Herbert to those
> of our own day. He did this as naturally as if he were
> thinking aloud, and their true and beautiful words were the
> best expression he could find for what he was thinking or
> feeling. To be sure he called Byron 'my lord Byrron' and
> pronounced the name of Goethe strictly in accordance with
> the English letters – 'As Goethe says, "Ye ever-verdant
> palaces" etc. Altogether, I never met with a man before or
> since, who had spent so long a life in a secluded and not
> impressive country, with ever-increasing delight in the daily
> and yearly change of season and beauty.

Sir Henry Holland records in his *Recollections* that it was said of
his grandfather that he 'could never be got to complain of the change
or distemperature of the seasons.'

Dinner at Woodley was eaten in a kitchen furnished with oak-
dressers and cupboards, a room 'which might have easily been made
into a handsome dark oak dining-parlour', and the visitors, after their
homely meal of duck and green peas, sat, not in the parlour which
was never used, but in 'a pretty sitting-room [which Mr Holbrook
called] the counting house, since he paid his labourers their wages at
the great desk near the door.' This room, as also in *Cousin Phillis,*
was full of books: 'They lay on the ground, they covered the walls,

they strewed the table' – so different from the Thornton's drawing room of *North and South* where a few books were set out for show.

In a second walk round the farm, this time accompanied only by Mary, and occasioned by the fact that 'he was obliged to talk to his men', Mary again describes Mr Holbrook:

> [he] strode along, either wholly forgetting my existence, or soothed into silence by his pipe – and yet it was not silence exactly. He walked before me with a stooping gait, his hands clasped behind him and, as some tree or cloud, or glimpse of distant upland pastures, struck him, he quoted poetry to himself, saying it out loud in a grand sonorous voice, with just the right emphasis that true feeling and appreciation give. We came upon an old cedar tree, which stood at one end of the house – "The cedar spreads his dark green layers of shade," Capital term – "layers." Wonderful man ... when I saw the review of his poems in Blackwood, I set off ... and walked seven miles ... and ordered them ... what colour are ash buds in March ... Black: they are yes – black, madam ... [Back at the farm-house] nothing would serve him but he must read us the poems he had been speaking of, which included Locksley Hall...[7]

But there are yet more surprises in Mr Holbrook. Calling on the Misses Jenkyns and bringing Miss Matty a book of poems she had liked, he announced a forthcoming visit to Paris, because he said, "I've never been there, and always had a wish to go; and I think if I don't go soon, I mayn't go at all; so as soon as the hay is got in I shall go, before harvest time." When we next hear of the old man, he has been to Paris and returned. But the expedition has cost him all his strength. He can no longer go round his fields but sits 'with his hands on his knees in the counting-house, not reading or anything, but only saying what a wonderful city Paris was!' Then came the news that Thomas Holbrook was dead and Miss Matty took to wearing a sort of widow's cap, 'something like that style' as she said to the little milliner of *Cranford*.

Though a "kindly town", as Mrs Gaskell had called Knutsford, *Cranford* is a society in which there are minute gradations of class of which everyone is aware and observant. If a social rule is broken, as occasionally it is for social convenience, in the case, for example, of the acceptance of Miss Pole, the prosperous retired dressmaker, into the highest 'echelon' of *Cranford* society, the reason is understood and appreciated. Everyone has his or her own place, knows it, and on the whole keeps to it. Though the Honourable Mrs Jamieson is a snob and socially ambitious, she is balanced by Lady Glenmire, 'a bright little woman', who, though a peeress, startles *Cranford* when she first comes there with her homely ways and causes Miss Pole to exclaim: 'My dear, ten pounds would have purchased every stitch she had on – lace and all!' But, though *Cranford* society is aware and observant of class, it is also aware and observant of the needs of individuals of every class. Not only the elderly aristocrats but servants, too, have rights, feelings, and even eccentricities that must be respected and allowed for. Even the Honourable Mrs Jamieson has a manservant of great dignity who would 'always ignore the fact of there being a back-door to any house' when delivering a message and 'did not like to be hurried' in his duty of preparing tea, so that the ladies had to wait on his pleasure. The rector is another eccentric, an old bachelor who fancies that all the females in *Cranford* are chasing him and finds 'all his interests among the poor and helpless.' It is he who treats the 'National School' boys to seats at a conjuring performance put on by a Signor Brunoni, whose appearance in the district at the same time as a couple of burglaries sparks off all the delicious nonsense of the ladies' schemes to protect their lives and property. Signor Brunoni, though he had an Italian name, spoke like a Frenchman and though he wore a turban like a Turk, one of the ladies had seen a print of Madame de Staël with a turban on, showing clearly that the French, as well as the Turks, wore turbans! There could be no doubt that Signor Brunoni was both a burglar and a French spy 'come to discover the weak and undefended places of England...'

But Signor Brunoni is eventually found to be plain Samuel Brown, with an English wife and child. He is discovered some time after the performance lying sick and in debt in lodgings. The *Cranford* ladies rally to the support of these total strangers. Lady Glenmire gets the doctor; Miss Pole makes herself responsible for finding and paying the rent of new lodgings; Miss Matty sends the famous sedan-chair to carry the sick man to them and later covers a penny-ball (which she had lately been rolling under her bed every night to make sure no burglar was there), with 'gay coloured worsted in rainbow stripes' as a play-thing for the conjuror's 'little care-worn child'; while Mrs

Forrester, a lady of very ancient ancestry, makes her famous bread jelly for the sick man, 'her highest mark of favour'. Of the latter, Mrs Gaskell asks, half-laughing and half-serious: 'Who says that the aristocracy are proud? Here was a lady, by birth a Tyrrell and descended from the great Sir Walter that shot King Rufus, and in whose veins ran the blood of him who murdered the little princes in the Tower, going every day to see what dainty dish she could prepare for Samuel Brown, a mountebank.' And then, quite seriously: 'But indeed it was wonderful to see what kind feelings were called out by the poor man's coming amongst us.'

However, it is in the matter of Miss Matty's losing almost the whole of her small income that we see the spirit of *Cranford* most vividly in action. Miss Matty goes to the principal shop in the little town to see the Spring fashions and purchase the material for a new gown. She shares the counter, it being market day, with a farmer who is choosing a new shawl for his wife. To his dismay, his five-pound note is refused by the shop-man on the grounds that the bank has failed[8] and he is asked for cash or a note of another bank, neither of which he has.

Bewildered and indignant, the farmer says: "It's hard upon a poor man ... as earns every farthing with the sweat of his brow ... You must take back your shawl ... yon figs for the little ones – I promised them to 'em – I'll take them; but the 'bacco, and the other things ..." Miss Matty hears the conversation and the name of the bank in which she is a shareholder and from which she had only that morning received a 'very civil invitation ... to attend an important meeting to be held in Drumble.' Innocent Miss Matty had thought it 'very attentive of them to remember' her and even now she does not understand why the farmer's note is useless. The shop-man tries to explain the matter to her, but she is not really interested in explanations or 'reasons' and gently cuts him off:

> Perhaps so ... But I do not pretend to understand business; I only know that if it's going to fall, and if honest people are going to lose their money because they have taken our notes – I can't explain myself ... only I would rather exchange my gold for the note, if you please.

If the matter is cleared up it will only mean waiting a few days for her new gown, but if not:

> Why, then it will only have been common honesty in me,
> as a shareholder, to have given this good man the money. I
> am quite clear about it in my own mind...

The farmer accepts her gold for his note, reluctantly but gratefully, for 'five pounds is a deal of money to a man with a family.'

Miss Matty, however, as we soon learn, has lost the whole of her income but for a few pounds a year and she must give notice to her faithful servant, Martha. But Martha, too, though only a servant, also has a mind of her own and is a "good manager". She refuses to leave her frail little mistress, insists on working for nothing, even cooks dishes paid for out of her own money. When 'reasoned' with, her answer rings out:

> I'll not listen to reason ... Reason always means what
> someone else has got to say. Now I think that what I've
> got to say is good enough reason; but reason or not ... I've
> money in the Savings Bank[9] and I've a good stock of
> clothes and I'm not going to leave Miss Matty. No, not if
> she gives me warning every hour of the day!

Her next bit of management is to bully her 'follower' into agreeing to marry her "off-hand" (i.e. at once), but, of course, with Miss Matty's permission. The episode in which she literally pushes the puzzled fellow into Miss Matty's presence, ending up with a breathless "and, please Ma'am, we want to take a lodger – one quiet lodger, to make ends meet...," is perhaps the most comic and yet moving scene in the book.

But what occupation can Miss Matty take up to earn even the minute income that is essential? Her education has been so scanty and unsuitable as to make teaching, the only occupation open to a lady, impossible. Miss Matty's friends have not been idle. Miss Pole, hearing that Miss Matty had 'lost all her fortune', called a meeting of the little circle of ladies with all the precautions of a secret society and to which she reports: "one and all of us have agreed that while we have a superfluity, it is not only a duty, but a pleasure – a true pleasure ... to give what we can to assist her ... Only in consideration of the feelings of delicate independence existing in the mind of every refined female ... we wish to contribute our mites in a secret and concealed manner..." Paper, pens and ink being provided, every lady wrote down the sum she could give annually, signed the paper, and sealed it. If their proposal is acceded to, Mary Smith, a regular visitor to Cranford, is to ask her father, a Drumble business-man familiar with Miss Matty's investments, to open the papers under a pledge of secrecy, the proposal being that Mr Smith should arrange for the money to be paid to Miss Matty without her knowing that it did not come from the remains of her investments.

After this meeting, the aristocratic Mrs Forrester apologised to Mary for the small amount of her contribution, even though it was, Mrs Gaskell tells us, "actually a twentieth part of what she had to live upon and keep house and a little serving-maid, all as became one born a Tyrrell", while another member of the circle, Mrs Fitz-Adam, (note that the Fitz-Nigels had been the Norman owners of Tatton Park) apologised for not having put down as much as she could afford and was ready to give for, though she was now "sister-in-law to a ladyship, she had once been nothing but a country girl, coming to market with eggs and butter" when Miss Matty had been "a fine young lady" and "she thought she could never look Miss Matty in the face again if she presumed..." Ignorant of all this activity, Miss Matty was preparing to leave her home.. It was:

> a relief to her to be doing something in the way of retrenchment, for, as she said, whenever she thought of the poor fellow with his bad five-pound note ... she felt quite dishonest, [but] if it made her uncomfortable, what must it be doing to the directors of the bank, who must know so much more of the misery consequent upon this failure...dividing her sympathy between these directors (whom she imagined overwhelmed by self-reproach for the mismanagement of other people's affairs) and those who were suffering like her. Indeed, of the two she seemed to think poverty a lighter burden than self-reproach; but which Mary Smith privately doubted if the directors would agree with her.

Finally, Miss Matty is set up with a little tea and sweet shop in her own front parlour, this being thought sufficiently genteel, the sweets part being her own idea.

We then learn that, having "some scruples of conscience at selling tea when the principal shop-keeper in the town, Mr Johnson, included it among his numerous commodities...she had trotted down to tell him of the project and to inquire if it was likely to injure his business." On hearing of this sort of business procedure, Mary's father called it a

> great nonsense [and] wondered how tradespeople would get on if there was to be a continual consulting of each other's interests which would put a stop to all competition directly. And perhaps it would not have done in Drumble, but in Cranford it answered very well; for not only did Mr Johnson kindly put at rest all Miss Matty's scruples and fear of injuring his business...but repeatedly sent customers to her, saying the teas he kept were of a common kind, but that Miss Jenkyns had all the choice sorts... It was really very pleasant to see how her unselfishness and simple sense of justice called out the same good qualities in others... But my father [Mr Smith] says "such simplicity might be very well in Cranford but would never do in the world." And I fancy the world must be very bad, for with all my father's suspicions of everyone with whom he has dealings, and in spite of all his precautions he lost upwards of a thousand pounds by roguery only last year.

Here, Mrs Gaskell's irony can hardly be called 'quaint'.

When Miss Matty's shop opens, 'The whole country round seemed to be all out of tea at once, and though she warned her customers of the digestive dangers she believed to be associated with the drinking of green-tea' and gave the children overweight in sweets but 'always told them to hold out their tiny palms, into which she shook either peppermint or ginger lozenges, as a preventive to the dangers that might arise from the previous sale', the people round about, as well as paying for their purchases, brought many a little country present to the old rector's daughter, 'a cream cheese, a few new-laid eggs, a little fresh, ripe fruit, a bunch of flowers. The counter was quite loaded with their offerings sometimes...'

In constructing this delicate little comedy, so praised by some critics for its literary qualities, so blamed by others for its whimsicalities, so loved by generations of ordinary readers, Mrs Gaskell is directing just as much social criticism against the values of the commercial world, its business practices, and its consequent social alienation, as in any of her works, and showing just as much preference as ever for the values of the old rural way of life with its culture and customs and its roots in the world of nature. But she had now discovered the weapon of laughter, one which she was to use again with such devastating effect in *Wives and Daughters*. But in *Cranford*, as Barbara Hardy points out, the story is told in such a way that, though at first it seems that her humour is turned against the inhabitants of the little town, the gradual revelations and shifts of the story elicit our sympathy, admiration and affection, whereas there is a consistent irony in the references to 'Drumble'. We also remember that, during the appearance of 'Cranford' in *Household Words* between 1851 and 1853, Mrs Gaskell was in close touch with the Christian Socialists, visiting their workshops and writing: "I do talk and lend my pamphlets to everybody I meet." *Cranford* is one of the most subtle pieces of literature, the didactic pill so daintily sugared, the social theory so cunningly woven into this part-real, part-fable picture of life and values in a small country town, where, at the end of the book and late on a summer evening:

> into the principal street ... the fragrant smell of the neighbouring hay-fields came in every now and then, borne by the soft breezes that stirred the dull air of the summer twilight, and then died away. The silence of the sultry atmosphere was lost in the murmuring noises which came from many an open window and door ... even the children were abroad in the street ... enjoying the games for which the day had been too hot.

And as this delightful parable, Lady Ritchie's "visionary country home", concludes, if any little coolness should arise in the talk that can be heard through the open windows on this summer night, they will soon be resolved by "the old friendly sociability in Cranford society..."

CHAPTER 11
Mrs Gaskell and France

Mrs Gaskell's statements in *Cranford* about women who were able to manage their own affairs, and Miss Debórah's opinion, expressed in that same story, that women were actually superior to men, though humorously expressed, represent an important theme in both her private and public writing. So too, Thomas Holbrook's visit to France has the ring of truth for, ever since the Reformation, Protestant dissenters had looked to the continent for inspiration, refuge, and practical encouragement such as the printing of Protestant literature. Thomas Holbrook and Ebenezer Holman make up a composite picture, not only of Samuel Holland, but of many of the old Presbyterian dissenters, sometimes conservative in politics and, like Thomas Holbrook, only in favour of change that had its "root deep down in humanity." But whether of the right or left, whether, like Samuel Holland, deeply attached to the land, or, like the Wedgwoods and Darwins, with connections in industry, business, science, and the professions, their interests and connections were cosmopolitan.

As we have already seen, Unitarians, with other dissenters, were barred from Oxford and Cambridge and from political power and social influence in England by their religion and therefore looked to like-minded groups in America and Europe. Large numbers of Huguenots, French Protestant dissenters, in flight from persecution after the revocation of the Edict of Nantes, also had a strong cultural influence on English dissent. As Donald Davie has pointed out in *A Gathered Church* (1978):

> English Dissent in the eighteenth century was not insular in
> the least. The full cultural consequences of the influx of
> Huguenots into England ... has I think never been assessed,
> nor indeed much studied ... a strong and sturdy 'French
> Connection' can be traced among Dissenting leaders from
> before the seventeenth century is out until after the
> nineteenth century is under way.[1]

Several distinguished Unitarian families such as the Martineaus were, in fact, of Huguenot descent. After the 'Bloodless Revolution' of 1688, which considerably added to political and religious freedom in England at a time when this was conspicuously absent in the rest of Europe, political and religious refugees began to come here either for a time or to make their homes here permanently.

But there was another side to social life in England at that time, rather different from that of the gentlemen scientists, Augustan poets and essayists so admired by Voltaire. This can be seen in the pictures of Hogarth, who mercilessly exposed the corruption and barbarity to be found at all levels of society, particularly in certain sections of the aristocracy and middle-classes. In his *Civilisation* (1969),[2] Lord Kenneth Clark compares one of Hogarth's prints, 'A Midnight Conversation', portraying noisy animal spirits, drink, and disorder, with a picture painted by de Troy, 'A Reading from Molière', and points out the immensely more cultured atmosphere of the French picture, its elegant yet comfortable furniture, its serene and intelligent faces. In the Hogarth print all the figures are men while in the French picture five are women and sees the great advance in the civilisation achieved in Europe not only in the twelfth and thirteenth centuries but also in eighteenth-century France as due to the recognition of the value to society of feminine qualities.

Though with the Reformation much of this feminine influence was extirpated from Protestant countries as 'papist' and, with the growth of capitalism, women tended to lose even more of their influence and functions, they were still influential in seventeenth and eighteenth century France, where Paris was the centre of the cultured world and, in the French salons, witty and learned hostesses entertained the most intelligent men and women from all over Europe. The portraits of these women, as Lord Clarke points out, show them as mainly middle-aged rather than young, intelligent rather than beautiful, sensible, kind-hearted, and tactful rather than sexually attractive and the men they entertained outstanding intellectuals of all kinds who wanted to see gradual reform in religion and government, their minds enlightened and stimulated by regular and varied conversation in the ideal setting of the salon. These 'philosophes' were later blamed for the unleashing of the atrocities of the French Revolution but actually they were very similar in outlook to the English Presbyterians, moderate and tolerant almost to a fault in the tradition of Montaigne, the cultured sceptic, with his well-known "Que Sais-je?", 'what do I really know?'

When, in 1847, Mrs Gaskell wrote an account of Emerson's lectures at the Athenaeum in Manchester, on 'Men Representative of Great Ideas',[3] she preferred that on Montaigne to others on Swedenborg and Shakespeare on the grounds that Montaigne held 'the balance between the Idealist and the grossly practical man.' She concludes her article with the idea of Montaigne as 'clinging to one central harmony, though all around might be whirl and discord.' Montaigne is also quoted in her 'Traits and Stories of the Huguenots', published in the December 1853 edition of *Household Words* which she heard from French Protestant refugees in London. His *Essays*, translated into English early in the seventeenth century, show him to have been a scholarly country gentleman of originality, intellectual curiosity, tolerant, not irreligious but sceptical of bigots, fanatics, and theologians, tending to the rejection of the idea of original sin, and of not trying too hard to penetrate the great imponderables of life and death, especially when expressed in theological doctrines about which, as Mrs Gaskell herself said: "I am more and more certain, we can never be certain."[4] In short, he had much in common with the English dissenter of the comprehensive type, as well as a prose-style which, informal, personal, and based on his own preferences and habits, was one later popularised in England by Charles Lamb, also a Unitarian of the comprehensive type. Mrs Gaskell's own essays have been compared with Lamb's,[5] by which they may have well been influenced, but it is just as likely that they were inspired directly by Montaigne's.

In her letters, her autobiographical story, 'My French Master' (1853), her essays, 'Company Manners' (1854), the nouvelle, *My Lady Ludlow* (1858), and three articles on 'French Life' in 1864, we have evidence of her continuing interest in French life and literature. But it was on the aristocratic French women of letters and 'esprit', the hostesses of the salons, that her interest was particularly concentrated. Of all the books on child-rearing, for instance, that were current at the birth of her first child, it was a French work, *Sur l'Education Progressive*, by Mme Necker de Saussure, which she called, in the only diary of hers to survive, 'much the nicest book I have read on the subject', quoting her approvingly on the subject of babies' crying:

> There are and always will be enow of disappointments to
> enure a child to bearing them, and they will increase with

years and the power of enduring...; all that can be averted by a little forethought ... without interfering with the necessary degree of quiet but resolute discipline ... I do not like the plan in fashion formerly of making trials for young children.[6]

Albertine Necker de Saussure (1776-1841), the daughter of a Swiss physician, translated Schlegel's lectures on drama and her *Sur l'Education Progressive* (1828-32) was much read and praised. She was cousin by marriage to Mme de Staël, separated wife of Baron de Staël Holstein, who received, in her salon in Paris in the years prior to the Revolution, the most progressive intellectuals in French society. Mme de Staël also wrote extensively and her most important writings were political, but in her literary criticism and particularly in her book *On Germany* she was we have already noted, the first to introduce the word Romanticism and the German literary and philosophical movement of the past fifty years into France. Mrs Gaskell seems to have been extremely interested in Mme de Staël, writing in 1852 of meeting a Mrs Rich, "who had known Mme de Staël" and in Paris meeting the granddaughter of Mme de Staël, "said to be very like her". Mme de Staël's works included memoirs and two autobiographical novels, *Delphine and Corinne*, and it must have been to one of these that Mrs Gaskell was referring when she wrote to Catherine Winkworth after her visit to Southport in 1848: 'Don't forget we left Mdme de Staël in the bed of Venus.'[7]

'Company Manners', too, begins with a reference to an article in the *Révue de Deux Mondes* by Victor Cousin, the French Idealist philosopher whom Mrs Gaskell was disappointed at being inadvertently prevented from meeting when she was in Paris. The article referred to is about a series of biographies he was writing of French women of letters and the hostesses of salons. Mrs Gaskell writes that she does not know if his biographies are 'a relaxation from, or a continuation of, his study of metaphysics', but his list includes Jacqueline Pascal, 'known at Port Royal as Sister Euphemia', 'a holy, pure, and sainted woman'; the Duchess de Longueville, 'that beautiful, splendid sinner'; and Mme de Sablé who, Mrs Gaskell writes:

had been an habitual guest at the Hotel Rambouillet, the superb habitation which was the centre of the witty and

learned as well as the pompous and pedantic society of
Paris, in the days of Louis the Thirteenth. When these
gatherings had come to an end after Madame de
Rambouillet's death there were several attempts to form
circles that should preserve some of the refinement of the
Hotel Rambouillet (and it is on Madame de Sablé), a
gentlewoman by birth; intelligent enough doubtless from
having been a friend of Menage, Voltaire, Madame de
Sévigné, and others in the grand hôtel, that Cousin bestows
the mantle of Madame Rambouillet, as having all the
requisites which enabled her 'tenir un salon,' for Cousin
the acme of praise.

Cousin had concluded his memoir of her in the *Révue de Deux
Mondes* not, as Mrs Gaskell says English people would have done, "in
praise of the morals and religion of the person" but in telling us that
Mme de Sablé 'was unremarkable in one thing or quality' except that
she knew how to "tenir un salon" – (Mrs Gaskell can find no English
equivalent for the phrase) – and to this 'single, simple fact' he
attributed the success of her life. Though, at first, after reading the
memoirs, she had felt this opinion to be exaggerated, she had to set it
against her own 'experience of English society – of the evenings
dreaded before they came and sighed over in recollection, because
they were so ineffably dull.' She then proceeds to paint a word-
picture of her own idea of the ideal salon and its hostess very
reminiscent of de Troy's picture 'A Reading from Molière': the chairs
'easy and comfortable,' without anything in the centre of the room
which would prevent

> visitors from drawing near to each other, or to the fire, if
> they so willed it [and] furnished with deep, warm soberness
> of tone; yet lighted up by flowers and happy, animated
> people, [amongst whom] conversation must have flowed
> naturally into sense and nonsense as the case might be ...
> It might have been that wit would come uppermost,
> sparkling, crackling, leaping, calling out echoes all around;
> or the same people might talk with all their might and
> wisdom, on some grave and important subject of the day,
> in that manner which we have got into the way of calling
> 'earnest', [but] whether grave or gay, people did not go up
> to Mme de Sablé's salons with a set purpose of being either
> one or the other ... I have visited a good deal among a set

of people who piqued themselves on being rational. We have talked what they call sense, but what I called platitudes, till I have longed, like Southey, in the *Doctor*, to come out with some interminable, nonsensical word ... as a relief to my despair... Only let me say that there is one thing more tiresome than an evening when everybody tries to be profound and sensible and that is when everybody tries to be witty. I have a disagreeable sense of effort and unnaturalness at both times; but the everlasting attempt, even when it succeeds, to be clever and amusing, is the worse of the two. People try to say brilliant rather than true things; they not only catch eager hold of the superficial and ridiculous in other persons and in events generally, but, from constantly looking out for subjects for jokes and 'mots' and satire, they become possessed of a kind of sore susceptibility themselves, and are afraid of their own working-selves, and dare not give way to any expression of feeling, or any noble indignation or enthusiasm. This kind of wearying wit is far different from humour... But as to the rational parties that are in truth so irrational, when all talk up to an assumed character, instead of showing themselves what they really are and so extending each other's knowledge of the infinite and beautiful capacities of human nature... I see the grave, sedate faces at a party [when] everyone had brought out his or her own wisdom, and aired it for the good of the company; one or two had, from a sense of duty and without any special living interest in the matter, improved us by telling us of some new scientific discovery, the details of each and all of them wrong, as I learnt afterwards ... [while at] another party ... at a very respectable tradesmen's house, [in] a well-warmed, handsome sitting-room, with block upon block of unburnt coal behind the fire...

and here Mrs Gaskell describes the evening of entertainment consisting of nothing but the endless stream of food described in the previous chapter.

Having once more dissected the Manchester society with which she was so familiar, Mrs Gaskell contrasts this with the French salon, where books (as in the homes of Thomas Holbrook and Ebenezer Holman) were:

its natural indispensable furniture; not brought out and strewed here and there when 'company' was coming, but as habitual presences ... the volumes she [the hostess] was reading ... someone might open a book and catch on a suggestive sentence ... But I cannot fancy any grand preparations for what was to be said among people, each of whom brought the best dish in bringing himself; and whose own store of living, individual thought and feeling and mother-wit, would be infinitely better than any cut and dried determination to devote the evening to mutual improvement. If people are really good and wise, their goodness and their wisdom flow out unconsciously, and benefit like sunlight. So, books for reference, books for impromptu suggestion, but never books to serve for texts to a lecture.

And she closes this long essay with an enigmatic reference to someone whose 'rich gold coins of thought' had been ignored at one of the social gatherings she so much disliked in England, but which 'would have been valued at Mme de Sablé's, where the sympathetic and intellectual stream of conversation would have borne [her] and [her] golden fragments away with it, by its soft, resistless, gentle force.'

In 'Company Manners', the social life of the French salon was a mutual education, grave or gay, an on-going process to which all freely contributed the best they could give in an atmosphere the tone of which was set by a woman, well-born, well-bred, 'and ... tolerably intelligent', who would be 'past youth yet not past the power of attracting ... by her sweet and gracious manners ...quick, ready tact..., keeping silence as long as anyone else will talk..., saying a kind thing here and a gentle thing there, and speaking ever with her own quiet sense, till people the most opposed learnt to understand each other's point of view, which is a great thing for opponents to do.' Of a proposed Manchester dinner-party in 1848, however, she had written: 'I wish myself well thro' it...'[8]

In 'French Life', ten years later, she reflected further on the French salons and their hostesses. 'Mme A', an old friend of Mme Mohl, English wife of Julius Mohl, a German Orientalist, with whom Mrs Gaskell often stayed in Paris, had told her of the customs of 'receiving' before the Revolution and Mme de Circourt, who also had the gift of 'tenir un salon', had recounted to her memories of the

142

Revolution, as well as telling her of a young aristocrat who had refused to sleep in a room where Mme de Sévigné had slept because she was a Jansenist and he had feared 'the contamination of heresy'. Mme de Sévigné was a woman who had long attracted Mrs Gaskell but it was not until 1862 that she wrote to W.S. Williams, a reader for Smith and Elder, her publishers:

> I began to write some articles which I intended to send to *All The Year Round* [the Dickens' periodical which replaced *Household Words*] as pictures of French Society in Paris and the provinces in the nineteenth (sic) century (I think what gave me the start was the meeting with a supposed-to-be well-educated young lady who knew nothing about Madame de Sévigné, who had been like a well-known friend to me all my life.) But I think my MSS promises to be very interesting ... My book is rather Memoirs elucidatory of the Life and Times of Madame de Sévigné. The sort of subjects are, 'Who was Madame de Sévigné?' 'Her friends in Paris and the Hotel Rambouillet,' 'Her Two Cousins, (Bussy-Rabutin and Emmanuel de Coulanges) with the history of Madame de Miramion,' 'Her widowed life and her children,' 'Her old age, – debts and death.) (Then as to society in the Provinces I should take that rather rare book Flechier's 'Grands Jours d'Auvergne, or de Clermont, I forget which.) Flechier was contemporary with Madame de Sévigné both at the Hotel de Rambouillet and in the later days which she spent with Madame de Grignan in Provence...[9]

The following July was spent in France collecting material on Mme de Sévigné, and in September she wrote to Smith of Smith and Elder that the "Life and Times of Mme de Sévigné [is] more in my head than out of it, but I think it will be good."[10]

That Mrs Gaskell in some ways modelled herself on Mme de Sévigné would seem to be implied by the description of her as a "well-known friend" and there are certainly some almost uncanny resemblances between them. Baroness de Chantal was born in 1627. Her father died when she was only a few months old and her mother five years later. Though legally the ward of her grandmother, St Jeanne de Chantal, co-founder with St Francis de Sales of the

Visitation Order of nuns, her upbringing was largely in the hands of an old uncle, the Abbé de Livry. Educated at home by private tutors, she had access to her uncle's library and the society of his learned friends. As well as birth and breeding, she had health, high spirits, wit, and a pleasing appearance. She danced well (as did Mrs Gaskell) and had a taste for singing. At eighteen she married the Marquis de Sévigné, but the marriage was not happy, he being "a braggart about his amours", and he was killed in a duel seven years later. Though only twenty-five, she remained a widow for the rest of her life, though the long widowhood was not out of love for her dead husband. Was this independence, one wonders, one of the qualities which Mrs Gaskell so admired?

The young widow devoted herself to her children, had already become celebrated for her letters, went occasionally to court, frequented in moderation the reigning literary circles and always manifested great respect for the King, Louis XIV. She had political and religious friends among the Jansenists, a religious community which was in some ways similar to Calvinism but of a greater spirituality; its educational text books were popular throughout Europe and Jansenism may perhaps be called the French equivalent of English Puritanism. She read Tasso, Ariosto, La Fontaine, Pascal, Nicole, Tacitus, the huge old romances, Rabelais, Rochefoucauld, the novels of her friend Madame de la Fayette, Corneille, Bourdaloue and Bossuet, Montaigne, Lucian, Don Quixote and St Augustine. These are, almost without exception, names and works mentioned and/or quoted from by Mrs Gaskell.[11] There are innumerable examples of the same pleasures, each derived from domesticity, informal entertaining, family music and gardens, their love for a particularly beloved daughter, their appreciation of the great preachers of their day, their visits to friends, theatres, convents, great houses, even industrial establishments; in short, the same "many Me's" to which Mrs Gaskell admitted, yet both of them always maintaining the most correct of reputations. Both had great powers of discernment and description. Both were at their best and happiest among congenial friends, again so reminiscent of de Troy's 'A Reading from Molière'. Both lived their life to the full even when old age, with its infirmities and disfigurements, encroached upon them, and Mrs Gaskell, like Mme de Sévigné, died "in her own house", as Thurstan Holland wrote to Charles Eliot Norton when acquainting him with her sudden death.[12]

Mme de Sévigné, then, followed closely by Mmes de Saussure, de Staël, de Sablé, de Circourt, 'Mme A', and finally Mme Mohl, hostess of one of the last of the intellectual Parisian salons, are the women Mrs Gaskell admired and on whom she seems to have modelled herself. In recent studies of Mrs Gaskell, the 'Mrs' has been dropped in favour of Elizabeth Gaskell or even Gaskell but she herself never dropped the 'Mrs', nor was there any male pseudonym for her such as Currer Bell or George Eliot. Yet the 'Mrs' did not, in her case, signify the dowdy-Nonconformist-minister's-wife image that it is now thought to be. Her literary ancestresses were the eighteenth-century poet Mrs Barbauld, poet and educationist, and Mrs Carter, translator of Epictetus and known by courtesy as 'Mrs' in later life though she never married. This is why Elizabeth Gaskell always chose to sign her work, when it was signed, 'Mrs Gaskell' – of Mme de Sévigné no one has ever thought to ask what her first name was! Perhaps the appellation that would have most appealed to her would have been that of Mistress Gaskell, the old English form of address for any woman of mature years, married or unmarried, which is found in Shakespeare and conferred on any woman of mature years and social standing. It is in French criticism too, that her name always appears as Mistress or Madame Gaskell and it was also in France that her literary works were perhaps most, in the fullest sense of the word, appreciated in her lifetime. All her works were translated into French from 1849, when an abridged version of *Mary Barton* appeared in a French periodical, and contemporary reviews were almost invariably favourable. As Annette Hopkins says in 'Mrs Gaskell in France. 1849-1890': "To have won and held a reading public for forty years in the France of George Sand, Hugo, Dumas père, Flaubert, Feydeau and Zola is no mean achievement..."[13]

In 1860, Mrs Gaskell wrote to George Smith about an article in *The National Review*:

> My dear Madame Mohl was the author of the Récamier article... I want a stronger and more practical opinion [than] my own... [i.e. Smith himself] to get her to write a book... She would do it well – has the sort of knowledge of good French and English society which few finely-observing women possess. I think she ought to write it out

of benevolence to her species – but do you think it would be 'acting to empty benches?'[14]

Mme Mohl never wrote such a book and perhaps Mrs Gaskell felt that her own 'Life and Times of Mme de Sévigné' must serve to draw attention to the part which an educated woman and an enlightened aristocracy could play in a truly civilised society. Sadly, even the little she wrote concerning Mme de Sévigné has not survived. It might well have further illuminated the shadowy and still controversial subject of her ideas on what we now term 'the woman question'. Nevertheless the many scattered references to the French women 'd'esprit' amongst whom we must include Mme Mohl, as well as Mrs Gaskell's own cosmopolitan English Presbyterianism, serve to throw some light on the subject.

CHAPTER 12
My Lady Ludlow: popular education and Coleridge's clerisy

One of the stories of the French Revolution which Mrs Gaskell heard in the salon of Mme de Circourt may well have provided the centre piece of *My Lady Ludlow* which appeared in *Household Words* between June and September 1858, though the story actually portrays an English aristocratic woman of the old school. Roundly condemned for its style by every critic who has bothered to notice it, the general attitude towards what is considered its main fault has been that its 'story within a story' is "its most obvious structural fault ... a long digression told by Lady Ludlow for the flimsiest of reasons [and with] every appearance of having been included to draw out the weekly numbers."[1] Actually, like *Cousin Phillis* and several other of the 'long-short' stories of Mrs Gaskell, it is a novella and one written in a particular style, that of the contemporary French Realist writer Prosper Mérimée.

One of the best-known writers in this genre, Mérimée habitually employed what is virtually the same technique as appears in *My Lady Ludlow*. In a style characterised by an unromantic economy and simplicity, he wrote romantic stories set against a flamboyant background and frequently dealing with violent events and emotions. As A.W. Raitt says, he "brings us to the very edge of the abysses which open up within our very being, allows us a terrifying glimpse into their depths, and then ... returns us to the apparent security of ordinary existence."[2] This is a perfectly valid description of *My Lady Ludlow*, though Mrs Gaskell utilised the technique for her own very different purposes. Mérimée's stories (which included 'Carmen'), are macabre and pessimistic, dealing almost invariably with passion and cruelty and are only relieved by an 'acid humour'. He frequented the court of Napoleon III and the Parisian salons, was a great admirer of England, wore English clothes, was a friend of Lord Brougham and Lord and Lady Holland, visited England, where he dined with the Whig politicians Gladstone and Lord John Russell, and even visited the Manchester Exhibition in 1857. He also had American friends such as the Storys, Childs, and Seniors (Mrs Senior being the sister of Thomas Hughes, the author of *Tom Brown's Schooldays*).

Mérimée had the reputation of admiring "high-minded and free-spoken English-women" and he had probably met Mrs Gaskell at Mme Mohl's salon in 1853 when the Gaskells stayed with the Schwabes, whom they had known in Manchester. During her visit of 1855 he invited her to take tea with him (with Meta as chaperone), but the meeting was obviously not to his liking for he recorded that "she drank some yellow tea and did not say three words"[3] He is also reported as having pronounced her work "unrealistic and provincial". But, in part of a letter to Mrs Senior, he said of *Ruth*:

> To tell the truth I'm afraid the subject is not so new for me as it must be for anyone English. We continentals have not so many prejudices as you, and what in England is considered audacity is something very simple in France. The source of the mischief is your church and something even further off. The idea was to make a sacrament of what ought never to have been anything but a social convention... It seems to me that in England the subjection of women is worse than anywhere else. I believe that women seldom take lovers because they fear to lose caste... There is [in *Ruth*] much talent and even natural feeling. The characters, at least those from spheres known to me, seem to be genuine and well drawn... In a word, it is very well done; but do you wish to know what my criticism is? Why is Ruth so unhappy? Not because she has had a child, but because she was too poor to treat herself to that whim. Give her five hundred pounds sterling, and she will go away to France, where she will be loved and made much of by everyone, lovable as she is... There is no conclusion to be drawn about *Ruth*, unless that it is very imprudent to have a child without being able to provide for it. Do you think it is not just as great a misfortune for a married woman...Mrs Gaskell told me that *Ruth* had been burnt in the name of morality. That is worthy of you puritans...[4]

Seldom can a writer and a novel have been more misunderstood from so many different points of view.

Though a social critic of many aspects of French life, Mérimée was a member of the school of writers then known as the 'laid' or 'ugly' school. Notorious for his own sexual promiscuity, amongst things he liked in real life he is reported as having included "making love as often as possible, and not too often to the same person", and he had little interest in poetry, religion, music, or family ties. In short, he was almost a French counterpart of Bellingham, the type of man pilloried by Mrs Gaskell in *Ruth*. He died in 1870 and his house in Paris was burnt down during the Commune in 1871. That Mérimée's amours had come to Mrs Gaskell's notice may well have been the reason for her visit to him in Paris in 1855 in order to study the man at closer quarters and, disliking both him and his stories, in 1858 set out to make use of his idiosyncratic style in a story which is also macabre and deals with passion and cruelty but its conclusion not one of disaster and death but of hope and reconciliation. It is worth noting that Mérimée, having visited the Manchester Exhibition the year before the publication of *My Lady Ludlow*, probably met Mrs Gaskell again, since she was one of its official hostesses and her dislike of him may well have been reinforced on that occasion.

Written at the same time as her friend Henry Green was writing *Knutsford, Its Tradition and History* (1859), *My Lady Ludlow* is the story of the 'education' of an English aristocratic woman very different from the French women Mrs Gaskell admired. The material to hand was ample, both from her own personal experience and in the annals of Cheshire on which Green was engaged. In these, Mrs Gaskell herself had some part, writing, for example, to James Crossley at the Chetham Museum in Manchester making enquiries on Green's behalf about "The Bold Ladie of Cheshire, one of the Chomondeley family said to have been knighted by James I."[5] The character, Lady Ludlow, is based partly on the eighteenth century Lady Jane Stanley who appears in Green's book. One of the notabilities of Regency Knutsford, she had lived at the now demolished Brook House opposite the Unitarian chapel, had walked out in state with a gold-headed cane, as does Lady Ludlow, and, like Lady Ludlow, had very strict ideas of propriety, leaving money to provide the still existing pavements down each side of King Street, only one flag-stone wide so as to discourage young couples from walking arm in arm!

But we have already seen that Mrs Gaskell was, from the earliest days of her marriage and almost certainly before it, a frequent visitor at Capesthorne Hall, one of the old feudal estates near Knutsford, the hereditary owner of which was Mrs Davenport. Mrs Gaskell had, in 1849, written to Eliza Fox, of Capesthorne as "a place for an artist to be in – old hall, galleries, old paintings & such a dame of a lady to grace them" and, two years later, Mrs Davenport visited the Gaskells in Manchester – Mrs Gaskell had written to Marianne: 'Don't you think I'm very bold to ask her?' In a crowded two days, Mrs Gaskell, Mrs Davenport and a Mr Crewe, 'a clergyman on the estate – interested in education', visited an industrial school at Swinton, had tea with Mr Morell, an inspector of schools, with whom they 'had a deal of talk about education', visited a Deaf and Dumb asylum and the Schwabe's calico-printing works, and entertained to dinner William Fairbairn, the engineer, Mr Shuttleworth, a cotton merchant, and his wife, and Mr Wright, the prison philanthropist.[6] When, the following year, Mrs Davenport married Lord Hatherton, the Whig politician, Mrs Gaskell became a visitor at Teddesley Park, Staffordshire, Lord Hatherton's country residence, as well as at their London house in Berkeley Square.

Other great houses where she also visited were Chatsworth, the great Derbyshire house of the Duke of Devonshire; the residences of the Nightingale family, immensely rich Unitarians, at Lea Hurst in Derbyshire and Embly in Hampshire; the Shaens' Crix in Essex; and Worleston, near Crewe, the country estate of the wealthy Manchester Jewish family, the Behrens. Of the last, she wrote to Marianne in 1859:

> Our visit to Worleston was charming ... the gentlemen hunted while the ladies watched from carriages... We dined at seven; turtle soup, green peas (at half a guinea a quart) iced pudding, duckling, chickens, lamb &c &c &c, then we worked [presumably at fine sewing and embroidery] & the gentlemen fell asleep.[7]

Mrs Gaskell had, therefore, an ample knowledge of both the ladies of the Tory and Whig aristocracy. The character of Lady Ludlow very obviously symbolises the old aristocracy, Tory and rural, maintaining the standards and traditions of 'old England' but not intellectuals and not open to new ideas and new needs, thereby blocking genuine progress, especially in the field of popular education.

In the same story, Mr Gray, a young clergyman, stands for the duty and opportunity of the established church to raise the social, religious, and educational conditions of the poor. Minor themes are represented by the Cranfordian character, Miss Galindo, an intelligent, elderly gentlewoman who cannot, because of social prejudice, exercise her real talents in a congenial occupation for which she is well-fitted, that of clerk to the steward of Lady Ludlow's estate; Bessy, the illegitimate girl, who can make a place for herself in society if accepted for her own qualities regardless of her origin; and Mr Brooke, an ex-Birmingham baker, a dissenter who has bought the estate adjoining Lady Ludlow's and is a representative of the contribution that middle-class industrialists of the better type might make to the improvement of agriculture and therefore to the standard of living in general.

My Lady Ludlow, like *Cranford* and *Cousin Phillis*, has a young narrator; in this case Margaret Dawson, who again both tells and takes part in the story. Margaret had been the daughter of a poor clergyman, whose wife was 'said to have good blood in her veins' and who, when she wished to maintain her position among 'rich democratic manufacturers', used to put on her old English lace ruffles, the only 'finery' she had. The clergyman had had a large family and when he died Lady Ludlow, an aristocratic connection of the widow, as an act of charity had taken Margaret into her own home, Hanbury Court. Jane Austen's Mansfield Park begins with a similar situation but no subsequent events or experiences of charity could be more different than that of Fanny Price and Margaret Dawson. Margaret is not the only poverty-stricken girl taken in by Lady Ludlow. She has four or five companions and all receive the most loving and courteous care, an old-fashioned education, and, if they marry, 'a wedding-dinner, her clothes and house-linen'; or, if they remain unmarried, they will inherit "a small competency" at Lady Ludlow's death. Margaret, soon after her arrival at Hanbury Court, becomes, through a fall, an almost useless cripple, but she is given even greater care and consideration until she decides, of her own free will and when he is able to support her, to live with her brother. This love and care Lady Ludlow also extends to forty-odd indoor and outdoor employees, several of whom she continues to maintain and keep in her service in spite of their inefficiency or incapacity and even when in financial difficulty herself. Though she continues to live as she always has done, in great state, with her gold-headed cane, her great lace cap, her special "chair of state", her exquisite china and antique furnishings, and in the autocratic rule of her estate, as befits the heiress of an ancient family, Lady Ludlow's is an austere, deeply pious life. Each evening after supper, one of her 'young ladies' is called on to read to

151

the assembled household the Psalms and Lessons of the day, though there are no prayers since Lady Ludlow is so orthodox in her religious views that she will have none but those in the Book of Common Prayer and not even those read by anyone less than a deacon!

It is while Margaret is living at Hanbury Court, that

the cry for education was beginning to come up; Mr Raikes had set up his Sunday Schools; and some clergymen were all for teaching writing and arithmetic, as well as reading. My lady would have none of this; it was levelling and revolutionary, she said. When a young woman came to be hired my lady would have her in, and see if she liked her looks and her dress, and question her about her family. Her ladyship laid great stress upon the latter point, saying that a girl who did not warm up when any interest or curiosity was expressed about her mother, or 'the baby' (if there was one) was not likely to make a good servant. Then she would make her put out her feet, to see if they were well and neatly shod. Then she would bid her say the Lord's Prayer and the Creed. Then she inquired if she could write. If she could and she had liked all that had gone before, her face sank, for it was an inviolable rule with her never to engage a servant who could write. But I [Margaret] have known her ladyship break it, although in both cases in which she did so she put the girls' principles to a further and unusual test in asking her to repeat the Ten Commandments. One pert young woman ... who had got through her trials pretty tolerably, considering she could write, spoilt it all by saying glibly at the end of the last Commandment: "An't please your ladyship, I can cast accounts." "Go away, wench," said my lady in a hurry, "You're only fit for trade; you will not suit me for a servant." The girl went away crestfallen; in a minute, however, my lady sent after her to see that she had something to eat before leaving the house; and indeed she sent for her once again, but it was only to give her a Bible, and to bid her beware of French principles, which had led the French to cut off their King's and Queen's heads. The poor blubbering girl said, "Indeed my lady, I wouldn't hurt a fly, much less a king, and I cannot abide the French, nor frogs neither, for that matter." But my lady was inexorable, and took a girl who could neither read nor

152

write, to make up for her alarm about the progress of
education towards addition and subtraction. (Ch I)

The main plot of Mrs Gaskell's story concerns this opposition of
Lady Ludlow to popular education which brings her into conflict with
the new young clergyman, Mr Gray, who preaches education "both in
the pulpit and out of it" and is prepared to bear the expense of a
suitable school-building himself, if he can obtain the land on which to
build it, since Lady Ludlow refuses him this and even the use of one
of her tenant-farmer's barns as was her legal right. It is not surprising
then that she is outraged when a small intelligent boy named Gregson,
the son of a local poacher and ne'er-do-well, repeats to her the
contents of a letter which he had been bidden by her steward, Mr
Horner, to deliver to her. The boy had lost the letter but had been
taught to read by the elderly steward, who had him in view as a future
foreman whose help he would need in his old age. Lady Ludlow
lectures the boy severely, dismisses out of hand his reply to her
accusation regarding the morality of reading other people's letters,
namely, that he had read it to keep his reading in practice since he had
so little other reading matter, and she sends him packing. When little
Gregson has gone, Lady Ludlow tells Margaret what she believes to
be a cautionary tale of the French Revolution, the story within a story
of which so many critics have complained, yet which is indispensable
to Mrs Gaskell's aim in writing it, i.e. to show that aristocratic fears
of popular education were unfounded. Though the villagers may
behave with respect and decorum when under 'my Lady's eye' there
was, in fact, much poverty, injustice, and brutality in the village
which could lead equally well to similar violence.

Mrs Gaskell analyses Lady Ludlow's fears, prejudices and
principles with sympathy and sensitivity, portraying her as motivated
not so much by fears for herself, nor even for her class, but for the
very fabric of civilised society and the Christian religion with its
ancient pieties and charities of which she is herself the epitome. The
tale which Lady Ludlow tells Margaret Dawson is of a tragic and
macabre event during the French Revolution when a friend of her
now-dead son, a charming young French aristocrat, Clement Crequvy,
and his cousin, Virginie, had both ended their lives on the guillotine.
Virginie's father had been a friend of the infamous (as Lady Ludlow
calls him) Jean-Jacques Rousseau and when Clement proposed

marriage to Virginie, the girl had told him, "When I marry…I marry a man who, whatever his rank may be, will add dignity to the human race by his virtues, and not be content to live in an effeminate court on the traditions of past grandeur", taking her principles, says Lady Ludlow, from her equally 'infamous' father, the "degenerate Dé Crequvy, tainted with the atheism of the Encyclopaedists", the philosophes who had produced the first encyclopaedia in an attempt to bring all knowledge together in an easily accessible form. Virginie had:

> a very noble and attractive presence. In character she was daring and wilful (said one set); original and independent (said another). She was very much indulged by her father who had given her something of a man's education, and selected for her intimate friend a member of the Bureaucracy, a Madame Knecker, daughter of the Minister of Finance. Mademoiselle de Crequvy was thus introduced into all the free-thinking salons in Paris; among people who were always full of plans for subverting society. (Ch V)

After his cousin's scornful rejection of his marriage proposal, Clement naturally withdrew to a sad and respectful distance and promised his mother (his father being already dead), 'that he should not again present himself at his uncle's salon.'

When the Revolution came, Clement and his mother, being 'the strongest possible royalists and aristocrats', were among those earliest to be termed 'proscrats', 'as it was the custom of the horrid Sansculottes to term those who adhere to the habits of expression and action in which it was their pride to have been educated', continued Lady Ludlow, but they escaped from France and, arriving in London in peasants' dress and almost penniless, had approached Lord and Lady Ludlow, old friends of theirs, who were staying at their town house. Clement had left France believing that Virginie and her father (her mother, like so many of Mrs Gaskell's heroines, also being dead), were quite safe, since her father was somewhat popular with the party in power, but soon they heard that even Virginie's father was guillotined and his daughter imprisoned by the licence of the mob whose rights she had always advocated. Though his mother was dying from shock and sorrow, Clement left her in the care of the Ludlows and returned to Paris to try to bring Virginie out of the country. The

154

rest of this story, which shows evidence of a detailed knowledge both of the geography of Paris and the course of the French Revolution, is taken up with her attempted rescue. Virginie is living under the surveillance of the concierge of an inn which had fallen into the hands of the woman's brother, a wine merchant named Morin, whose son has an ambition to marry Virginie, to possess a girl 'far above him in rank.' It is the unwitting co-operation of the young son of the concierge and his ability to read a letter from Clement to Virginie that causes the failure of the attempted rescue and brings the young couple to the guillotine. The tragic dénouement of this story within a story, as gripping as anything in *A Tale of Two Cities*, culminates in the reconciliation in prison of the two cousins before their death on the same guillotine. As Virginie dies, young Morin, standing in the watching crowd, shoots himself, an incident very similar to Mérimée's macabre stories.

Lady Ludlow, as we return to the quiet English country house, sees the literate young son of the French concierge for what he was, the innocent dupe and instrument of a 'petit-bourgeois' trying to raise himself above his station, but also as a symbolic threat of violent, ignorant forces subverting society. She replies to Margaret's comment: "It is a sad story your ladyship," with:

> "Yes it is. People seldom arrive at my age without having watched the beginning, middle, and end of many lives and many fortunes...young people should remember that we have had this solemn experience of life on which to base our opinions and form our judgements, so that they are not mere untried theories...I am thinking of Mr Gray, with his endless plans for some new thing - schools, education...he has not seen what all this leads to...a young man like him, who, both by position and age, must have had his experience confined to a very narrow circle, ought not to set up his opinion against mine; he ought not to require reasons from me, nor to need such explanations of my arguments (if I condescend to argue)...as going into relation of the circumstances on which my arguments are based... why should he be convinced?... He has only to acquiesce...I am the lady of the manor... But it is with Mr Horner that I must have to do about this unfortunate lad Gregson. I am afraid there will be no method of making him forget his unlucky knowledge. His poor brains will be

intoxicated with the sense of his powers, without any counterbalancing principles to guide him. Poor fellow! I am quite afraid it will end in his being hanged!" (Ch IX)

But little Gregson does not end up on the gallows and it is Lady Ludlow herself who receives a surprising education. In this novella, there is a neat little history of the Anglican parson from the late eighteenth to the mid-nineteenth century. Lady Ludlow remembers that, in her grandfather's day, "Parson Hemming was family chaplain too and dined at the Hall every Sunday. He was helped last and expected to be done first." On Margaret's arrival at Hanbury Court, the clergyman had been Mr Mountford, who loved good food, hunted regularly, and preferred to give food or money to sick parishioners rather than make both himself and them miserable by visiting them. But a new breed of parson was coming to prominence in Mrs Gaskell's time, deeply earnest and spiritual young men, both Anglicans and Dissenters, who drove themselves relentlessly in their spiritual and educational work for the poor, sick and ignorant. Such a one is Mr Gray. Representative of both a living type and an ideal figure of the clergy, he obviously owes much to Maurice and other Christian Socialist clergy, as well as to the fictional Mr Tryan, a young clergyman in George Eliot's *Scenes from Clerical Life*, which had appeared in Blackwood's the previous year and of which Mrs Gaskell had written to the author: "I never read anything so complete, and beautiful in fiction in my whole life before... Janet's Repentance [in which Mr Tryan appears] perhaps most especially of all... [I] went plodging through our Manchester streets to get every number, as soon as it was accessible from the Portico reading table."[8]

In *Janet's Repentance*, 'Mr Tryan's most unfriendly observers were obliged to admit that he gave himself no rest. Three sermons on Sunday, a night-school for young men on Tuesday, a college-lecture on Thursday, addresses to school teachers, and catechising of school-children, with pastoral visits, multiplying as his influence extended beyond his own district ... would have been enough to severely tax the powers of a much stronger man... On some ground or other, which his friends found difficult to explain to themselves, Mr Tryan seemed bent on wearing himself out. His enemies were at a loss to account for such a course...' But at Mr Tryan's funeral, 'every heart was filled with the memory of a man, who through a self-sacrificing life and in a painful death had been sustained by the faith which fills [the] form with breath and substance.'

The life of Mr Gray in *My Lady Ludlow* is equally self-sacrificing and sustained by a deep and earnest spirituality but, although he lies sick for some time with an illness, Mrs Gaskell allows him to recover and in the end to enjoy the fruits of his labours. After many vicissitudes he convinces Lady Ludlow of his sincerity, mainly through his personal example and his labours on behalf of the little community, pressing home Mrs Gaskell's alignment with the views of Coleridge, Arnold and Maurice on the clergy as the principal means of education throughout the land. But she also presses home, in *My Lady Ludlow*, the point that the clergy who were willing to take a positive lead in this work could not do so unless they received the support and co-operation of the aristocratic patrons of their livings, who, like Lady Ludlow, were immensely powerful influences in every sphere of local life. Although *My Lady Ludlow* is similar in many ways to *Scenes from Clerical Life*, Mrs Gaskell emphasises much more insistently than does George Eliot the needs and rights of the intelligent poor child, the sad difficulties of the illegitimate child, the possibilities for good in even the most apparently 'undeserving' poor as seen in the poacher, Gregson, and the need for an aristocracy not only of old-fashioned piety and 'noblesse oblige' patronage towards their 'inferiors' but one with a much greater openness to the facts of reality and the changing needs and aspirations of the times, and the much greater intellectual curiosity and vigour which she saw in the best elements of the French aristocracy.

Far from viewing the influence of an 'enlightened' aristocracy as leading to violent revolution in England, Mrs Gaskell sees them, particularly the women, as indispensable to social and religious progress and the reconciliation of classes. Lady Ludlow is a woman of great piety and good-will and it is not long before, under the tutelage of the young and nervous but obstinate and determined young clergyman, she begins to see her estate and its village with new eyes. She learns that 'duties' include responsibility "for all the evil [we do] not strive to overcome"; that justice does not include sending a man like Gregson to prison "for being a vagabond, for no specific act, but for his general mode of life", thus leaving his wife and children without support. Even the poacher's twelve-year-old lad, described by Mrs Gaskell, as he first appeared before Lady Ludlow, as

> a lithe, wiry lad, with a thick head of hair standing out in
> every direction as if stirred by some electrical current, a
> short, brown face, red now with affright and excitement,
> wide resolute mouth and bright, deep-set eyes which
> glanced keenly and rapidly round the room, the brightest
> and sharpest (of the farm-lads) although by far the raggiest
> and dirtiest...(Ch IV)

Even he has rights as well as duties, particularly to education, the satisfaction of which may lead him to become a more useful member of society, rather than to the terrible scenes of the French Revolution acted over again in England.

It is not from the efforts of the young clergyman alone that Lady Ludlow learns new ideas and new ways but also from her new steward, Mr James, a representative of the new generation, who replaces the aged Mr Horner. An ex-naval officer friend of Lady Ludlow's son, wounded at Trafalgar, he has been chosen by her on grounds of family, class, and as a kindness to an impecunious and ailing man who had served his country. But, though a young man, he has had experience of life in the outside world among men of many backgrounds and, to Lady Ludlow's horror, though he holds opinions even more 'Church and King' than her own, he seeks from Mr Brooke, the Baptist ex-baker from Birmingham, agricultural advice, friendship, and, finally, his daughter's hand in marriage. Mr Brooke, having made a fortune in Birmingham and purchased the estate adjoining Hanbury Court, had made varied and extensive improvements to it. Miss Galindo, the intelligent, educated and impoverished part-time companion of Lady Ludlow, has much to say about Mr Brooke. An eccentric spinster in the habit of employing as her domestic helps the most grotesquely unemployable females in the village, she points out to Lady Ludlow in one of Mrs Gaskell's most delightful passages of tongue-in-cheek naïvety:

> we must have bread somehow, and though I like it better
> baked at home in a good, sweet brick oven, yet, as some
> folks never can get it to rise, I don't see why a man may
> not be a baker. You see my lady, I look upon baking as a
> simple trade, and as such lawful. There is no machine
> comes in to take away a man's or woman's power of
> earning their living, like the spinning-jenny... There's an

158

invention of the enemy if you will. [The combination of steam-power and the spinning-jenny were the means of introducing the first mass-production in England]. ... But baking bread is wholesome, straightforward elbow-work. They have not got to a contrivance for that yet, thank Heaven. It does not seem to me natural, nor according to Scripture, that iron and steel (whose brows can't sweat) should be made to do man's work. And so I say, all those trades where iron and steel do the work ordained to man at the Fall, are unlawful and I never stand up for them. But say this baker Brooke did knead his bread, and make it rise, and then that people who had, perhaps, no good ovens came to him, and bought his good, light bread, and in this manner he turned an honest penny and got rich; why all I say my lady is this – I dare say he would have been born a Hanbury or a lord if he could; and if he was not, it is no fault of his, that I can see, that he made good bread (being a baker by trade) and got money, and bought his land. It was his misfortune, not his fault, that he was not a person of quality by birth.

"That's very true," said my lady, ... "but, although he was a baker, he might have been a Churchman. Even your eloquence, Miss Galindo, shan't convince me that that is not his own fault." "I don't see that, begging your pardon my lady ... when a Baptist is a baby, if I understand their creed aright, he is not baptised; and consequently he can have no god-fathers or god-mothers to do anything for him in his baptism ... don't let us be hard upon those who have not had the chance of god-fathers and god-mothers. Some people ... are born with silver spoons, – that's to say, a god-father to give one things, and teach one's catechism and see that we're confirmed into good church-going Christians, – and others with wooden ladles in their mouths. These poor last folk must be content to be god-fatherless orphans, and Dissenters, all their lives; and if they are tradespeople into the bargain, so much the worse for them; but let us be humble Christians, my dear lady, and not hold our heads too high because we were born orthodox quality." (Ch XIV)

Again, as in *Cranford*, in a passage which will bear comparison with the speeches of Shakespeare's fools, Mrs Gaskell uses the weapon of laughter against unreasonable social and religious prejudice, while, at the same time, recognising the goodness and sincerity of many of those who held them. Indeed, she clearly sympathises with the old aristocracy in England who feared anything, such as working-class education, which might lead to revolution, for only ten years earlier, almost the whole of Europe had again been aflame, while in 1789 the enlightened philosophes and their families had been swept away with the reactionary aristocrats.

Plot and sub-plot of this novella are integrated by the existence of the two young boys who are able to read letters not intended for their eyes. Though contrived, this pin-points Mrs Gaskell's concern as to the importance of the social and religious milieu in which popular education takes place. In the French episode the boy is the unwitting victim and product of revolutionary atheism but in the main story the education of little Gregson and his life becomes a vehicle towards social harmony.

Miss Galindo, writing to Margaret Dawson after the latter had left Hanbury Court, reports with relish an afternoon tea-party that had been held there, the first that Lady Ludlow had given since the death of her husband and son many years previously. She had dressed in her black velvet and old lace, and at the party were all the local clergy, the farmers and their wives, the Baptist ex-baker, Mr Brooke, and his wife, and Captain James and his wife, the former Miss Brooke. Miss Galindo writes that she thought Mrs Brooke "a rough diamond" who had "never learned manners" and the "parsonesses", as she calls the clergy wives, had been highly amused when she took out

> a clean Bandana pocket-handkerchief, all red and yellow silk [and] spread it over her best silk gown before drinking her tea. [As one of the parsonesses was] right down bursting with laughter...my dear Lady Ludlow...takes out her own pocket-handkerchief, all snowy cambric, and lays it softly down on her velvet lap...and when one got up to shake the crumbs into the fireplace, the other did the same... Mrs Parsoness of Headleigh scarce spoke for the rest of the evening...and Mr Gray, who was before silent and awkward in a way which I tell Bessy [the illegitimate, former village school teacher, now Mrs Gray] she must cure him of, was made so happy by this, pretty action of my lady's that he talked away all the rest of the evening and was the life of the company.

Lady Ludlow's "tea-drinking" is, of course, a modest English 'salon', amusing, perhaps naïve, but deeply moving, and envisaging the mutually-educating and civilising process so evident in the picture of 'A Reading from Molière' and so absent from Hogarth's 'A Modern Midnight Conversation'. In the latter, the women have been banished, either altogether, or to the 'withdrawing' room. At Worleston the men, after dinner, were asleep and the women sewing. But in the French picture and at Lady Ludlow's tea-party, the women are an integral part of the group. In the latter, as in the French salon, the central and inspirational figure is an 'enlightened' as well as aristocratic woman.

Even so, when a school-house is actually built with the approval and assistance of Lady Ludlow, on the village green and just by the church, she still expressed:

> her strong wish that the boys might only be taught to read and write and the first four rules of arithmetic; while the girls were only to read, and to add up in their heads, and the rest of the time to work at mending their own clothes, knitting stockings and spinning. My lady presented the school with more spinning-wheels than there were girls, and requested that there might be a rule that they should have spun so many hanks of flax, and knitted so many pairs of stockings, before they were taught to read...(Ch XIII)

reflecting the fact that Mrs Gaskell herself detested women who had 'accomplishments' but could not do the practical work of a good housewife,[9] but Miss Bessy, illegitimate but educated, whose existence had not previously even been admitted by Lady Ludlow, is soon teaching the children more than the three Rs...

In the distant future, when Mr Gray and Lady Ludlow are both dead, the daughter of Miss Bessy and Mr Gray will marry 'little' Gregson, by then the Reverend Henry Gregson returned from Cambridge to be the new vicar of Hanbury. In the meantime, we are left with the Hanbury Court tea-party which has, at least for an hour, brought all classes and both sexes, Church and Dissenters, clergy and lay-folk, male and female, old and young, legitimate and illegitimate, intelligent and stupid, into the same room, sharing a modest meal and conversing together. It is, of course, once again a scene of personal, class, and religious reconciliation but also one representative of a 'clerisy', an expression first introduced by Coleridge in his *Church and State,* an educating élite to which all classes would contribute under the tutelage of a national Church. Henry Chadwick, writing on *Church and State* in 1977 almost provides a commentary on *My Lady Ludlow:*

> Society, for Coleridge, had to keep a balance between the vitality of free energy [little Gregson] and the ordered forms of institutional, organized power [Lady Ludlow].[10]

It is in *My Lady Ludlow,* a story almost entirely disregarded by modern critics, that we see most clearly Mrs Gaskell's view that the English aristocratic woman should add to her traditional role of 'lady bountiful' and guardian of a valuable though limited culture, a new one as reconciler and educator in society and so make a real contribution to the growth, not of atheistic revolution, but an harmonious, educated Christian society. One can only hope that, in real life, her "boldness" in 1851 in inviting to her home in Manchester that "dame of a lady" Mrs Davenport (later Lady Hatherton, hereditary mistress of the ancient hall, Capesthorne, and wife of a Whig politician,) was worth the exhaustion produced by those two days of conducting her and Mr Crewe, the clergyman on her estate, on the tour of Manchester schools and factories, and that the tea-party at which they "had a deal of talk about education", and the final dinner-party which included Unitarian industrialists and Mr Wright, the prison philanthropist, bore some worthwhile fruit. To Marianne, she wrote afterwards: "I was so busy with Mrs Davenport all Monday and Tuesday, and so very much tired yesterday that I could not write being quite worn out."[11]

CHAPTER 13
Some social themes in *Wives and Daughters:* education, science, and heredity

Let us move on to *Wives and Daughters*, now recognised as Mrs Gaskell's masterpiece. It can, like all great novels, be read on several different levels. It is a sparkling comedy of manners, a delightful study of provincial society in the tradition of Jane Austen and Trollope. It is a deeply penetrating enquiry into personal relationships which has been seen by one eminent critic as extremely sad and perhaps reflecting the disappointments at the end of Mrs Gaskell's own personal life.[1] It is a study of the influence of heredity, early environment, and education on character and hence on social values. It examines the landscape of contemporary society and considers the question as to what are the lasting values in society and what may be done to improve them. By 1864, when the novel began to appear in *The Cornhill Magazine*, Mrs Gaskell's techniques as a writer had immeasurably improved and the plot develops with great complexity and subtlety. Nevertheless, the 'carpentering' on the ideological level is quite clear, especially to a reader who has made a close study of Mrs Gaskell's letters. While the social and religious themes are very cunningly interwoven so that it is difficult to separate them from the literary aspects of the novel, the general opinion that this is Mrs Gaskell's least didactic work is soon seen to be far from the truth.

Always having probed the place of reason and feelings, intuition and imagination (for Mrs Gaskell was venturing into the psychological novel where definitions are notoriously difficult), in *Wives and Daughters* this is continued with variations and developments in accordance with the pre-occupations of the 1860s. Apart from the cotton depression at the beginning of the decade, 'the condition of England' was beginning to improve, poverty was not so rife, popular education had greatly improved and at the end of the decade was to be made compulsory. In 1859, Darwin's *Origin of Species* had focused attention on questions of heredity and evolution and *Essays and Reviews*, in the following year, on the relevance of science and the Higher Criticism of the Bible, to religion and, therefore, to the life of the nation.

Molly Gibson, the heroine and central figure of *Wives and Daughters*, left motherless at an early age, has been brought up by her father, the local doctor, until she is sixteen when the novel begins. We learn that Dr Gibson is a man who:

> did not give way to much expression of his feelings [and] took a pleasure in bewildering her infant mind with his badinage. He had rather a contempt for demonstrative people [and] deceived himself into believing that still his reason was lord of all because he had never fallen into the habit of expression on any other than purely intellectual subjects. Molly, however, had her own intuitions to guide her. Though her papa laughed at her in a way which the Miss Brownings [Cranfordian spinsters who had been friends of her mother] called "really cruel" ... Molly took her little griefs and pleasures and poured them into her papa's ears... The child grew to understand her father so well and the two had the most delightful intercourse together... (Ch III)

What 'mothering' Molly could not get from her father she has found in the rough but loving arms of Betty, their old servant, "that kind-hearted termagant" of whom she had been "her charge ... her plague and her delight" since she was three years old. She often rides with her father on his country rounds, waiting for him on her pony while he makes his visits at remote farms and hamlets. But because he often has to leave her at home, when Molly is eight, he engages Miss Eyre, the respectable daughter of a shop-keeper in the town, as a daily governess. Dr Gibson gives Miss Eyre (cf Jane Eyre) her instructions. She is not to:

> teach Molly too much; She must sew and read and write and do her sums, but I want to keep her a child, and if I find more learning desirable for her, I'll see about giving it to her myself. After all, I'm not sure that reading and writing is necessary. Many a good woman gets married with only a cross to her name; it's rather a diluting of mother wit, to my fancy; but we must yield to the prejudices of society, Miss Eyre, and so you may teach the child to read! (Ch III)

It has only been by fighting and struggling hard that Molly persuades her father to let her have French and drawing lessons and, 'once a week, [she] joined a dancing-class at the assembly rooms ... and read every book that came her way, almost with as much delight as if it had been forbidden. For his station in life, Dr Gibson had an unusually good library...' Later, Molly continues her education in the old library at Hamley Hall, a small hall similar to the real Sandlebridge and Dam Head House, where there were also "many old books and a few new ones" and, when staying there, Molly reads Scott's *Bride of Lammermoor*. Miss Eyre, however, remains in the Gibson household as a sensible and kind companion to Molly until she is called away by sickness and a death in her own family.

Though Dr Gibson's remarks on the education of women may well represent a barbed comment on Mrs Gaskell's part, aimed at the general attitude of even intelligent men to this subject, Molly has had the security of an upbringing in a stable situation, in close contact with a basically kind and consistent if somewhat unemotional and unimaginative parent, an old affectionate servant, a morally good and sensible governess, and all of these within the cohesive community of a small provincial town, Hollingford, and its rural background. Her early education has been in her own home and limited to the tools of education, the three R's, and sewing, the essential and practical skill of all women at that time. Later these are embellished with the 'accomplishments' of French, drawing, and dancing. And, finally, what 'higher education' she had has been placed within her reach but achieved by her own efforts. A close textual study of the first few chapters of *Wives and Daughters* reveals interesting comparisons and contrasts with Mrs Gaskell's own background and education, and that of her daughters, as well as similarities between the fictional Dr Gibson and Dr Peter Holland and William Gaskell.[2]

With this background and education behind her and "her own intuitions to guide her", Molly sallies forth into adult life to do battle with and, at the last, to triumph over the lack of sympathy, imagination, and moral integrity of many different types of people.

Mrs Gaskell uses Cynthia Kirkpatrick, who becomes, in the course of events, Molly's step-sister, to illustrate the results of a very different background from Molly's. Cynthia, the same age as Molly, has been brought up from an early age in various boarding-schools and when the story opens is spending two years at a school in Boulogne with a view to becoming a governess. She, like Molly, has only one parent. Her father was an Anglican clergyman who had died leaving his widow and small child virtually penniless. Cynthia, therefore, has had all the more need of a mother's love and companionship. "A child should be brought up with its parents," she says; but not only has Mrs Kirkpatrick been forced to become an untrained governess, ultimately at the great house, Cumnor Towers, in the vicinity of Hollingford, in order to support herself and so causing Cynthia to be sent away to school, this mother actually prefers her child's absence to her presence. Contrasted strongly with Molly's parent, 'Clare' (the 'maiden' name by which Lady Cumnor always prefers to call her), had kept herself aloof from her daughter. Clare is a "superficial and flimsy" creature, a complete egocentric who sees everyone and every event only in relation to her own interests and comfort, 'an unperceptive person, except when her own interests are dependent on another person's humour', quite unable even to comprehend moral integrity or the needs of others. When Molly, for example, after Clare's marriage to Dr Gibson, becomes seriously ill through grief and the misunderstandings of others, Clare says her illness is "more tedious than interesting" and of herself as having "nursed [Molly] daily, almost nightly, – wakened times out of number by Dr Gibson getting up and going to see if she [had] her medicine properly!"

Addicted to 'dirty, dog-eared novel[s] from the circulating library', 'the leaves of which she turned with a pair of scissors', and with 'a superficial skill in the choice of and arrangement of her words, so as to appear as if the opinions that were in reality quotations, were formed by herself from actual experience or personal observation', she is quite incapable of real thought, has no respect for the truth, and her whole moral equipment operates throughout the novel quite differently from that of Dr Gibson and Molly. A vain woman, wishing to look younger than her age and with a flair for clothes (which is inherited by her daughter), she has kept Cynthia in the background so that she could enjoy the sort of social life in which Cynthia was an encumbrance. She even finds it "inconvenient" and "expensive" for Cynthia to travel from Boulogne for her wedding and so the girl is not present on that occasion. Later, Cynthia says: "Oh Molly, you don't know how I was neglected just when I wanted friends most. Mama does not know it; it is not in her to know what I might have been if I had only fallen into wise good hands. But I know it..." For, whereas Molly is sensitive, loving, loyal, and has a deep sense of duty and moral integrity, Cynthia is given to small deceits, is unable to form deep, loyal relationships, and it is her defective moral sense which causes Molly to become an object of gossip on the part of the whole community, to the great displeasure of her dearly-loved 'papa'. She also causes Molly herself intense suffering, loneliness and, in the end, her breakdown in health. Cynthia will always be a natural pleasure-seeker, unreliable, shallow, unimaginative, given, like her mother, to deceit, a reckless flirt, what modern social workers would call emotionally and psychologically crippled, unstable and insecure. Yet by the end of the novel she is to become the wife of a London barrister and, in the natural course of events, the mother of his children...

But, of course, these four characters are not so black and white as I have painted them. If they were, the novel would be merely a moral tract. The plot develops out of Dr Gibson's attempts to be both father and mother to Molly and, owing to the fact that one of his resident apprentices has begun to address secret love-letters to her and, following Miss Eyre's departure, his decision to provide Molly with what he considers a necessary second 'mother'. He admits to little desire to re-marry but when he meets Clare at Cumnor Towers, where she is on a social and he on a professional visit, he is attracted by her elegant appearance and proposes to her in a business-like yet precipitate and unthinking manner. On her part, Clare, who had by that time been set up in a school of her own by the Cumnors in a house belonging to them, their own children now no longer requiring her services, when Mr Gibson, now her fiancé, has departed, bursts into tears – of relief that she will no longer have to earn her living but be able 'to sit in her own drawing-room.'

This incident of Dr Gibson's proposal and subsequent marriage represents his first failure of feeling, sympathy, imagination or intuition. He has failed to see that their relationship is infinitely precious to Molly, that his omitting to discuss the matter with her or even to mention it until it was a fait-accompli, is a serious blow to Molly's emotional security, a 'young lady' of sixteen who has thought of herself as mistress of the household. Her grief and disappointment at the thought of an unknown woman 'taking her place' in her father's affections and in the house is intense and the beginning of what proves to be a disastrous situation. Molly at once sees what sort of person

Clare is and is made uneasy by her knowledge, although it is a year before Clare's moral inadequacies are forcibly brought home to Dr Gibson by her serious misuse of professional information obtained by eavesdropping at his surgery door. Henceforth, though not a man "to go into passions", with Clare "he became hard and occasionally bitter in his ways, preferring to cut short a discussion by a sarcasm, or by leaving the room."

Yet Clare is not all bad. She does not bear malice, is conscientious about paying her debts, is kind to the poor, and Mrs Gaskell is careful to point out the difficulties she has had as a poor clergyman's widow thrown on the world to fend for herself and a daughter, who, like her mother, also has beauty, "a careless perfection of dress", clever fingers and an impulsive generosity, as well as on Cynthia's part, an affection for Molly and respect for Dr Gibson. Cynthia also recognises her own faults, replying to Dr Gibson's "what faults you have fallen into have been mere girlish faults at first – leading you into much deceit..." with "Don't give yourself the trouble to define the shades of blackness... I'm not so obtuse but what I know them all better than anyone can tell me..." On the other hand, Clare's exquisitely amusing reactions to the situations and moral problems of everyday living make her perhaps the supreme Gaskellian character while Cynthia is a very attractive one. But Mrs Gaskell most carefully analyses and demonstrates the deleterious effects that Clare's inadequacies as a teacher, as well as a mother, have had on her past pupils, in the person, for example, of Lady Harriet, one of the new generation of Whig aristocrats, at Cumnor Towers, who, 'taught' by Clare, now feels quite inadequate to face her own considerable social responsibilities and entirely disinclined to marry owing to her childhood subjection to Clare's indiscreet confidences about her flirtations with visiting dancing masters and other such men. Clare's deficiencies are amply demonstrated throughout the novel and they have, of course, borne most heavily and poignantly on Cynthia, so that when she has told her step-sister of the events which led up to Molly's involvement in the unhappy deceit that had brought her (Molly) so much suffering (and the part Clare had played in precipitating them), 'Molly was struck by the aged and careworn expression which had temporarily taken hold of the brilliant and beautiful face; she could see from that how much Cynthia must have suffered...' In fact, Clare's deficiencies, in the 'present' of the novel, and in her various rôles, spread like a noxious gas so that the whole community is infected.

The influence of early education has now been seen at work in the Kirkpatrick, Cumnor, and Gibson families. It is also to be seen, in a wider sense, in the Hamley family of Hamley Hall. Squire Hamley, though of ancient lineage, 'who might have visited at every house in the county', 'was very indifferent to the charms of society' because he himself had received an unsuitable and inadequate education. His father, having been 'plucked' at Oxford, had sworn that none of his children should ever become a member of either university, and he had been educated at:

> a petty provincial school, where he saw much that he hated... [;] imperfectly educated ... and aware of his deficiency ... awkward and ungainly in society, he kept out of it as much as possible and was obstinate, violent-tempered and dictatorial in his own immediate circle. However, he was also generous and true as steel; the very soul of honour ... and had so much natural shrewdness that his conversation was always worth listening to, although he was apt to start by assuming entirely false premises... (Ch IV)

– in short, he was a good man spoiled by a bad education. Of the same generation as Dr Gibson and Clare, Squire Hamley's unsatisfactory education has two dire results. His wife is a "delicate, fine London lady" with a taste for poetry and strong social and intellectual interests – (the new books in the library are hers). Though proud of his wife's abilities and there is a great love between the two, the Squire's obstinate unwillingness to entertain and accompany her to London to visit theatres and so forth, whence, if she goes, she goes alone, result in such feelings of deprivation and isolation on her part that this charming lady becomes an invalid and dies, in spite of Dr Gibson's efforts to save her which include the provision of his own daughter as a companion.

The Squire's two sons, Osborne and Roger, are both sent to Cambridge but again the Squire's refusal to entertain their social equals when they are at home means that they do not feel able to accept invitations and so they too are deprived of suitable companionship during their vacations. This has the effect on Osborne, the elder and weaker of the two, of his spending his vacations in London and abroad, falling into debt, and entering into a secret, unsuitable marriage with a French Catholic 'bonne', the equivalent of an English nursery-governess, a girl who is a symbol of all those qualities of class, nationality, and religion that were an abomination to the Tory squire, his father. The secret marriage leads to Osborne's deceit, further debt, deteriorating relations with his father and, despair working on a not robust constitution, to his death from a heart disease. So the Squire's bad education may be said to have led, indirectly, even to the death of his wife and son.

Osborne had been the darling of the Hamley family. The heir, something of a poet like his mother, 'carrying away many of the prizes at school' (Rugby), and 'thought to be clever', he was somewhat spoilt by his mother and both parents had had extravagant expectations of his future career as a Fellow at Cambridge. 'His appearance had all the grace and refinement of his mother's – He was sweet tempered and affectionate, almost as demonstrative as a girl', whereas, of Roger, 'clumsy and heavily built... square, grave and rather immobile of face,... good but dull', winning no prizes at school but bringing home favourable reports of his conduct, there has even been some discussion as to whether he should go to Cambridge at all, but, remembering his own regrets, the Squire had insisted. Roger, however, goes on to become a Senior Wrangler while Osborne's career at the university is a complete failure.

At Rugby, Osborne's second-rate literary talents had been praised and rewarded while the scientific genius of Roger had been entirely missed. This reflects contemporary feeling about Rugby. In 1821, a Bill had been presented to Parliament which had pressed for more practical, scientific, and even business subjects to be included in the curriculum of the public schools, a Bill which, though not passed, had expressed a strong desire for change and which had resulted in the appointment in 1828 of Dr Arnold as headmaster of Rugby. It had been confidently expected that his appointment would change the face of education as a whole but this had been wrong as far as the curriculum went. Arnold's strong personality only served to entrench the classical emphasis more deeply, believing as he did that the study of Latin and Greek, which gave a picture of a whole civilisation and its values, was an adequate preparation for personal and public life.

He did not see science as helping in this even though he was living at the beginning of the scientific age.

Mrs Gaskell had been, as we have already seen, an admirer of Arnold and the sermons in which he had chastised the rich for their neglect of the welfare and education of the poor. He had seen the public schools, where the sons of the rich were educated and which had become largely nurseries of vice, lying, idleness, drunkenness and gangsterism, as an instrument for the production of Christian gentlemen who would know their private and public duties; and he had a great success in this, many of them being, again as we have already seen, among the 'younger' men who admired Mrs Gaskell's works and were prominent in the Christian Socialist movement. Nevertheless, by 1865 Mrs Gaskell had obviously come to believe that the current education of both men and women, who were born to social responsibility in society, was inadequate for the needs of the times. The profession of 'civil engineer', for example, which Roger Hamley's parents had originally thought a suitable career for him owing to what they thought were his inferior abilities, was not in 1865 (and is still not) thought of as a profession for a public school 'gentleman'. Mrs Gaskell, however, had never thought of engineers as 'inferior' and in her letters speaks with respect and admiration of Sir William Fairbairn, James Nasmyth, and Holbrook Gaskell, while Paul's father, also an engineer in *Cousin Phillis*, invented out of interest in the problems involved, not with a view to profit. The portrayal of Osborne and Roger Hamley can be seen as her final view that, though of vital importance, the education of upper-class boys to be men of integrity, sensitive in their personal relationships and to their social and economic responsibilities, is still not quite enough. She had written long before to the young Marianne – who, on leaving her London school, had decided to take on part of the education of her two youngest sisters for a period – that, as well as the music, drawing, painting, dancing and foreign languages which played the largest part in the education of all the Gaskell girls, there must also be "hard and correct" work, "the dry bones of knowledge".

Reason had never at any time been abandoned by Mrs Gaskell but it had to be kept in its proper place and guided by intuition, sympathy, imagination, and all bound together in a moral integrity, particularly in the leaders of society, for only they had, in her view, the power to initiate measures for social betterment.

Nor had Mrs Gaskell ever been ignorant of, or hostile to, science as such. The interests of the 'Unitarian cousinhood', the Holland-Wedgwood-Darwin group, would have seen to that from her childhood. The Literary and Philosophical Societies too, founded very much under Unitarian auspices, had always had a scientific bias. The one founded in Manchester, closely associated with the famous John Dalton and visited by the young Coleridge, was famous throughout the country, met at Cross Street Chapel, and William Gaskell was one of its chairmen. There had been working-men scientists in *Mary Barton*, weavers who threw their shuttles with Newton's *Principia* propped up on the loom and who knew the Latin names of every plant within miles of Manchester. In *Cousin Phillis*, Mr Holman, the minister-farmer, was also interested in mathematics.

In *Wives and Daughters* there appears a whole group of gentlemen scientists, among them Dr Gibson, of course, a doctor interested in science for its own sake and anxious to improve his medical knowledge for the benefit of his patients, some of whom he treats without charge. He is welcome at Cumnor Towers when Lord Hollingford, the heir, is at home, since he too is a scientist who contributes 'papers' to 'learned journals' and has a laboratory at the Towers. Welcome there also is Roger Hamley, the central male figure in the novel, whose career Mrs Gaskell admits is based on that of Charles Darwin.

In 1851 she had dined in London with Darwin and described him as "a cousin ...who has been round the world',[3] and in 1864 wrote to Smith, Publisher of The Cornhill, in which *Wives and Daughters* was to appear, that the character Roger "works out for himself a certain name in Natural Science – is tempted by a large offer to go round the world as a naturalist."[4] Unlike the fictional character, however, Darwin was paid nothing for his voyage on the Beagle and his expenses were met by his uncle, Josiah Wedgwood.

Mrs Gaskell had remarked in 1861 about "not being scientific", and, of course, this was so in the conventional sense of the word, but she was referring to the meeting in that year of the British Association in Manchester. Her husband was responsible for the organisation of this particular meeting and she was expected to entertain a houseful of guests which would include Henry Smith, Savillian Professor of Geometry at Oxford and Augustus Harcourt, assistant to Professor Brodie, Professor of Chemistry at Oxford, and to sit through a series of lectures, and, 'not feeling very strong', she expressed the wish that the meetings were over. Her own scientific interests were more in tune with those of the Wordsworths, (Dorothy was an excellent botanist), Coleridge and Ruskin, minute observers of nature in whom nature and religion fused into a social philosophy of great spiritual intensity. She even seems to have preferred to look after her garden and the small-holding she had established in a field opposite Plymouth Grove, which included a cow and pigs, to writing. In 1864, Smith sent her a hand-drawn Valentine card showing himself on his knees begging for the copy for *Wives and Daughters* while she, with her back to him, is contemplating her cow. The house in Plymouth Grove can be seen in the background.[5] Coleridge's own attempts in the direction of rural production had been ineffectual but Mrs Gaskell produced good butter and milk for her family at a time when these were unobtainable in Manchester. Coleridge, too, was the first to exhibit in his *Biographia Literaria*, that awareness of the body-mind relationship which is so evident in Mrs Gaskell's *My Diary*, the day-to-day study of her first child, written between 1835 and 1838 (thus predating Darwin's own similar study,[6] and worked out with great complexity in *Wives and Daughters*.

We can, however, turn to a very different source of information as to Mrs Gaskell's interest in and attitude towards science, especially Darwinian materialism. Of all the Victorian poets it was Tennyson who had the greatest interest in science. In 1850, Mrs Gaskell had written to Eliza Fox, on the publication of *In Memoriam*, that it was "a book to brood over." It was a borrowed copy that she had read; she was triumphant when she managed to get a copy of her own, and the number of quotations from it in her works almost rival those from Wordsworth and Coleridge. In 1858, she chose to inscribe for Isabella Banks, the Manchester-born writer and antiquary, as an autograph, the following lines:

> O yet we trust that somehow good
> Will be the final goal of ill
> To pangs of nature, sins of will
> Defects of doubt, and taints of blood;
> That nothing walks with aimless feet
> That not one life shall be destroyed,
> Or cast as rubbish to the void
> When God hath made the pile complete [LIII, 1-8]

173

From Tennyson's 'In Memoriam'
E.C. Gaskell
April 10th 1858

These lines may be taken as the motif of *Wives and Daughters*. Mrs Gaskell had a long struggle against "the never-ending sorrow" of her son's death and the wasted, stunted and wantonly sacrificed lives in the Manchester cotton-factories. It was in *In Memoriam* that Tennyson had also tried to come to terms both with the death of his friend Hallam and the clash between Christianity and scientific facts and theories. It is one of the few poems in which an attempt is made to see man as a biological phenomenon with a past, a present and a future; evolution (nine years before Darwin's *Origin of Species*) as shifting from natural selection to a spiritual growth which is partly man-controlled, a Christianity without bigotry and sectarianism as compatible with the world-view of science. Questions of heredity, the influence of early environment on character, and various aspects of the 'struggle for survival' are all explored with great subtlety in *Wives and Daughters* (which could as easily have been called *Fathers and Sons*), but with an emphasis on the development of the moral integrity which is essential for the further evolution of man and society. In this last novel of Mrs Gaskell's, the sheep and goats are divided, insofar as they are divided, on this question of moral integrity and its possibilities of development and survival in society.

Molly, the central female figure, has to struggle hard for her survival, needing all her quality of "simple goodness", as it has often been called by critics, and which, as has been admitted, Mrs Gaskell makes both charming and credible. But Molly also has endurance and courage and inner resources. These are seen at work from the beginning of the novel, when her father tells her of his proposed remarriage and she feels that "It was as if the piece of solid ground on which she stood had broken from the shore, and she was drifting out to the infinite sea alone", to the overcoming of her illness at its end. On the other hand, Roger, though somewhat obtuse and not seeing Molly's true qualities until he has had his fingers burned by Cynthia's more obvious charms, also has sterling qualities and a deep self-sacrificing love for his father and brother. The 'European republic of learned men', scientists (not what we would now call technologists), who meet at Cumnor Towers, though "without polished manners...very much in earnest about their own subjects and not having much to say on any other", are also kind and unassuming. And one feels sure that Mrs Gaskell is putting her own thoughts into the mouth of Dr Gibson when he says of their scientific ideas that he would like if it were possible, to have lived 'till their reality was ascertained and one saw what they led to.'[8]

By the end of *Wives and Daughters*, Osborne Hamley, weak in body and mind, has been eliminated in favour of the more robust Roger, who, as Frederick Greenwood, the then editor of *The Cornhill*, says in the few pages needed to complete the novel (which he wrote for the January 1866 number based on what Mrs Gaskell had told her daughters of her intentions), "will marry Molly, and that is what we are most concerned about." They are to live in London, where Roger is to take up an important scientific position. We know that Mrs Gaskell had no love for London society, except for the theatres and literary life which the fictitious Mrs Hamley had also longed for, and we can presume that Roger and Molly will symbolically help to counteract the undesirable effects on the nation's capital of the second-rate Cynthia and her equally second-rate barrister husband.

Squire Hamley, who, at the beginning of the novel, had rejected out of hand the idea of Molly as a daughter-in-law on the grounds of her inferior class, is now devoted to her and is also learning to love his French, even lower class and Roman Catholic daughter-in-law, Aimée, for her own very real qualities – her name, of course, meaning love. She has borne Osborne a child and the Squire is delighting in the grandson who will inherit the old hall and its poverty-stricken, and therefore neglected, estate. The child has been born of love and, less romantically, of a human cross-fertilisation which will, hopefully, produce a healthier man than his father had been, physically, mentally, and, morally – and for good measure Mrs Gaskell has given him, for a mother, an experienced and pious nursery-governess who tactfully thwarts the old Squire's attempts to spoil the child!

But it is a tribute to Mrs Gaskell's genius that the 'carpentering' on this level of the novel is never allowed to obtrude and it is only when we make a conscious effort to 'go back-stage' that the ideological 'props' of this, her last and greatest novel, are revealed.

CHAPTER 14

Wives and Daughters: **social values of the 1860s**
and 'old England' compared

Though Mrs Gaskell set *Wives and Daughters* in a period about
1820, the "half a life-time ago" which was a favourite phrase of hers
and which she used to denote a remembered past, the novel is, on
another of its levels, a melancholy commentary on the turgid stream
of money which flowed through and dominated the society of the
1860s. This society was in effect early Edwardian as the young
Prince of Wales began to set up his own 'court', separate from that of
his parents. Mrs Gaskell was well aware of the Prince's 'ménage'
and in 1859 had refused an invitation for herself and Meta to join an
incognito house-party in the Trossachs, an invitation due to her
friendship with Lady Augusta Bruce, one of the Queen's ladies-in-
waiting, who, in 1863, had married Dean Stanley, and was sister to
Colonel Robert Bruce, the Prince's recently appointed 'governor'.[1]

This same stream of money is in Dickens' *Our Mutual Friend*,
published at the same time as *Wives and Daughters* and symbolised in
Dickens' novel by the River Thames as it flowed through London. In
both novels we see the desire in the 1860s for money and particularly
the acute need of it for anyone 'in society'; the arrogance of those
who have it personified by Lady Cumnor, who has been called the
first Edwardian hostess in English fiction; and the struggles of those
who do not have it in the persons of Clare, Cynthia, Molly and the
Hamley family. In 1863, Mrs Gaskell had written, in *Fraser's
Magazine*, of the "Shams" of contemporary society and in *Our Mutual
Friend* Dickens named his nouveau-riche family the Veneerings. In
the following year, Mrs Gaskell's old friend, Max Müller, who had
serenaded her in German in the Lake District nearly twenty years
previously,[2] wrote: "I should not like to live in London... this
skirmish... this trying to out-do each other in pretence and conceit is
quite sickening."[3]

In *Wives and Daughters*, it is in London that the Cumnors spend
most of the year in various frivolities which "cannot be missed", and
of which Clare, on hearing of Cynthia's engagement to a London
barrister, exclaims in ecstasy that her daughter will "live in Sussex
Place and keep a man and a brougham and I don't know what ... in

this generation there are so many more rich young men than there were when I was a girl."[4] In *North and South*, Margaret Hale, listening to the talk of the business-men over the dinner table in Milton Northern, had been appreciative of their energy after the "vapid" conversations she had heard over London dinner-tables. In *Cranford*, Mary Smith's father, though a representative of Drumble, the industrial city on the horizon of the story and himself contaminated by its utilitarian values, had, nevertheless, agreed to become part of the compassionate scheme of Cranford's elderly ladies to provide Miss Matty with a small income after the failure of her bank. But in *Sylvia's Lovers, Cousin Phillis*, and *Wives and Daughters*, all written in the 1860s, Mrs Gaskell seems, at first sight, to have forgotten the industrial city and its qualities, whether good or bad, though we know from her letters that this was not in fact the case.

It was in the early 1860s that Mrs Gaskell, far from forgetting Manchester, had made herself ill with relief-work during the cotton-depression brought about by the American Civil War. She knew well all the reasons for the depression from her correspondence with Charles Eliot Norton, whom she plied with questions and whose answers she preferred to anything she read in *The Times*. She was, indeed, invited but refused to write a series of articles on conditions in Manchester in *The Daily News*, saying that she had little to comment on except to commend the cotton-workers' "patient spirit of endurance."[5] It was also to Eliot Norton that she cried out in pain in 1863:

> I cannot tell you what a nightmare last winter was - and at the last we seem to have done more harm than good – not 'we' alone – perhaps 'we' less than most; but the imposition, the deterioration in character &c &c were so great ... people who were good and hard-working before, & at the beginning of the 'relief,' people we knew & had respected, were found paying a man 6d a week to answer to their name, & claim relief for them in different districts[.]... One local Relief Committee – consisting of small shop-keepers were found to have supplied themselves with great-coats out of the Funds entrusted to them &c &c &c...[6]

The causes of the distress and the corruption of the cotton-workers had shifted from the industrial city of the provinces to London and even across the sea to America. And so we see, in *Sylvia's Lovers*, that the oppression of the common-folk comes from the House of Commons in London via the local civil and military authorities, i.e. the whole apparatus of the state; and Mrs Gaskell actually contrives that Philip, the ambitious young shop-assistant, visits London (by sea) on behalf of his Quaker employers. In *Cousin Phillis*, tragedy comes to the small rural community in the person of Holdsworth, a representative of the 'new young men', who, after disturbing the peace of that community, departs for Canada, for there, on his own admission, he will be paid more than he could command in England. In *Wives and Daughters*, a similar young man, a bailiff of Lord Cumnor's, corrupts the young Cynthia, by 'lending' her a considerable sum of money, in return for the promise of her secret engagement to him, when she is abandoned at school during the summer holidays by her mother without sufficient funds. In these novels then, the real sources of evil in society lie in the power of the state, the power of money itself and the power of the type of people who have it or are determined to get it, i.e. the nouveau-riche and the ruthlessly ambitious.

In the Cumnor family, money-power has invaded the country to a greater extent than it had ever done before and the great Whig mansion dominates the countryside. Even so, as distinct from the towns, something of the feudal values and social cohesion of 'old England' still remains, 'the Earl' still representing to the local people the great feudal lords of the past; and no man would dream of voting against 'his' candidate in the Parliamentary elections, (in this case his heir, Lord Hollingford), whether or not they agreed with his politics, – and this not from any feeling of compulsion but from a feeling of loyalty. The Cumnors also do a deal of good in various ways for the people of Hollingford and the surrounding area. Lady Cumnor has established a school on the estate (as did the Egertons at Tatton Park even if Mrs Gaskell calls it an 'industrial school' which merely teaches the three Rs and turns out 'capital' estate employees. The Earl, too, when in residence, shows considerably more personal concern for his tenants (even against the advice of his estate manager, old Mr Goodenough, a hard man who dislikes his masters' "pottering" as he calls it) than the average manufacturer in the towns. It is significant that it is on one of these 'pottering' expeditions amongst his farms that he first meets the young Molly, sitting on her rough pony, waiting for her father who is making a sick-call. The Cumnors, in return, are dependent to a large extent on the ordinary folk of the area for their services and supplies. The social cohesion of the small community is perhaps most amusingly and perceptively described in the visit of the whole Cumnor family to the ball at the Assembly Rooms, another vivid evocation of Georgian Knutsford before the coming of the railway.

It is also at Cumnor Towers that the scientists of the novel meet, men who are interested in the greater understanding of nature rather than her exploitation. In February 1864, when the novel was being written – it began to appear in *Cornhill* the following August – Mrs Gaskell was staying with Professor G.J. Allman, a botanist and Professor of Natural History at the university of Edinburgh. He and his wife, a sister of William Shaen, were old friends and she describes him to Charles Eliot Norton as "the most charmingly wise man I ever met with ... full of deep thought & wisdom & knowledge and also like a child for unselfconsciousness and sweet humility. You would so like and value him". And, at the end of the letter, she asks Norton to try and locate an American scientific book which Dr Allman very much wanted, adding that Agassiz, an eminent evolutionist (though he took a different view of it from that of Darwin to whom Allman was known), would perhaps help in the search.[7] Even so, in the following May, she wrote to George Smith, outlining the plot of *Wives and Daughters*, that Roger was "rough and unpolished",[8] the same qualities of which she had complained, in 1860, of the young men of the day who were lacking in "those higher qualities[,] the spiritual qualities as it were, which those must appreciate who would think of my daughters."[9]

One sees much of Charles Darwin in Roger. On Molly's first visit to Hamley Hall, we read of his seeking a rare plant,

> one which he had long been wishing to find in flower...
> he... went with light and well-planted footsteps in search of
> the treasure. He was so great a lover of nature that,
> without any thought, but habitually, he always avoided
> treading unnecessarily on any plant; who knew what long-
> sought growth or insect might develop itself in that which
> now appeared insignificant?[10]

179

His father, too, though not a scientist, is also a lover of nature and an admirer of his son's knowledge and, on Molly's very first day at the Hall, he shows her a small island in the middle of a stretch of water, which he promises to let her visit some time but not on that occasion because the use of a boat would disturb the young coots and grebes which were "still in the nests among the reeds and water-plants..." He recounts with pride, while giving a detailed description of the wild-life of the estate, Roger's bolting:

> into a copse because he saw something fifteen yards off, some plant maybe, which he'd tell me was very rare, though I should say I'd seen its 'marrow' at every turn in the woods, and if we came upon such a thing as this, touching a delicate film of cobweb upon a leaf with his stick as he spoke, 'why he could tell you what insect or spider made it, and if it lived in rotten firewood, or in a cranny of good sound timber, or deep in the ground, or up in the sky or anywhere.'[11]

In fact, nature plays as significant a part in *Wives and Daughters* as it had in any of Mrs Gaskell's earlier works. On the first page of the novel, we find Molly standing at her bedroom-window in Hollingford, where, at six o'clock on a summer morning, the air is sweet, the dew 'already on the flowers in the garden below but still rising from the long hay-grass in the meadows directly beyond', while the pleasant, brisk ringing of the church bells 'is calling everyone to their daily work, as they had done for hundreds of years' and the 'little puffs of smoke ... already beginning to rise from many a cottage chimney' show that some housewives are already preparing breakfast for 'the bread-winner of the family'.

Though Molly is made miserable on her first visit by the magnificence of Cumnor Towers, the gardens are "really lovely" and, riding across the park at night with her father, (another hint of 'young Werther') she

> struck her pony and urged him on as hard as he would go... exclaiming, "oh! I am so glad to be here! It is so pleasant riding here in the open, free, fresh air crushing out such a good smell from the dewy grass."[12]

Hamley Hall, however, remains, from soon after the beginning to its end, the real focus of the novel, and descriptions of its natural surroundings are a continuing commentary on what goes on there. Of Molly's first journey to the old hall we read:

> At length they came to a village; straggling cottages lined the road, an old church stood on a kind of green, with the public-house close by it; there was a great tree, with a bench all round the trunk, and the little inn. The wooden stocks were close to the gates... They swung in [Molly was travelling the seven miles from Hollingford to Hamley Hall in the Hall carriage] at the gates of the park ... and drove up through meadow-grass, ripening for hay – it was no aristocratic deer-park this – to the old red-brick hall; not three hundred yards from the highroad. [Looking from her bed-room window there, Molly could see] a flower-garden right below; a meadow of ripe grass just beyond, changing colour in long sweeps, as the soft wind blew over it; great old forest trees a little on one side, or by putting her head out, if the window was open, the silver shimmer of a mere, about a quarter of a mile off. On the opposite side to the trees and the mere, the look-out was bounded by the old walls and high-peaked roofs of the extensive farm-buildings. The deliciousness of the early summer silence was only broken by the song of the birds, and the nearer hum of bees. Listening to these sounds, which enhanced the exquisite stillness, and puzzling out objects obscured by distance or shadow, Molly forgot herself.[13]

This minutely-observed small hall and its surroundings is not Sandlebridge but it may very well be the red-brick Dam Head House of Mrs Gaskell's ancestor, William Holland, and the village, that of Mobberley, some seven miles from Knutsford and where there are Hollands buried in the churchyard.[14]

In addition to the great tree on the village green at Hamley there stands another on the lawn near the house, a cedar beneath which Mrs Hamley establishes an 'open-air summer parlour ... where there were chairs, table, books and tangled work.' Such a cedar still stands on the lawn at the back of Heathfield, Mrs Gaskell's girlhood home. It is under such a tree that Ruth is buried and under another such, in the short story, 'The Sexton's Hero', that a group of holiday-makers listen

181

to a tale of true heroism, moral courage, and the sacrifice of self for a loved-one. It is under the tree at Hamley Hall that Molly learns from Mrs Hamley a love of poetry.

On Molly's first visit to Hamley Hall, when Dr Gibson calls to see her:

> It was a brilliantly hot summer's morning; men in their shirt-sleeves were in the fields, getting in the early harvest of oats; as Mr Gibson rode slowly along, he could see them over the tall hedge-rows, and even hear the soothing measured sound of the fall of the long swathes as they were mown.[15]

When he had told Molly of his forth-coming marriage, it was to the terrace with its seat 'almost surrounded by the drooping leaves of a weeping ash – on the long broad terrace walk on the other side of the wood that overlooked the pleasant slope of the meadows beyond...' that the girl ran and flung herself 'on the ground – that natural throne for violent sorrow – and leant up against the old moss-grown seat...' And it was here that Roger, returning from a scientific dredging of ponds and ditches, found her and did his clumsy-kind best to comfort her, bringing her a drink of spring-water in a 'broad green leaf, turned into an impromptu cup. Little as it was, it did her good.'

Autumn, in *Wives and daughters*, is not the dreary season as it is so often portrayed, but "the bright solemn fading of the year", the season of:

> The golden corn-harvest, the walks through the stubble-fields, and rambles into hazel-copses in search of nuts; the stripping of the apple orchards of their ruddy fruit, and the joyous cries and shouts of watching children; and the gorgeous tulip-like colouring of the later time [which came] with the shortening days. There was comparative silence in the land, except for the distant shots, and the whirr of the partridges as they rose up from the field, [and Molly gathered] a nose-gay of such leaves as struck her for their brilliant colouring [while] thick holly bushes shone out dark green in the midst of the amber and scarlet foliage.[16]

Even when Mrs Hamley is dying the sad scene indoors is contrasted with that outside; the

lovely tranquil winter's day; every branch and every twig
on the trees and shrubs ... glittering with drops of the sun-
melted hoar-frost; a robin was perched on a holly bush,
piping cheeringly...[17]

Near the end of the novel, when Molly is recovering from her
illness, a great basket of flowers comes for her from Hamley Hall.
She is now well enough to arrange them herself and she comments on
the white pinks which were Mrs Hamley's favourite, the bit of sweet
briar which, though it has pricked her finger, "quite scents the room",
the rose, "very rare", which she recognises as the one which grew "in
the sheltered corner of the wall, near the mulberry tree", which Roger
had bought for his mother and which he had brought to Molly's notice
on one of her visits to the house.[18]

But, in fact, on hearing of Molly's illness, the whole Hollingford
community (as in *Cousin Phillis* and *Cranford*) had rallied to her
support, Cynthia returning from a visit to London, the Cumnors' again
sending fruit, flowers, and the "latest caricatures", the *Cranfordian*,
Miss Brownings, and Mrs Goodenough, all hovering anxiously in the
background, the "humble patients" of Dr Gibson leaving their
"earliest cauliflowers" and "their duty to Miss", "each in his or her
own way [showing] kind interest in her". Yet:

> The last of all, though strongest in regard, most piteously
> in earnest, came Squire Hamley ... to hear the smallest
> detail... Every resource of his heart, or his house, or his
> lands was sacked and tried, if it could bring a moment's
> pleasure to her...[19]

It was also from the neglected terrace at Hamley Hall with its
weeping ash-tree, that Molly had seen the pleasant slope of meadows
beyond and the 'sunny, peaceful landscape, with trees and a church-
spire, two or three red-tiled roofs of old cottages, and a purple bit of
rising ground in the distance.' Here, for the last time we see Mrs
Gaskell contemplating the archetypal scene of 'old England' with its
small hall, farm, church and cottages all closely integrated with each
other and with the landscape, an image representative of a way of life
only ended, finally, by the General Enclosures Act of 1845.

183

Yet Mrs Gaskell had never over-idealised country life. Margaret, in *North and South*, had warned Higgins, the cotton-operative, discontented with the conditions of his work, that he would find, after the companionship and mental stimulus of his work-mates, the life of a country labourer monotonous and less well-paid. In *Cumberland Sheep-Shearers*, she had discussed the diseases of sheep and agricultural rents as well as admired the beauty of clear-eyed boys riding the rams. She was not blind to the faults of 'the country gentlemen', in *Wives and Daughters* represented by the old Tory, Squire Hamley, who were often unwilling to try new ideas, often arrogant, prejudiced, and with a limited education, their relative poverty and the low productivity of their land very much their own fault. But at Hollingford, with its hinterland of villages, hamlets, great and small halls, and isolated farm-houses, the class-alienation and poverty of the industrial city and the state-power and cash-nexus of London, are both, in the last resort, absent or much diminished.

The Earl's absence from his estate for the greater part of the year is mitigated by his 'pottering' expeditions and it is at his house that a wide variety of people meet to mingle and exchange ideas, scientific and otherwise, as evidenced by later scenes at Cumnor Towers when even Molly, under the kindly protection of Lady Harriet, feels more at ease. Lady Cumnor's frivolity is off-set a little by her school and the annual 'school-scrimmage' at the Towers to which the lesser ladies of Hollingford who help in the school, look forward with quite palpitating eagerness and excitement, as well as other of her small 'condescensions'. Squire Hamley's neglect of his land and lack of courage and progressiveness in this area, which result in his having to 'turn off' a few of his estate-workers because he cannot pay them any longer, do not have the dreadful effect of such dismissals as occurred in Manchester. And, when this Tory squire receives a message from an old estate-worker who is dying, he knows and fulfils his immemorial duty of visiting him and giving what comfort he can; a far cry from the deaths of Davenport and John Barton in *Mary Barton* and young Bessie in *North and South*, the death of the last from "the fluff", a preventable disease, which passes quite unnoticed by her former employer.

In fact, it is to Hamley Hall that, in *Wives and Daughters*, we return again and again. Though, especially at the beginning of the novel, the Squire is represented as a crusty and in many ways

184

misguided old man, also from its beginning, we are told: 'There was a dignity in [his] quiet conservatism that gained for him an immense amount of respect from high and low.' As various members of the Hollingford community point out: "no one ... knew the time when the Hamleys had not lived at Hamley", "Ever since the Heptarchy," said the vicar, an opinion shared by the Squire himself, who calls himself "a Hamley of Hamley, straight in descent from nobody knows where – the Heptarchy they say... sometime before King Alfred, because he was the King of all England..." Miss Browning says: "I have heard there were Hamleys of Hamley before the Romans", and Mrs Goodenough came in with the still more startling assertion: "I have always heerd", said she with all the slow authority of an oldest inhabitant, "that there were Hamleys of Hamley afore the time of the pagans."[20] Is this, one wonders, a Knutsford folk-memory of Plantagenets as referring to the Hollands?

Squire Hamley describes himself and his sons as follows:

> here am I, of as good and as old a descent as any man in England, and I doubt if a stranger, to look at me, would take me for a gentleman, with my red face, great hands and feet, and thick figure, fourteen stone and never less than twelve when I was a young man; and there's Osborne, who takes after his mother, who couldn't tell her great great grandfather from Adam, bless her; and Osborne has a girl's delicate face, and slight make, and hands and feet as small as a lady's ... Now, Roger is like me, a Hamley of Hamley, and no-one in the street will ever think that red-brown big-boned clumsy chap is of gentle blood.[21]

In the same chapter as this passage occurs, as well as in the letter to Smith about the plot of the novel, Mrs Gaskell is at pains to say that, though Hamley is a squire, he lives "more as a yeoman, when such a class existed, than as a squire of this generation."

In contrast with the magnificent interior of Cumnor Towers, which is described in great detail, at Hamley Hall there are "none of the luxuries of modern days". Here, the furnishings are old-fashioned and austere; in fact we see again the "elegant economy" of Cranford. Everything is 'well-preserved' and, though often thread-bare, 'exquisitely clean', the wooden floors of 'finely grained oak'. In the simple bed-room which Molly occupies, 'the climbing honey-suckle outside the open window scented the air more exquisitely than any toilette perfume.' In the equally austere drawing-room with its ancient furniture, there are "stands of plants", and "great jars of flowers" and here the Squire and Molly play cards each evening. Here, too, family prayers are said at the close of the day – 'the old butler came in with a solemn look, placed a large prayer-book before his master... [,] the maids and men trooped in to prayers, – the windows still open and the sounds of the solitary corn-crake and the owl hooting in the trees, mingling with the words spoken.' It is again a scene reminiscent of *My Lady Ludlow* and *Cousin Phillis*, one of simple piety lived in close contact with nature and in which class exists but is transcended.

In fact, the 'carpentering' on this level of the novel is as easily recognisable as that in the previous chapter. The 'ham' in Hamley is the Saxon word for a settlement. The Heptarchy was a confederation of seven Anglo-Saxon kingdoms in the seventh and eighth centuries and the Holland family had held land in South Lancashire in Saxon times. Compared with the Hollands, the Egerton family, with their new and magnificent Tatton Park (still being added to in 1862), were incomers, "mere muck of yesterday", as Squire Hamley describes the Cumnors at the beginning of *Wives and Daughters*, whose ancestor had begun "his fortune through selling tobacco in King James' reign." The Egertons had made a large fortune in industry through shrewd industrial investment.

In choosing the name of Hamley for the village which Molly saw from the neglected terrace of the old hall, all the evidence is that Mrs Gaskell saw it as representing the remains of the lifestyle which existed in Saxon times, when the land was held in common and yet on an individual basis. Moreover, it was held, not for money, but for service to the rest of the community, to the feudal lord and to the king. Each village was, in fact, a single farm in which the humblest cotter had more security than the modern land-owner. All decisions were made by the elected 'moot' or council, a form of democracy which has never been improved upon and to which even the yeoman (Old English 'yeme-mann', the free-holder owning as well as working his sizeable holding and living in his small hall, the aristocrat of the peasantry) was subject.

H.J. Massingham, 'the modern Cobbett', returned, in the present century, again and again to the concept of the Saxon village and the yeoman, seeing in this ancient image "the base of the apex which we call civilisation"; the Peasants' Revolt in the fourteenth century as the culmination of grievances caused by the long occupation by the Normans, whose manorial system bore far more heavily on the peasants than had ever been the case previously, the Commons as having betrayed the 'commons' of England and, four centuries later, destroying them. In Massingham's opinion, if the peasants had won in the fourteenth century England would not have mislaid her soul in that "avid pursuit of wealth which is the history of the nineteenth century."

The yeoman, who stood between the high aristocracy and the common people, and reaching his 'grand siècle', in the seventeenth century (Shakespeare was of yeoman stock), was, according to Massingham, noted for

> his patriarchal relation with his men, his intimacy with their labour, his full-blooded generosity...his use of the vernacular, his field-learning, his homeliness... His sense of devotion to the land made him the trustee of it, and this quality of personal responsibility was the greatest of his gifts to the national character – the reverse of that centralization; committee rule and bureaucratic control to which we have pinned our faith since his decline.[22]

The yeomen, then, became the guardians of the liberty both of the people and the country. That well-known term, 'the yeomen of England' calls up an immediately recognisable image and it is one that fits exactly Squire Hamley and his son, Roger, with their red faces, thick-set bodies and unshakeable integrity. Yet it is also at Hamley Hall that, as we have already seen, there is the possibility of new life growing out of the decay of the old in the figure of Roger's little nephew, "a sturdy chap" as the Squire calls him.

By the end of *Wives and Daughters*, we have found the principle of 'reconciliation on a higher level' at work yet again and also the culmination of an exaltation of the rural scene which constitutes a vision of the Golden Age, not only recalling the values of 'old England' in a decade when they had never been more strongly attacked, but also seeking to envisage a future in which the best of the past shall be enriched by the new insights of the present. It has been said that a Golden Age never existed and never can exist. It is, nevertheless, a concept which has existed in the mind of man since the beginning of recorded time. Mrs Gaskell was one for whom it had as much reality, on its own terms, as the concepts which promoted the Industrial Revolution itself and she saw that any civilisation which lost sight of it would decay and die.

CHAPTER 15
"A purer aether, a diviner air": Italian influence on
Cousin Phillis

Towards the end of the 1850s, to the list of Mrs Gaskell's men-friends had been added a name with which we are already familiar, that of Charles Eliot Norton (1827-1908), the American whom she and her two eldest daughters met in Rome at the beginning of her three months visit in the spring of 1857. She was then forty-seven and he thirty, a Unitarian by birth and conviction, though of a very different type from his father Andrews Norton, a rich Boston business-man who was also a prominent lay-theologian and president of Harvard, at that time a Unitarian academy. Charles Eliot Norton was one of the first to foresee and support the northern states on the question of slavery. Extremely cultured and much travelled, he was an intellectual leader of great strength. Editor of a distinguished journal, *The North American* and a contributor to *The Atlantic Monthly*, a New England magazine of literature and politics, he numbered amongst his friends Emerson and several of the New England Transcendentalists, most of whom were or had been Unitarians (and whom Andrews Norton called 'infidels'). Though he made but a small contribution to literature, he became Professor of the History of Art at Harvard (1875-98) and described himself as one whose aim was to arouse in his countrymen, "the sense of connection with the past and gratitude for the effort and labours of other nations and former generations."[1] He wrote and lectured extensively on twelfth and thirteenth century Italy.

Mrs Gaskell and Norton met only once after the Roman spring of 1857. Later that summer, he visited Manchester on his way back to America, partly to see the Art Treasures Exhibition (by which Manchester hoped to put itself on the cultural map) and partly to see the Gaskells, with whom he stayed several weeks. But the relationship between Norton and Mrs Gaskell was one of the 'romantic friendships' of the period. They corresponded for the rest of her life and though, again no doubt owing to the activities of Meta Gaskell, relatively few of Norton's letters have survived compared with Mrs Gaskell's, at his death forty years after hers, he was found to have kept every line she wrote to him, including the pencilled notes

189

arranging outings in Rome in 1857. They were not published until 1932.[2]

During the wounding controversy about her *Life of Charlotte Brontë*, which met her on her return from Rome, Norton wrote to his fellow-American, James Russell Lowell, who had also met Mrs Gaskell in Rome. Norton had escorted her and her daughters as far as Venice by way of Sienna and Florence on their way home, and of the book on Charlotte Brontë, said that it was:

> almost as much an exhibition of Mrs Gaskell's character as of Miss Brontë's – and you know what a lovely and admirable character she has. Seeing her as intimately as one sees a companion on a journey, I learned every day to feel towards her a deeper affection and respect. She is like the best things in her books; full of generous and tender sympathies, of thoughtful kindness, of pleasant humour, of quick appreciation, of utmost simplicity and truthfulness, and uniting with peculiar delicacy and retirement a strength of principle and purpose and straightforwardness of action, such as few women possess.[3]

Though with perfect propriety, their correspondence was carried on in an almost love-language: "To think that you will really touch this bit of paper", writes Mrs Gaskell to "My dear Mr Norton" and she is "My dearest Mrs Gaskell". She turns to him for all sorts of information and advice on her affairs, both private and public; he is the confidant of all her thoughts and activities. Three years before her death, he asks:

> Does the drawing-room look as it used to do, – the piano & your table in the same place, – the 'flowers still blooming in the little conservatory, – the same landscape over the fireplace – the same centre table with the books and work on it as of old? How long ago & yet how fresh seem the days I spent with you! There are some weeks that occupy a great space in one's life, – & that was one of them.[4]

In 1862, when he decided to marry and wrote to acquaint her of this, he asked her to let his future wife share in the affection which he relied on "as one of the permanent blessings of life."[5] Her reply included the words:

> I have often thought that of all the men I ever knew you
> were not only the one to best appreciate woman, but also
> ... to require along with your masculine friendships, the
> sympathetic companionship of a good gracious woman.[6]

He named his second daughter Elizabeth Gaskell Norton.
Mrs Gaskell had an almost desperate nostalgia for Italy, lamenting:

> It was in those charming Roman days that my life at any
> rate culminated. I shall never be so happy again. I don't
> think I was ever so happy before. My eyes fill with tears
> when I think of those days ...[7]

and Norton, when he heard in 1863 that she was actually in Italy
again, wrote:

> I revisit in imagination the places to which we went
> together, I recall our drives & the beauties of the
> Campagna, I hear your words, & altogether I am passing a
> very delightful morning with you in Rome ... The blue
> violets remind me again of Rome, they are as blue &
> almost as abundant as those you are gathering in the grass
> at the Borghese villa.[8]

In 1859, Norton had sent her a copy of his translation of some of
the earlier poems of Dante's *Vita Nuova*, a collection of poems which
are concerned with Dante's love of Beatrice and fore-runner of *The
Divine Comedy*, the great religious, philosophical and literary work of
the Middle Ages and which Norton was also to translate in 1895. He
gave to the earlier work the title of the *New Life of Dante* and when
Mrs Gaskell received it she replied that she had always wanted a copy
of her own since she had read it in manuscript when they were both in
Rome. Furthermore, in 1865, only weeks before her death, she
thanked him for a book "on the portraits of Dante" which, "it [is] a
pleasure even to open ... the faces themselves seem to carry one so up
into a purer aether, a diviner air."[9]

Here she is misquoting from memory a passage in Wordsworth's
'Laodamia', a story of the Elysian fields, a place where only the soul
that is "as kind as resolute and good and brave", was worthy to walk
"the paths of upper air" –

191

In happier beauty; more pellucid streams
An ampler ether, a diviner air.
And fields invested with purpureal gleams;
Climes which the sun, who sheds the brightest day
Earth knows, is all unworthy to survey. (104-108)

Wordsworth's lines are, in their turn, almost a direct translation of a passage in Virgil's *Aeneid*: – "largior hic compos aether et lumine vestit purpureo solemque/suum, sua sidera norunt" (VI, 641) which C. Day Lewis has translated as:

What largesse of bright air, clothing the vales in dazzling
Light, is here! This land has a sun and stars of its own.[10]

Only at this point do we find how devious a writer Mrs Gaskell was, how deeply embedded in her texts were her emotions and her social and religious ideas. The key to the cipher here is Virgil's "purpureo", which Wordsworth clung to in his version, rendering it as "purpureal gleams" rather than merely 'purple'. The reason is simple. The Latin word purpureus does not, when used in its poetic sense, mean the colour purple, but brilliant and beautiful in an unearthly fashion. Gray had used it in this sense in his heavily mythological 'Progress of Poesy' where Venus has "The bloom of young Desire, and purple light of Love". Pope, in his 'Pastoral', had, before him, written: "And lavish Nature paints the Purple Year", a note being given to the word 'purple' in an edition of 1751 as "used in the Latin sense, of the brightest, most vivid colouring in general, not of that peculiar tint so called." Donald Davie, in his article, 'Hardy's Virgilian Purples' (1976),[11] describes Virgil's "Purpureus" as "a light that is not any terrestrial light ... the light of an alternative cosmos" and associated with 'a Divine Mind'. He also points out that the image of this light (note C. Day Lewis' translation above) was taken up from Virgil by Dante in *The Divine Comedy* where, in the 'Inferno', the writer, having lost his way in a gloomy forest, is hindered from climbing a mountain by wild beasts which represent luxury, pride, and avarice. He is met by Virgil, 'the good pagan', who promises to show him the punishments of Hell and that he shall then be conducted by Beatrice, the real yet ideal woman, to Paradise where he will behold the Beatific Vision. And when Beatrice makes

192

her appearance in the shades of Purgatory, it is "within a cloud of flowers ... by angelic hands tossed upward ... wreathed, o'er a white veil, with an olive stem [and] under, a cloak of green apparelled in the hue of living flame."[12]

It is quite impossible here to elaborate, in any remotely satisfactory way, on the intertwining themes of Virgil's feelings for the Italian countryside, the 'light' in which he and Dante saw it, the Dante and Beatrice relationship as it appears in Dante's poetry, Mrs Gaskell's and Charles Eliot Norton's deeply emotional but almost entirely unspoken thoughts on the subject; Professor Davie's article on Hardy and Eliot Norton's introductory essays to his own *Vita Nuova* are extremely enlightening in this respect.

An unusual number of examples of the use of the word purple appear in Mrs Gaskell's own writings, both in her letters and her fiction. Naturally, the moorland heather at Haworth and in Scotland is purple, the red rocks above the Derwent in Derbyshire are streaked with "misty purple". But the great dome of sky and "purple hill-shadows" at Silverdale also remind her of the Roman campagna and at Heidelberg there is "a rain-mist, all soft and golden before the purple hills."[13] In her fiction it is always associated with her landscapes and her heroines. On the first few pages of Ruth's story, describing the house where she worked "... over all these changes from grandeur to squalor, bent down the purple heavens with their unchanging splendour!". When she walks, in love with her lover, among spring flowers, she exclaims "at the evening glory of mellow light which was in the sky behind the purple distance." In North Wales with him, she sees, "the purple darkness on the heathery mountainside".[14] In *Wives and Daughters*, Molly sees Hamley Hall in the distance as a "deep purple" house and the landscape which she sees from the neglected terrace includes "a purple bit of rising ground in the distance".[15]

In *Cousin Phillis*, the field, in which Paul first sees Mr Holman, his labourers and Phillis sing their evening psalm, is set against a landscape of:

> upland common, full of red sand-banks, and sweeps and hollows bordered by dark firs, purple in the coming shadows, but near at hand all ablaze with flowering gorse... which seen against the belt of trees appeared brilliantly golden.[16]

It is in *Cousin Phillis*, also, that we find almost all the references to Virgil and Dante in Mrs Gaskell's fiction. Virgil, as we have already noted, is among the books on the shelf for regular reading and Phillis and her father read Virgil in the evening together. Holman says that one of the Calvinist ministers had told him that "a poor little quotation I was making from the *Georgics* savoured of vain babbling and profane heathenism." But he quotes

> a line or two of Latin, "It's wonderful," said he, "how exactly Virgil has hit the enduring epithets nearly two thousand years ago and in Italy; and yet how it describes to a T what is now lying before us ..."[17]

and on another occasion:

> tapping the old vellum-bound book he held; "in the first *Georgic* [he] speaks of rolling and irrigation; a little further on he insists on the choice of the best seed and advises us to keep the drains clear. Again, no Scotch farmer could give shrewder advice than to cut light meadows while the dew is on them, even though it involves night-work. It is a living truth in these days." He began beating time with a ruler on his knee, to some Latin lines he read aloud...[18]

It is in the *Georgics* that Virgil writes of the real landscape and its cultivation while in his *Eclogues* he presents the image of a Golden Age.

Finally, Phillis, who reads Dante's *Inferno* by herself with the aid of an old Italian dictionary while doing her household tasks, says to Paul: "I knew something about Dante before; and I have always liked Virgil so much ... [I wish] I could make out this old Italian ..." And Holdsworth, the ambitious, less than scrupulous engineer who has been to Italy, draws Phillis as Ceres, with loosened hair, to the girl's confusion, and says to Paul as he picks up a volume from the shelf: "You don't mean to say they take Virgil for gospel?"[19]

Mrs Gaskell's use of the word purple is invariably associated with the natural (in the sense of the wild) and the rural landscape, of which (as in Hardy) her heroines are an integral part, creating a symbiotic spiritual world indicating something timeless behind the transient physical appearance of Nature and which is again associated with woman.

The character of the heroine, Shirley, in the book of that name, in whom Charlotte Brontë portrayed, at least in part, her sister Emily, also sees Nature in its highest sense as a woman and Eve, the first woman, as 'heaven born', the mother of the Titans and gods, wearing on her head, "the consort-crown of creation".[20] In a letter written in 1853, Mrs Gaskell had said that Emily herself "must have been a remnant of the Titans who used to inhabit the earth,"[21] giving the impression that she was particularly familiar with the above passages.

We can also be almost certain that *Cousin Phillis* was begun in Florence, a few months before it began to appear in the *Cornhill* in November 1863. In the Uffizi Gallery in Florence hangs a picture by Botticelli (1446-1510) which we know as 'Primavera' (Spring). In contrast to the artist's later 'Venus', which is naked, Primavera is depicted as a young girl, fully clothed in a gauzy, bluish-purple dress, standing in the centre of a wood and surrounded by graceful attendant spirits on whom her hand is raised in blessing, while at her feet flowers spring from the earth. She is a goddess of love, not merely in the sexual sense, but as symbolic of the love which blesses and brings forth all the creative powers of body, of spirit, and of the whole world of nature.

Paul, the narrator of *Cousin Phillis*, is a young man who, throughout the story, has observed her from a certain distance (as Dante observed Beatrice, meeting her face to face only on two occasions and as was coincidentally also the case with Eliot Norton and Mrs Gaskell). Meta Gaskell was to remember, long after the event, how in Rome with her mother:

> we were to see the great day of the Carnival – Shrove Tuesday ... Suddenly against this turbulent background there stood out the figure of a young man just below the balcony, smiling up at my mother... [he] caught at some confetti that Mama was dangling on a long stick ... and Mama said 'Oh look what a charming face!' and Mr Story said 'Oh, that's Charles Norton ...'[23]

Let us consider again the Latin *purpureo*, rendered by various translators as 'hue of living flame', 'dazzling light', 'a light that is not any terrestrial light'. In Paul's descriptions of Phillis:

The westering sun shone full on her and made a slanting stream of light into the room within. She was dressed in dark blue cotton of some kind up to her throat, down to her wrists, with a little frill of the same, wherever it touched her white skin. I have never seen the like. She had light hair, nearer yellow than any other colour. She looked me steadily in the face with large, quiet eyes ...[23]

On another occasion:

Inside the house sate Cousin Phillis, her golden hair, dazzling complexion, lighting up the corner of the vine-shadowed room.[24]

And again:

Virgil, Caesar, a French grammar ... and Phillis Holman's name in each of them ... although she was sitting at her work (knitting worsted stockings) quietly enough, ... her hair was looking more golden, her dark eyelashes longer, her round pillar of a throat whiter than ever ... I went to bed and dreamed that I was as tall as cousin Phillis ... and had a still more miraculous acquaintance with Latin and Greek.[25]

Finally, he sees her in Spring:

standing under the budding branches of the grey trees, over which a tinge of green seemed to be deepening day after day, her sun-bonnet fallen back on her neck, her hands full of delicate wood-flowers.[26]

Phillis is both beautiful and good, scholarly yet capable of performing all the practical and womanly tasks on a farm. And after the serious emotional crisis which threatens her life, the loss of Holdsworth, with the usual toughness of Mrs Gaskell's heroines she determines to return, with a new maturity, to the even tenor of her former life of what Wordsworth had called, "natural piety". Her "I can and I will" are the closing words of the story.

Cousin Phillis is not only Mrs Gaskell's blueprint for a Christian Socialist society, an exquisite evocation of English country life and the rural landscape, in Mr Holman yet another portrait of the yeoman, Massingham's 'apex' of a true civilisation, but also Mrs Gaskell's most inspirational and idealised view of woman. Paul will never aspire to marriage with his cousin, as his father had urged on him from a worldly point of view, but she will be the measure by which he will judge other women and his own attitude towards them, as Eliot Norton admitted his debt in this respect to Mrs Gaskell. Phillis has therefore, the qualities of both an English Beatrice and an English Primavera, the gauzy blue dress of Botticelli's Primavera finding its echo in the simple blue dress which Phillis wears throughout the story, charmingly illustrated by M.V. Wheelhouse in the edition of 1910, the centenary of Mrs Gaskell's birth.[27]

In the National Library of Scotland there are two manuscript letters written by Mrs Gaskell in 1863 in reply to one from George Smith of Smith and Elder, publishers of the *Cornhill Magazine* in which *Cousin Phillis* was appearing in monthly instalments. Smith had expressed the wish that the story should end before she had expected. She sketches out an ending omitting a final scene in which Paul, the narrator of the story, visits the Holman farm again after some years.

Mr Holman is dead, her mother an invalid and Phillis is running the farm herself. Paul finds her superintending the draining of a marshy field, which may be one of the causes of an epidemic of fevers and is using technical sketches shown to her and her father by Holdsworth. With her are two children orphaned by the epidemic, whom she had adopted, thus reinforcing the truth of what she says at the end of the story as it is now in the published version which Mrs Gaskell never altered when the story appeared in book form. "We will go back to the peace of the old days. I know we shall; I can, and I will!"[28]

CHAPTER 16
The woman question

It was in the last few months of her life that Mrs Gaskell secretly purchased, at Holybourne near Alton in Hampshire, just such a house, as Hamley Hall. Its name, The Lawn, derived from the Middle English 'laund', an open space between woods, is an apt description of its situation. Formerly an old hostelry, The White Hart, it had been noted as 'a good stopping-place for man and beast'. In 1865, it had a large drawing-room with French windows opening onto spacious lawns, flower-gardens, a vegetable garden, and a stream which, crossed by a small wooden bridge, led to an orchard, paddock, and a piece of agricultural land; three or four acres in all, as she informed Charles Eliot Norton. Like Hamley Hall, the house stood on the edge of a village green where there was a large tree, a few cottages, and a church. The village took its name from a river which flowed through it and the fact that, in the Middle Ages, it had been one of the places of call for pilgrims on their way to the shrine of St Thomas à Beckett at Canterbury. Having acquired The Lawn, in the month before she took up residence, Mrs Gaskell was selling her surplus apples at one and sixpence a bushel, informing the future tenant of the land she proposed to let, that her predecessor had made over nine tons of hay off it the previous year, "besides the aftermath [second crop]", and that nine or ten women had made the hay in three days. She also invited Thurstan Holland to come down from London, partake of bread, butter and cheese, cold meat, "excellent milk", Alton Ale, and to give her his advice on the garden.[1]

That she had set her heart on this house there is no doubt.[2] Her health was failing quickly and there was little she could now do in Manchester that was of any practical help to cotton-workers after the depression, though she continued to write letters on behalf of would-be emigrants and to find situations in domestic service for country girls where they would be safe from corruption and the dangers and economic uncertainties of factory life. Her daughters were now grown women, her husband absorbed in his own work, and she had an efficient housekeeper in Hearn, a woman who had been in her household for half a century and was now a valued friend. As she felt her physical powers waning, her powers as a writer were growing and she was already spending more and more time away from Manchester (to the surprise and curiosity of her husband's congregation) in search of peace and quiet. The country houses of friends, the seaside and foreign hotels, no longer satisfied this need, if ever they had done so. The Lawn would be a place where she could not only rest and write but, as Mrs Chadwick claims, 'have her own pony-carriage, in order to enjoy drives around to such places as Selborne, the birthplace of Gilbert White, and to Chawton, associated with Jane Austen, and to the many other historical spots within a short distance of Holybourne.' It would also be a home of her own where, for at least part of the year, she could be her "own woman", entertain her own friends, live the sort of country life which alone seemed to satisfy her deepest aspirations, and, being in the south, it was away from the curiosity and social obligations of the Knutsford area.

Moreover, the situation of Holybourne was extremely healthy. In the valley of the Wey, yet some three hundred feet above sea-level amidst chalk hills, it was a place, again according to Mrs Chadwick, where the water from its springs was noted for its purity. The springs would have been an important factor in Mrs Gaskell's choice of The Lawn. All through the long hot summer of 1865 she had been plagued by the long standing problem of the unhealthiness of their house in Manchester. From Dieppe at the beginning of October where she, Meta, and Julia had gone for a short rest amidst all the preparations regarding The Lawn, she wrote to Marianne, in charge at Plymouth Grove:

> I am so sorry about the smell. I enclose a piece for you to read to or give Papa, as you see best at the right time. And now, I will tell you my theory by whh I account for the pestiferous smell. You see the contents of WC& C go into a cess-pool at the corner of the yard near the coal-cellar & stable, & going under both. A drain goes under the house out into the garden & into the cesspool in the field. Adjoining both drain and cess-pool is the cistern under the pantry, from which the water goes (or ought to go) to the scullery tap. Now this tap has been dry ever since July. Rowlands said at first that it was owing to the dry summer, but after filling it with town's water (it is usually filled with rain) the scullery tap was still dry, showing that it leaked somewhere. Now where it leaked out the smells must come in from the cess pool or drain adjoining if the cistern

is not quite sound. When it is quite sound the flag [stone] with the ring in it ought to be CEMENTED down. As it has been all summer it has been a gulley-hole inside the house [.] I am sure it is most seriously injuring our health. I had done all I could before I left, with Mr Coates and Rowlands; but still the scullery tap did not run; until it does the smell will go on. The whole system of drainage is bad. It was so in the Nicholls' time; they left in consequence – I always thought until this last summer, that it had been remedied – Both Charlie [Crompton, her son-in-law] & Georgina have perceived the smell in the drawing room & spoken about it. However, one does not expect to have to write about drains from Dieppe, does one?[3]

Quite so. The Gaskells had rented the house, in the prestigious Manchester suburb, Victoria Park, for fifteen years and for about the same time Mr Gaskell had been a prominent and respected member of the Sanitary Committee in the city. Yet it is his wife who has to master the details and shortcomings of the sanitation of the house in which his family lived (one is tempted to wonder about his nose, since even visitors had noticed the smell!) But what is significant is that Marianne had to write to her mother about it even though she was abroad and then Mrs Gaskell had to write a note for Marianne to "read or to give Papa", as she saw "best at the right time."

That the Gaskell marriage was happy in its early years is obvious. A handsome couple from a similar background with mutual interests in literature and music, he was a minister in need of a wife and she a portionless girl in need of a husband, if she were not to face the prospect of earning her living as a teacher, or, marriage outside the Unitarian circle being difficult, remaining a dependent spinster for the rest of her life as were many of the Holland women. Each, therefore was something of a 'catch' for the other. The honeymoon in North Wales was indeed idyllic, providing the material for the similar experience of Ruth. In due course, the young father romped in the drawing-room with his little girls, while their mother played the piano, and he snowballed and flew kites with them out of doors.

The young wife was also proud and delighted when her husband began to lecture on poetry to the Mechanics' Institutes. But in letters to her sisters-in-law, Ann Robson, and her own namesake, Elizabeth Gaskell (née Holland), and later, in the letters to Marianne not published until 1966, we find evidence of a different element in the marriage, one which would suggest that it was not quite so 'blissful' as it was said to be in her funeral sermon at Cross Street Chapel and as has been quoted by all subsequent writers except Aina Rubenius.

Hannah Lumb had seen the dangers of the match on her first meeting with Gaskell which, rather curiously, did not take place until after the engagement: "why Elizabeth how could this man ever take a fancy to such a little giddy thoughtless thing as you?" and "many other equally pretty speeches"[4] on the subject. One tends to agree with Mrs Lumb after having seen the many portraits of Gaskell, but the happy bride-to-be quoted the remarks with glee. Yet, within a few years of her marriage, she is complaining of Gaskell's lectures on poetry in 1838 that "if [he] had taken time to it he would have done it capitally – as it is I fear his usual fault of procrastination will prevent him doing justice to it"[5] a tart remark which perhaps throws light on the reason why the proposed series of poems for Blackwoods' in 1837 never got farther than the first. Later in 1838 she writes:

> When I had finished my last letter Willm looked at it, and said it was slip-shod – and seemed to wish me not to send it, but though I felt it was not a particularly nice letter I thought I wd send it, or you would wonder why I did not write. But I was feeling languid and anxious and tired, & have not been over-well this week, and the consciousness that Wm may at any time and does generally see my letters makes me not write so naturally & heartily think as I should do. Don't begin that bad custom, my dear![6]

Though, in the same letter, she admits that she is happy in her married state, she says she can be "more open with Sam", Gaskell's brother, then a doctor at the Infirmary in Manchester, than she "dare be with William". In 1841, she writes to Ann Robson that she is "all alone, and not feeling over & above well". She is anxious about Marianne's health, "and Wm[,] I dare say kindly[,] won't allow me to ever talk to him about anxieties, which it would be SUCH A RELIEF often. So don't allude too much to what I've been saying in your answer." She expresses fears as to what may happen to her two little girls in the possible event of her death: "we all know the probability

201

of widowers marrying again" and, as she has no sister or close relative, she begs Anne, "as much as circumstances permit", to watch over them: "I do often pray for trust in God, complete trust in Him – in regard to what becomes of my children. Still let me open my heart sometimes to you, dear Anne, with reliance on your sympathy and secrecy."[7]

It has frequently been said that Gaskell was right to discourage her from talking to him about her anxieties regarding childish illnesses on the grounds that she made too much of these. But the same attitude from Gaskell is apparent twenty years later regarding the drains at Plymouth Grove. The enjoinment to secrecy in the early letters quoted above and the instructions to Marianne as to the manner in which she was to communicate to him about the drains, "as you see best at the right time", do not make pleasant reading. In the early letter to Ann Robson, quoted above, Mrs Gaskell also says that, though her husband feels "most kindly towards his children, [he] is yet most reserved in expressions of either affection or sympathy." This 'reserve' has also been made much of with regard to, in later years, his shutting himself up in his study even when there were distinguished visitors in the house. Though she knew he was a busy man, the closed study door obviously puzzled and distressed Mrs Gaskell, for she mentions it several times in letters to intimate women friends and relatives. So also the fact that, apart from the German holiday of 1841 and occasional short visits to relations and to Silverdale, he insisted on taking his holidays alone or with a male companion. This 'reserve' did not prevent him from pursuing an extremely active social life in Manchester amongst people of his own choice, such as "dining with a world of professors and college people at Mark Philips'", the latter being the first M.P. for Manchester, a bitter campaigner against the Ten Hour Bill, and, of course, a Unitarian/Utilitarian.

Gaskell's virtual withdrawal from family life was a never ceasing heartache to Mrs Gaskell, as well as an affront to her personal dignity as a successful woman in her own right. It was probably a contributory factor in her determination to set up an establishment of her own. Only six months before her death, again to Ann Robson, she writes:

I never know what makes him so busy... And when
he is at home, we only see him at meal-times; so that
it is not the giving up of family life to him, that it
would be to many men... He does not like any of us
to go with him when he goes from home, saying it
does not give him so much a change.[8]

Of a visit he had recently made to Rome, arranged by her with her
American friends, the Storys, she says in the same letter:

I had got money enough (from my writing) both to
pay for his going, & for Meta's or mine, or both of
us, with him but he quite declined it, giving the
reason as above... He always goes to the Edmund
Potters in his holiday; wherever they take a house,
generally in Scotland; this year I believe it will be in
Wales. Mrs Potter says she has often asked me (in
her letters to him) to accompany him; but if she has,
he has never told me of it... (ibid)

The hurt and humiliation is clear. This 'reserved' man merely
reserved his sociability for people of his own choice and these did not
include his famous wife, so attractive to many distinguished men of
her time, nor his daughters once they were grown women. Moreover,
there is evidence that this 'reserved,' scholarly and upright man, as he
has unanimously been presented was, with other women, actually a
vain, rather silly and embarrassing flirt and, like many Victorian men
of his type, was also attracted to little girls and to other men. To his
closest male friend, John Relly Beard, first principal of what is now
the Unitarian College, Manchester, he wrote little notes on ministerial
affairs to a man he was seeing almost every day, and addressed to
"My friend, philosopher and guide", "Vir erudissime et amicissime",
one signed "Goosequill", and another strange note, written in 1864
reads:

Υψιστε και κροτζτε τνραυυ [most high and mighty
master] Let not thy countenance be turned away from me,
but credit thy slave when he says that it was absolutely out
of his power to obey thy behests as he is ever delighted to
do, one moment sooner. He humbly craves, at thy hands,

the small modicum of time in which to disport himself at the approaching Saturnalia, that thou wilt find inscribed on the next page [this page is missing] Submissively casting himself at thy feet, he remains

δουλος σου ταπεινοτατε

Your humblest slave

W.Γ. (γαμμου;)

The initials above are, of course, W.G.: the word in brackets is a transliteration in Greek of the English 'gammon' – nonsense?

In another letter, he apologises for not having visited his friend on a particular occasion, having missed the train, "owing to a young lady (Drat 'em,) they're always in mischief."[9] This can only apply to his daughters. Julia, the youngest was, at the time of writing, nineteen.

His fondness for his own little girls had long since been replaced by a fondness for other people's. As Mrs Gaskell said, when writing to the Storys, he was "very fond of children, playing with them all day long, not caring for them so much when they are grown up..."[10] Two little girls of whom Gaskell was particularly fond were Margaret, the daughter of William Shaen, and the famous author of children's books, Beatrix Potter. It was from the Potter house-parties in Scotland and Wales that Mrs Gaskell claimed, on May 1865, only a few months before her death, that her husband had deliberately excluded her (though Beatrix was not born until the year after Mrs Gaskell's death).[11] It was during the houseparties of the 1870s that the father of Beatrix, Rupert Potter, a keen amateur photographer and a son of Edmund Potter (1802-83), a wealthy calico printer, took two photographs of Gaskell with Beatrix. In one, she is about seven and is sitting on Gaskell's knee with his arm round her. In the second, taken when she was about nine, he is seated and she is standing by his side. He has one of his arms round her and is also holding her hand. The photographs are reproduced in *The Tale of Beatrix Potter* (1946) by Margaret Lane and *The Journal of Beatrix Potter* (1966) edited by Leslie Linder. In the journal edited by Linder, Beatrix frequently mentions Gaskell (who also stayed with them at their London home), their correspondence, and what she calls the "deep child-like affection" between them.

Of greater interest is his relationship with Margaret Shaen who was about eleven years old when Mrs Gaskell died. Her parents, William and Emily Shaen, (the latter a sister of Catherine and Susanna Winkworth) were Mrs Gaskell's closest friends and a number of her letters are written from their London home. In a letter to Elizabeth Haldane, one of Mrs Gaskell's early biographers, in 1929 Margaret Shaen wrote: "I wonder if you will want to say much about Mr Gaskell – I cd in talk tell you a good deal about him, more than I cd write. Those sheets & sheets of love affairs are now all safely burnt – pitiful – I shld have burnt them on receipt!"[12]

The following year Margaret Shaen wrote, (again to Elizabeth Haldane), about Gaskell's vanity having led him to believe that her aunt, Susanna Winkworth, would have liked to marry him. This is borne out by one of Mrs Gaskell's letters in 1852, though, perhaps from pride, she words it rather differently.[13] To Anne Shaen, another aunt of Margaret's, she (Mrs Gaskell) had, some four years earlier, written:

> Wm seized the letters saying he was sure they were for him; but perceiving that yours and Mrs Shaen's were for me, he said this is Louey's and this I know is for me. You see he thought all that sitting by her at the piano had not been without due effect...[14]

The rest of the sentence has been erased by an unknown hand. The tone is light but, as Elizabeth Haldane says in her biography, there is a hint of jealousy on Mrs Gaskell's part, certainly in the case of Susanna Winkworth.

With regard to "Those sheets & sheets of love affairs" which Gaskell had written to Margaret, it was in May 1864 that Mrs Gaskell outlined the plot of *Wives and Daughters* to George Smith when Margaret Shaen would be about ten years old. It is in this novel that Mrs Gaskell writes of the reserved Mr Gibson, so like Gaskell in appearance and even accent, being attracted by the faded elegance of Clare, and of Lady Harriet of Cumnor Towers, now of marriageable age, expressing herself as being quite repelled by the idea of marriage owing to the highly unsuitable tales told to her when she was a child by Clare about her flirtations with the visiting masters who had supplemented her own meagre talents. It is not beyond the bounds of possibility that the child, Margaret, innocently, or her mother, jokingly, had recently shown Gaskell's letters to his wife, and, far from being amused by them, she had been hurt and humiliated. She had always been a proud woman and there are numerous cases of her 'getting her own back' on people who had offended her, in her novels. Even *Cranford* had been thought a little too near the truth by certain people in Knutsford. And, as Barbara Hardy has said, *Wives and Daughters*, on the personal level, is a sad book, every love relationship being, in some way or at some time, frustrated.[15]

It seems reasonable to believe, therefore, that Mrs Gaskell's views on 'the Woman Question' were, therefore not unnaturally, influenced by her own relationship with her husband. Though the actual subject of marriage is rarely mentioned in her novels, they all concern themselves with the differences between men and women on the mental and emotional level, on their rôles in society, and, in *Wives and Daughters*, she chronicles the compromises of most marriages and the disaster which failure to compromise brings about. Gibson and Lord Cumnor learn to tolerate their wives, the Earl having already done so before the novel opens, Gibson by its end. But Squire Hamley, however much he loves his wife cannot change in the way she desires and she dies.

Mrs Gaskell's fear of dying in child-birth and of her husband marrying a woman who might not be a suitable or loving step-mother to her children was eminently reasonable in those days of over-frequent child-bearing and primitive obstetrics. She, herself, was never in as good health, as she said, after she began to have children, her own mother was ailing after her (Elizabeth's) birth and had died when she was only fourteen months old, after which she spent the next twenty years without a stable home and with an infrequently seen father who quickly remarried and founded another family. We see this deeply traumatic experience mirrored in the characters and the situations of Mr and Mrs Gibson, Molly, and Cynthia thirty years later in *Wives and Daughters*, as well as in the trail of motherless girls strewn all the way through the stories that came before it.

As regards the apparent peculiarities of her husband's character, he had married in the expectation of acquiring a pretty, attractive, well-educated young wife with a taste for literature similar to his own but who would become the usual type of minister's wife. Very few men would have liked to be outshone either in society or intellectually by a wife who became a brilliant conversationalist as well as a charming hostess and who entertained and was deeply respected by such men as Carlyle, Maurice, Dean Stanley, Jowett, Dickens and many others. Nor had he expected a wife who would set the members of his congregation by the ears with novels so extremely controversial that one of them was burnt by the father of a family as unfit to be the subject of a novel, nor one whose social and political ideas (though she never sat on a public platform) were so alien to those of the majority of the men in his congregation, amongst whom were members of Parliament and holders of municipal office and spent months at a time away from the manse and the chapel. Yet Gaskell obviously supported her, read her proofs, corrected her spelling, and handled much of the business side of her writing. He too was deeply involved in his own ministerial work, his private tutoring, his work in the setting up and eventual Principalship of the Home Missionary College for the training of Unitarian ministers in the industrial areas, when the dissenting academy moved from Manchester to London in the 1850s, his membership of the Manchester Literary and Philosophical Society, the Statistical Society and the British Association for the Advancement of Science. So perhaps his wife's frustration at the closed study door, his attacks of fatigue which she mentions in her letters, as well as his general preference for male society are understandable.

The truth is almost certainly that the Gaskell marriage was no better and no worse than most marriages, modern and Victorian. The stresses and strains of the present day are somewhat different from those of the Victorians owing to reliable contraception, careers for married women and easy divorce, but their existence is still very real. Few men, even today, like to be outshone in any way by their wives and prefer one who will be a help to them in their own careers.

As for Gaskell's loss of interest in the society of his daughters as they grew up and his predilection for other people's little girls, as well as his close friendships and holidays with other men, this was a feature of the social life of even the most academic and respectable of the men of the period. At Oxford, Charles Dodgson was photographing and telling, as Lewis Carroll, *Alice's Adventures in Wonderland* to the little girl, Alice Liddell and at Cambridge Tennyson suffered his intense and tragic friendship with Hallam. Summer reading parties of males only with what we might call a guru were part of undergraduate life, those of the unmarried Jowett being particularly well-known. Even John Relly Beard, the close friend of Gaskell to whom Gaskell wrote the strange letter that has already been quoted, a highly dedicated and respected Manchester minister, always seems to have spent his holidays apart from his wife.

There is no doubt that, though women suffered from unwanted sexual intercourse which so often led to the annual baby and/or 'women's ailments', men must have suffered considerable sexual deprivation and repression in marriages where the wife was strong-minded enough, when a reasonable number of children had arrived, not to be prepared to risk life, health and outside interests. Religion, morals, social convention and even the law, too, were all against any form of dissolution of the marriage, or even any obvious evidence of disharmony within it. And Mrs Gaskell was the last woman to admit openly even to the latter, except perhaps to one or two close women friends and her eldest daughter Marianne, who became her confidante (and often her substitute at the manse), regarding the difficulties of combining her marriage with her career as a professional writer. Nevertheless, there is also evidence in her letters that she was fond of her husband and took care, as far as he would allow it, for his health and comfort. But the strain and frustration become more and more evident as her life drew to its close.

We do not know the recipient of a letter in 1856, in which Mrs Gaskell says:

> I would not trust a mouse to a woman if a man's judgement was to be had. Women have no judgement. They've tact and sensitiveness and hundreds of fine and lovely qualities, but are angelic geese as to a matter requiring serious and long scientific consideration. I'm not a friend of Female Medical Education.[16]

Yet she was a friend of Florence Nightingale, indeed admired her almost to the point of idolatry except for her "want ... of love for individuals" and, two years after the letter on 'Female Medical Education', she spent a whole morning reading Miss Nightingale's privately printed *Notes on Matters Affecting the Health, Efficiency, and Hospital Administration of the British Army*. She wrote at once to tell the author how much she appreciated the "deep wisdom and quiet continual devout references to God" in the book. It is inconceivable, therefore that she would have neglected to read the still more famous

Notes on Nursing[17] from the same pen and available to the general public in the following year.   According to Miss Nightingale's biographer, C. Woodham-Smith, this book "caused a mild sensation" and had a large sale.   A small book, it was primarily written for women who had the care of children and the sick, but it is much more.   In it, for example, she denounced the scanty education available to the Victorian girl.   But she was no feminist in the usual sense of the word.   She did not believe, for example, from the available evidence that the position of women in general would be much improved under the existing social and economic system and *Notes on Nursing* ends with an attack on:

> the jargon about the rights of women ... which urges
> women to do all that men do, including the medical and
> other professions, merely because men do it, and without
> regard to whether this is the best that women can do; and of
> the jargon which urges women to do nothing men do,
> merely because they are women ... you want to do the
> thing that is good whether it is suitable for a woman or not.

Though Mrs Gaskell was "not a friend of Female Medical Education", this can only have meant the training of women as doctors, for she gave Meta permission to train as a nurse if she still so wished when she was thirty, doing "the thing that is good"; the whole subject of personal vocation, meant much to her.

To Eliza Fox, one of many friends involved in the Women's Movement, she wrote in 1850:

> If Self is to be the end of exertions, those exertions are
> unholy, there is no doubt of that – and that is part of the
> danger in cultivating the Individual Life; but I do believe
> we have all some appointed work to do, whh no one else
> can do so well; wh is our work; what we have to do in
> advancing the Kingdom of God; and that first we must find
> what we are sent into the world to do, and define it and
> make clear to ourselves (that's the hard part) and then
> forget ourselves in our work and our work in the End we
> ought to strive to bring about.[18]

The purchase of the house in Hampshire, in the last months of her life, may be seen, therefore, in several lights: as the one great rebellion against her husband, her marriage and the demands of the Manchester manse, or as a compromise to save both her marriage and her personal life, or as a return to her roots and as an eventual secure home "in the middle of a pretty village, so that it won't be a lonely place for the unmarried daughters who will inherit."[19] She certainly intended the latter to have property of their own and the independence that goes with it. But it was not to be, in spite of all her efforts to bring it about.

It was Smith, her publisher, who lent her £1,000 towards the cost of The Lawn. This she expected to 'write off' in the next three years during which part of the house was to be let to two ladies. William Shaen, Thurstan Holland and Charles Crompton, all lawyers, arranged the legal details. Everything was kept a complete secret from William Gaskell who was in Scotland at the Potters' late summer house-party. This was supposed to be on the grounds that, when the house was paid for, it was to be a surprise retirement present to him. Until then he was to think the house a rented one. Even Mrs Chadwick, her devoted admirer, could not forbear to remark that this seemed "strange" and that "Mr Gaskell was so firmly attached to Manchester, that he would have had very little use for it." In August, she wrote to Thurstan Holland:

> If trustees are necessary I shld like none better than you and Charlie, but I wd rather do without trustees IF possible. Mr Shaen I fancy suggested some way in whh they might be done without – [20]

William Shaen, founder of the first building society, a 'moral-force' chartist and founder of the Bedford College for women, was a firm believer in women's rights. But did these three men, in whose 'judgement' Mrs Gaskell had such faith, advise her rightly, taking into account all the circumstances? So great was the strain of all that was involved in acquiring and furnishing The Lawn, before the uncertain date of her husband's return to Manchester, that she burst out on several occasions during the last few months of her life that she was not sleeping, she was "quite worn out", she was so tired she hardly knew what she said, that she was "nearly dead for want of food and rest", even, to Marianne,

–it's an unlucky house. I believe I was a fool to set my heart on the place at all. For it will be a perpetual worry, finding tenants & replacing furniture & worry tells on my writing power. Yet writing will be the only way to pay off the debt ... then next week Papa may come home any day...[21]

CHAPTER 17
'Look to the past, the present and the future':
some conclusions

The Holland family motto, 'Respice, Aspice, Prospice', 'Look to the Past, the Present and the Future', was peculiarly realised in Mrs Gaskell. Her descent from an ancient aristocratic family – one near to the throne and Protestant before the word existed, one still socially recognised by the aristocracy of Cheshire and Lancashire in her own time, and one still rural-based – these facts undoubtedly were the origin of social and religious ideas which changed little in essentials over her fifteen years as a writer and social reformer; ideas which arose not only from her background but from deeply philosophical historical ideas of her own which have been ignored by her critics, both contemporary and modern.

Her northern-bred independence of mind and character, her very real practical skills and the support of her religion also stood her in good stead when she came to encounter the 'culture shock' of mid-Victorian industrial Manchester and her letters present vivid pictures of her bracing herself against its impact, – yet her religion has been consistently misunderstood and denigrated as a 'blot' on her literary work.

Her excellent education and 19th century nonconformist conscience were inherited from a Puritan tradition that male and female were, if sometimes only in theory, equal in the sight of God; their women had had not only a better than normal education but also a considerable degree of moral freedom. Hence, perhaps, Mrs Gaskell's "I don't believe William would ever have commanded me."[1] Puritan women had conducted household prayers when the husband was absent, even if other men were present, had instructed their children and servants, had been permitted even to reprove their husbands in moral and religious matters if they saw fit.[2]

Mrs Gaskell was, therefore, from the beginning, in temperament and in upbringing very much her "own woman" (though Charlotte Brontë, in her own then single state, had wondered about this), and her statement to her husband's congregation regarding the duties of a minister's wife, on her first coming to Manchester, is an example of this independence of mind.

212

The comprehensive tolerance of the old Presbyterian tradition which comes out strongly both in her letters and work (though by then it had become somewhat overshadowed by the development of sectarianism within the Unitarian body), has also been much misunderstood by her critics and, though always loyal to the Unitarian principle that Christ was not God, she regretted the rationalism, the lack of spirituality and ritual in the movement and was able, again in the old tradition of the 'Church Puritans', to remain close to and participate with pleasure in the services of the Established Church and to alternate between the Church and Dissent in her writing. Though called a rationalist e.g. by Coral Lansbury in her *Elizabeth Gaskell: the Novel of Social Crisis* (1975), Mrs Gaskell's idea of Christ as "a divine being" not "a mere man", made her, as she herself says, "not (Unitarianly) orthodox",[3] nearer to Arianism than Humanitarianism,[4] and she called herself 'a true Christian'[5] though this was, of course, denied by orthodox Christians of other denominations.

The most important aspect of her religious ideas, as we have seen, is her keen interest and participation in Christian Socialism, a very definite philosophical and practical challenge to nineteenth century capitalism. From the late 1840s to the end of her life her enthusiasm for this was unabated. Yet because of the suppression of almost all of her correspondence until 1966, she has been ignored in the works relevant to the movement, except for a brief statement by S.C. Carpenter in his *Church and People 1789-1889* (1933) that the Christian Socialists saw in Mrs Gaskell an "ally". So also has this same strong theme both in her letters and works been all but ignored by modern literary critics and biographers, who have seen her politics as middle-class Liberalism.

Perhaps again because of her own secrecy and that of her family, Mrs Gaskell has been consistently patronised by modern critics. T.S. Eliot, for example, himself coming from an American Unitarian family background, in reviewing *The Letters of Mrs Gaskell and Charles Eliot Norton* in 1933, claimed that she was not "a European", that she "came from a parsonage in Manchester", that William Gaskell was "an earnest, conscientious somewhat humourless Unitarian pastor [who] never absented himself voluntarily from Manchester [and] took an annual holiday at Morecambe Bay but even that was in the same county." Eliot implies that Mrs Gaskell's visit to Rome in 1857, where she first met Eliot Norton, was her only venture into Europe, a holiday taken alone to which she was "entitled" since she had borne 'a number of children' and 'devoted herself, and in the end sacrificed herself, to her husband.' Her sense of humour, according to Eliot was 'timid and fluttering', and her unsatisfied love of beauty, gaiety, and civilisation '... profited by her visit to Italy and by Norton's explanation of the art of Titian.' He concludes that Mrs Gaskell 'was not George Sand; but the best of her writing is perhaps more permanently readable, for she is among those English (and American) writers who have known how to make a literary virtue out of provinciality and in her case, simple goodness.'6

In fact, all the Gaskells regularly visited London and travelled extensively in Europe, even William Gaskell 'bachelorizing' with a male companion or alone, not only in Scotland but in Italy and Switzerland, a far cry from Eliot's reference to what was only one, if a favourite, holiday centre of the family, 'at Morecambe Bay', actually Silverdale. Mrs Gaskell's visit to Rome in 1857 was, not taken alone as a relief from domestic burdens, but with her two eldest daughters (then aged twenty-three and twenty) and her friend Catherine Winkworth, in a desperate determination to be out of England when the reviews of her *Life Of Charlotte Brontë* appeared. Eliot's condescending conclusions on Mrs Gaskell's provinciality might have been forgiven on the grounds of a superficial knowledge of only the best of her writings, but it is unforgivable in a professional review of the correspondence between her and Eliot Norton, to miss references to the Gaskells' European visits and, for example, her allusion to 'Göethean theories of self-development' a European expression if ever there was one.

It must be admitted that Mrs Gaskell's writings, which have a superficial appearance of provinciality, together with the similarly superficial background of the 'parsonage in Manchester', the destruction of her notebooks and diaries and all but a handful of the letters addressed to her, and the fact that those of her own letters which have survived were only published in 1966; all have conspired to hide the real Mrs Gaskell. As early as 1841 she was moving serenely through a Heidelberg ballroom with a wreath of flowers in her hair, already aware of the implications of the historic names represented amongst the dancers, and sorry that, owing to the fatigue of dancing every dance (or her husband's mild disapproval?), she missed the one that she might have had with Göethe's grandson. It is noteworthy, too, that in Paris in 1855, when a soirée was given in her honour, owing to this party "for grandeurs, titles and dresses", she was disappointed at being prevented from attending a dinner-party to meet Victor Cousin, friend of Hegel and the great French popularizer of German Idealist philosophy.[7]

David Cecil in 1948 saw her as a minor "lady Victorian novelist", once again provincial, "unable to bear unhappy endings", and whose "moral exhortations" and "liberal pieties" marred her work.[8] Others have accepted her as a useful reporter of industrial facts which could be used to grind their own various political and historical axes.[9] Among modern critics, only Annette Hopkins, writing in 1946 on Mrs Gaskell's conflict with Dickens because of her unwillingness to re-shape *North and South* to the requirements of *Household Words*, makes the cryptic statement that Dickens did not understand the "philosophical basis" of the work,[10] and Martin Dodsworth, in his introduction to the 1970 Penguin English Library edition, calls it a "bildungsroman", though he does not refer to the fact that this genre originated with the novels of Göethe. That Mrs Gaskell is still so misunderstood, may have been as I have said, up to a point, her own fault. Apart from the destruction of the usual sources of relevant information, she was a proud and private person who, even in letters to intimate friends, rarely revealed the deepest sources of her work nor ever defended herself publicly against the attacks of critics, even though they often made her ill.

She was, what F.D. Maurice called himself, a "digger": one who tried to penetrate, within the limitations of her times, the very springs of human behaviour, both on the basis of her own experience and observation and an eclecticism which sought for information and inspiration wherever it might be found, not only through reading but conversation and correspondence with that great variety of people, from all walks of life, who crowd the pages of her letters.

This is particularly prominent in her attitude to 'The Woman Question'. Her background had given her, before she came to Manchester, an extremely elevated view of the position of women. What she actually saw of women in Manchester was probably her most traumatic experience of the city; poor women as expendable factory fodder; rich women, wives and daughters of self-made manufacturers, sitting idle in their drawing rooms, unable, because of their 'social' position, to occupy themselves with useful household tasks yet deprived of truly creative leisure by their lack of education; poor 'genteel' women who, unmarried, had to seek the only work open to women of their class, the mainly uncongenial and humiliating position of governesses in 'trade' families. She grieved indignantly over the first, was somewhat contemptuous of the second, did all she could, practically, for the third, and became one of a group of women who were, as well as providing first aid projects, exploring, in various ways, the true nature and possibilities of their sex.

It was from her own experience and observation that, she came to believe that for the majority of women, motherhood, in its fullest sense as the creation and rearing of new life and the heart of that indispensable social unit, the family,[11] was woman's true vocation and fulfilment. She therefore disapproved of women working in factories since this resulted in their exploitation and the general neglect of proper house-wifery and child-care. Yet she was realistic enough to approve of public nurseries for the children of women factory workers.

She believed that all women, especially the unmarried, must have suitable opportunities of employment, though these were, for her, more limited than those of Florence Nightingale, but we have reason to believe that she agreed with her that women's positions in society would not improve much without great changes in the economic and social bases of society. As to her idea of the nature of woman as a reconciler in society, closer to the natural and spiritual world than man, to whom she was inspirer and companion, equal but different, we cannot say exactly how much was due to her Puritan background, her own innate qualities, her studies of Göethe, Dante, Mme de Sévigné and her compatriots, her feelings towards her husband, Eliot Norton, and men friends such as William Shaen. But it is noteworthy that she is much closer to the modern French women's liberation movement, which recognises and rejoices in 'la difference', than to the Anglo-American which sees every mention of this difference as in some way a degradation rather than an elevation of women.

This attitude however, seems to be beginning to moderate slightly in view of Betty Friedan 's book *The Second Stage* (1982). Twenty years ago her book *The Feminine Mystique* opened the door to the American women's liberation movement: in *The Second Stage* she suggests that American women have gained the world but are in danger of losing their souls. It advocates a return to thinking about love and child-bearing as well as jobs and rights, though she does not advocate giving up the latter. This has caused a furore amongst hard-line American feminists but has been greeted by many other women with relief.

Mrs Gaskell, then, in her thoughts on the subject of woman's place in society, looked 'to the past, the present, and the future'. Looking back to our Saxon roots, to the image of the yeoman and the social and sexual cohesion of pre-industrial society, to the best of French society of her own day, we see her preoccupation with all that she considered undesirable in contemporary English life and with the possibilities of change in the future. Her musings on such subjects as natural sciences, heredity, social cross-fertilisation, and general education all show that she regarded some changes as inevitable, indeed desirable, but she did not regard all change and novelty as good in itself. She was no "mutaphilic", as Professor Grüber dubs Charles Darwin. What was best in the past she treasured, and felt that it must not heedlessly be thrown away and lost forever but be incorporated into the social fabric of the present and preserved for the future.

What haunted Mrs Gaskell's mind endlessly was 'the unhappy state of things between those so bound to each other by common interest, as the employers and the employed must ever be ...' as she wrote in the preface to *Mary Barton,* i.e. the social alienation brought about by mass-production, especially on a capitalist basis. Her description of the Spottiswoodes' printing venturer, "so like a happy family"; Miss Galindo's thoughts on the bakery which would benefit a local community: Hope Farm, where the employer felt an ethical responsibility for his workers, where each contributed according to his ability and work problems could be talked out long before there was any possible escalation to the strike, which was, in Mrs Gaskell's day, the workers' only weapon; all these look forward to the 'small is beautiful' movement, to the small business, to intermediate technology rather than the image of mass-production which Miss Galindo saw as the root of all evil.

John Lucas, in 'Mrs Gaskell and the Nature of Social Change' (1975),[12] claims that Phillis, in the end, sadly, and 'tacitly' admits "the inevitability of the change that Holdsworth and all he stands for has wrought in her" by her wish for a (temporary) change of scene and that therefore, Mrs Gaskell herself finally admitted the necessity and even desirability of social change, presumably of any sort. Yet,

217

as we have seen, the very last words of Phillis and of the story are that, after the change of scene, "Then – we will go back to the peace of the old days. I know we shall; I can and I will!"

This story like all Mrs Gaskell's major works, has a strong allegorical element in it. Phillis' last words are curiously emphatic and would seem to indicate that though Mrs Gaskell felt, as has been admitted, that some changes were inevitable even desirable (such as the popular education originally so opposed by Lady Ludlow), eventually society would return to a more stable, simple way of life, more based on rural, religious and cultural values, which values she saw as harmonising and ennobling influences, rather than those of materialism. Surveying the decay of our urban centres with their empty factories, breeding grounds of unemployment and violence, who is to say that she will not be proved to have been right?

We know that, through her writing, Elizabeth Gaskell has had a lasting influence on English social thought. In her own self, and in her social work, she has also been a lasting figure in Manchester life and its traditions. In a paper given to the Manchester Literary Club in 1932, 'the centenary of the settlement in Manchester of "the charming Mrs Gaskell"', W. Henry Brown ended with a reference to her as 'bringing people of varied views and battling instincts together [so that] as individuals they would get to understand and most likely to love each other the better they knew one another.'[14] But it was an old Manchester factory worker who, in 1910, caught the secret of her influence and the nature of her ideas on class reconciliation.

> In the district round the old school building in Lower Mosely Street sixty years ago (and more) there was a teeming population, houses inhabited from cellar to garret, hand-loom weaving rooms as well as gigantic mills and with many other kinds of workshops scattered amongst them. Mrs Gaskell saw and knew that mixture all too well, and realizing what was then to many in such a seething population, homes of want, dens of many evils, she sought to rescue from a multitude of temptations a band of youngsters who would prowl these streets or gather indolently at the corners as loungers. Truly, a dreadful banditti, ever ready to snap at the unwary and draw them aside into the wake of wrong.
>
> Gathering between forty and fifty of these boys, who were all about fifteen years of age, she entertained them by

218

singing, story-telling, playing games: and to come in
contact with her personal presence, to listen to her voice
and watch her graceful manner ... was a paen of joy and
unspeakable comfort to lads pinched by poverty and
struggling for the bread of life ... Her manner was spirited
and attractive, her voice was clear and her tone expressive.
She was indulgent and painstaking with all of us, and so it
was that on our wayward minds she made a great
impression, and brightened our lives with her affectionate
regard and hope, and we gathered round her like young
troupes with loyal devotion. [15]

Elizabeth Gaskell wrote, half jokingly, to Charles Eliot Norton "I
am Medieval and unManchester and unAmerican." The old cotton-
worker wrote, some sixty years after her death, of her as what was, in
fact, a symbol of the mediaeval 'lady' with her knights and
troubadours, so much a civilising influence in Europe from at least the
middle ages until the French salons of the mid nineteenth century the
latter to which Elizabeth Gaskell was so much drawn. She, too, with
her writing, her social work and her place in the closely integrated
European religious and philosophical movements of the times, was a
civilising influence in Victorian Manchester and on contemporary
society as a whole with her emphasis on the need for reconciliation
between the classes and sexes, between the social cohesion of 'old
England' and the urgent need for social reform of various kinds,
popular education, more social mobility with its class fertilisation, a
greater understanding of natural science, of the connection between
mind and body, matter and spirit. As I have touched on at the end of
my chapters on *Wives and Daughters*, which she was still writing at
the time of her death, she cryptically brings all these together and
expresses them as the age-old idea of the possibility of a Golden Age,
an idea which has appeared in one form or another from recorded time
up to the present. Though most modern writers would say the latter
never existed and never could, one might think that this recurring
image may well represent man's instinctive desire for a civilisation in
which all human beings might live in peace and dignity and to their
best and fullest potential, unimpeded by greed and oppression. In this
sense, the image may be seen as having, as well as mere nostalgia, an
objective reality as real as material and scientific progress, but one

which, as Coleridge wrote in his *Church and State* (1830) would include the necessity

> to preserve the stores, to guard the treasures, of past civilization, and thus to bind the present with the past; to perfect and add to the same, and thus to connect the present with the future but especially to diffuse through the whole community, and to every native entitled to its laws and rights, that quantity and quality of knowledge which was indispensable both to the understanding of those rights, and for the performance of the duties correspondent.'[16]

On the 18th November, 1865, Thurstan Holland wrote to Charles Eliot Norton:

> My Dear Norton,
> I have to break my silence to you by the sad news which will call out all your sympathies and regrets, for I know that you held Mrs Gaskell one of your dearest friends & loved her as she did you ...
> She died at the little village of Holybourne near Alton in Hampshire on Sunday afternoon last the 12th inst & her death was terribly sudden & quite unexpected. She was sitting in the drawing-room after an early tea about a quarter to six in the afternoon with all her daughters but Minnie [Marianne] round her ... when suddenly she fell forward and died at once in a moment without any pain or struggle ... she had always wished & often spoke of her wish to die a sudden painless death like this and we all believe that her end was particularly happy ... she had just realized a plan of which the last year she had been full, which was to buy a house in the country with her own money and hand it over as a present to Mr Gaskell, and it was in her own house that she died. She had been there for the past fortnight busily engaged in arranging the furniture & planning how she could best please him & she had just got everything into order and readiness & was rejoicing in the carrying out of her wish when she was suddenly taken away. Her end was peaceful and happy and painless & came as she had wished it to come: & all this is a great comfort to those who loved her.
> We buried her at the little town of Knutsford in Cheshire yesterday afternoon ... Knutsford I do not doubt you know

220

is her 'Cranford'. Was it not fit that she should be buried there? ...

I feel her loss very deeply for all who knew her well must have loved that kind sympathetic heart which shared every one's joys or griefs, that fresh intellect, that powerful imagination, that kindly interest that she took in everyone about her ...

Yours most truly,

E. Thurston Holland[17]

NOTES

CHAPTER 1

As no complete edition of Mrs Gaskell's works exists, various editions and their introductions have been utilised as indicated.

1. 'Mrs Gaskell'. Mat Hompes, *The Gentleman's Magazine* vol 279 1895, pp 124-138.
2. *A Quest of Ladies,* Phillis Hicks, Birmingham, 1949. All material on Avonbank other than in Mrs Gaskell's letters is based on this.
3. *The Autobiography of Mrs Fletcher*, Ed. Mary Richardson, Edinburgh, 1875, p 23ff.
4. *Memorials of Two Sisters* Ed. Josephine Shaen, London 1908 p 23ff.
5. *My Literary Life,* Eliza Lynn Linton 1899, p 92ff.
6. *The Lancashire Hollands,* Bernard Holland, London 1917. Material in Chapters 1 and 2 taken from this and from a Holland pedigree assembled by John Unsworth and in the possession of the present writer.
7. *Conversations of Göethe with Eckermann,* Trans. John Oxenford, Ed. J.K. Moorehead, Everyman Edition, 1935.
8. GL384:p492.
9. GL401:p5l5.

CHAPTER 2

1. Chapter XVII. *Ruth*: The World's Classics, O.U.P. Ed. by Alan Shelston 1985.
2. Introduction to *Cranford*, Lady Anne Thackeray Ritchie, MacMillan, 1891, passim.
3. *The Story of Knutsford* C.R. Bennett, The Knutsford Society, 1976, passim.
4. GL8:pl5.
5. *Mary Howitt: An Autobiography* Ed. Margaret Howitt, William Ibister, 1889 vol II, p28.

6. *Mrs Gaskell's Observation and Invention* J.G. Sharps, Linden Press, 1970, p3O.

7. GL12:p28

8. Preface to *Mary Barton*, Penguin English Library Edition, 1970, p37.

9. GL314:p418.

10. GL32:p64.

CHAPTER 3

1. For my description on Manchester in this section see:
Bentley's Miscellany vol 11, 1840; *Report on the Sanitary Conditions of the Labouring Population* 1842; *Mrs Gaskell, a Manchester Influence*, Henry W. Brown, *Papers of the Manchester Literary Club*, vol LVIII, 1932; *Our Sewer Rivers*, report read to the Manchester Statistical Society 1833-1933; T.S. Ashton, M.U.P., 1934; *Journeys to England and Ireland*, Ed. K.P. Mayer, M.U.P., 1958; *Victorian Cities*, Asa Briggs, 1968, Pelican Edition, pp88-138 passim.

2. *Mary Barton*, Penguin English Library Edition, Ch 9, p 98.

3. Asa Briggs, op cit pp 184-240.

4. GL453:p598.

5. *Mrs Linnaeus Banks: Author of The Manchester Man etc.*, E.L. Burney, Manchester, 1969.

6. GL384:p488.

7. GL7:p13, GL10:p23, GL11:p24f, GL100a:pp840, GL116a:p846, GL134p:201, GL175:p261, GL251:p354f, GL278a:p381a, GL419:p540.

8. Sharps, p153.

9. *Ruth,* World's Classics O.U.P. 1985: p153, p188, p210.

10. Introduction to *Ruth* by A.W. Ward in the Knutsford Edition.

11. *North and South* Penguin English Library, 1970 Chs. XV and XX.

12. 'William Rathbone Gregg and Mrs Gaskell,' David Shusterman, *Philological Quarterly* XXXVI, 11 April 1957.

13. GL12:p28f, GL27:p58f, GL55:p91, GL81:p132, GL82a:p133, GL97:p154, GL167a:p250f, GL185:p274, GL200:p294, GL394:p506, GL421:p544, GL443a:p901, GL453:p597f, GL461:p607, GL560:p743ff, GL565:p751.

14. I have this from my late dear friends, Misses Catharine and Ruth
Herford, daughters of Dr Travers Herford.

CHAPTER 4

1. GL33:p64.
2. 'Letters addressed to Mrs Gaskell by Celebrated Contemporaries'
Ed. R.D. Waller, *Bulletin of the John Rylands University Library,
Manchester*, January 1935.
3. GL37:p68.
4. GL38: p69
5. GL39:p70. For a study of 'Earnestness' and Carlyle see the first
two chapters of *A Victorian View of Literature*, Geoffrey Tillotson,
Oxford, 1978.
6. Printed in the introduction by A.W. Ward to *Mary Barton*,
Knutsford Edition, 1906.
7. Printed as Appendix 2, Penguin English Library Edition of *Mary
Barton*, 1972.
8. GL1:p1.
9. GL13:p34.
10. GL4:p5ff.
11. GL384:p487f. GL403:p516. GL414:p531 - note: *Round the Sofa*.
12. GL418:p534.
13. GL418:p 535
14. GL25a:p56f.
15. *Lyrical Ballads* Ed. R.L. Brett and A.R. Jones, 1968, Appendix c,
p 333.
16. ibid p337.
17. *The Later Wordsworth* E.C. Batho, 1933, p 342.
18. GL12:p 33.
19. Chapter L, *North and South*, Penguin English Library, 1970.
20. GL255:p256.
21. Preface to *Mabel Vaughan*, Susanna Cummins, London, 1857.
22. HHS, p224.
23. *Memorials of Two Sisters*, op cit and *The Correspondence of
Henry Crabb Robinson with the Wordsworth Circle*. Ed. Edith
Morley, vol. 11, 1927, Oxford, pp700, 705.

CHAPTER 5

1. GL39:p70f.
2. D.N.B.
3. For a study of this spirituality see *Lady Lettice, Vi-Countess Falkland*, John Duncon (1649) Ed. M.F. Howard, London 1908.
4. *Heads of Unitarian History*, Alexander Gordon, London, 1895, p20.
5. *The English Presbyterians*, Allen and Unwin, section by Roger Thomas, Allen and Unwin 1968, p 47.
6. *Puritanism in North West England*, R.C. Richardson, M.U.P., 1972, p 125.
7. *North and South*, Ch.IV. p67/68, Penguin English Library, 1970.
8. *The Rise of the Old Dissent*, Joseph Hunter, 1842, passim.
9. GL198a: p860.
10. 'The Nonconformity of the Old Parish of Rostherne including Knutsford and the adjacent parishes,' signed H.G. (Henry Green), Presbyterian Memorials, no. 16, *The Unitarian Herald*, Oct. 18, 25, Nov. 1, 8, 15, 1862.
11. *Reflections of Unitarianism in Mrs Gaskell's Novels*, unpublished doctoral thesis, Arthur Boggs, University of California, Bodleian Library, Oxford, microfilm, passim.
12. GL485: p648ff.
13. 'The Importance of the Seventeenth Century in Unitarian History,' H.L. Short, *U.H.S.T*, vol IX, no 4. p 199.
14. GL418: p537f.
15. *Lancashire Authors and Orators*, John Evans, London, 1850.
16. *Ruth* Ch. XIV, p 151, World's Classics O.U.P. 1985.
17. *The Unitarian Movement in the Religious Life of England, (1700-1900)*, H. McLachlan, George Allen and Unwin, 1934, p 285.
18. *Socinianism in Seventeenth Century England*, H.J. McLachlan, O.U.P., 1951, p 310 - quoted.
19. D.N.B.
20. John's First Epistle, ch 5, verse 7. Authorized Version, 'For there are three that bear record in heaven, the Father, the Word and the Holy Ghost; and these three are one.' The Revised Version omits this verse and it is generally admitted to be a late interpolation.
21. GL405: p520
22. GL485: p648.

23. GL593: p784f, undated letters.
24. 'The Founding of the British and Foreign Unitarian Association.' H.L. Short, *U.H.S.T.* Supplement to vol XVI, pp 4, 22.
25. Boggs, op. cit.
26. 'Priestley and Martineau,' H.L. Short, *Hibbert Journal* vol 60, no3.
27. *These Eighty Years: The Autobiography of a Unitarian Socialist,* Henry Solly, vol 1, London, 1893.
28. Holt, p 82
29. GL84: p136

CHAPTER 6

1. GL15:p41.
2. See Previous chapter.
3. Frau von Pickford with whom the Gaskells were staying.
4. Continuation of GL15 to be found on p820, *The Letters of Mrs Gaskell* op cit.
5. GL90:p143 GL181:p267 GL503:p681
6. *Collected Letters of Samuel Taylor Coleridge* Ed. Griggs, vol 11, 1966 edition, p 459.
7. *The Unitarian Movement in the Religious Life of England. (1700-1900).* H. McLachlan, 1934, pp50,51. quoted.
8. op cit p183
9. GL100:p158
10. GL286:p389
11. GL29:p61, GL30:p62
12. GL192:p282
13. GL217:p316ff.
This letter is designated as 'from a printed source' (see footnote to the letter GL217). The source is Elizabeth Haldane's *Mrs Gaskell and her Friends*, 1929, pp90-97, and it omits passages contained in the Symington Collection, Box 19, Leeds Archives Dept., Shaen Papers. One of such omitted passages reads - 'Yes! I have read Carlyle's W.M. once or twice, - and I thought it wonderfully clean and suggestive and disagreeable and I remember the Hamlet criticism particularly &c ...' 'Two Versions of a Gaskell Letter', Anna

Unsworth, *Notes and Queries*, 1982, Pembroke College, Oxford, New Series, Vol 29, No 4, p308.
14. GL418:p539

CHAPTER 7

1. *Sylvia's Lovers*, Everyman Edition, 1964, Ch. XXII, p22.
2. e.g. 'The Moorland Cottage', *My Lady Ludlow*, 'Six Weeks at Heppenheim' et al.
3. *Wilhelm Meister*, Vol 1. trans. H.M. Waidson, John Calder, 1977, passim.
4. Op cit Book IV, Ch VI, passim.
5. *Mary Barton*, Penguin English Library Ed. 1972 Ch XXII, p 298.
6. *Kubla Khan and the Fall of Jerusalem*, Elinor Shaffer, C.U.P. 1975, Introduction pp 1-15, also section on Coleridge, passim.
7. GL61:p98.
8. See 'Ruth, Mrs Gaskell's Neglected Novel' A.J. Sheltston Bulletin of the *John Rylands University Library Spring Edition*, 1976.
9. *Memorials of Two Sisters* op cit, p103.
10. *North and South*, Penguin English Library Ed. 1972 Ch. 11 p22.
11. *Ruth* Ch 23, p244, op cit.

CHAPTER 8

1. GL383:p485.
2. 'How the Unitarian Movement paid its debt to Anglicanism,' D. Wigmore-Beddowes, *U.H.S.T.*, volXXXI, Oct. 1964, quoted.
3. GL461:p608.
4. *Yesterday's Radicals: A Study of the Affinity between Unitarianism and Broad Church Anglicans in the Nineteenth Century*, D.G. Wigmore Beddowes, 1971, James Clark, p28 quoted.
5. GL461:p609.
6. 'How the Unitarian Movement paid its debt to Anglicanism,' *U.H.S.T.* 1964, quoted.
7. *Memorials of Two Sisters* op cit. pp 103, 104.

8. *These Eighty Years: the Autobiography of a Unitarian Chartist* Henry Solly, 1893, vol 1. MS letter referring to Shaen's Chartist Sunday School at Carter Lane Chapel, London. Symington Papers, Box 19, (uncatalogued), Leeds City Archives.

9. GL526:p706.

10. *Church and People*, 1789-1889, S.C. Carpenter, 1933, S.P.C.K. p 326.

11. S.T. Coleridge *Lay Sermons* (1817) Ed. by J.R. White, Princeton University Press, *Coleridge Collected Works* (Vol 6) pp 189, 190.

12. *Coleridge* ed. Stephen Potter, Nonsuch Press, 1971, p476 quoted.

13. GL130:p195f.

14. GL393:p502.

15. GL443a:p901.

16. 'Coleridge and the Manchester Academy,' John Unsworth, *The Charles Lamb Bulletin* October 1980.

17. *Sermons and Society,* Ed. P. Welsby, Penguin Edition, 1970, pp 210, 212, quoted.

18. ibid Chapter 15.

19. ibid Chapter 19.

20. GL47:p79.

21. *These Eighty Years*, op cit Vol 2. p125.

22. GL418:p537ff.

23. GL540a:p720.

24. GL67:p104f. In 1835 Mrs Gaskell spent an evening with the Maurices in London. 'Mrs Gaskell: an Unpublished Letter'. *Notes and Queries*, September 1988, Anna Unsworth

25. Holt, op cit, page 137, quoted.

26. *Sermons and Society*, op cit, pages 244,245.

27. *Memorials of Two Sisters*, op cit. page 42; The Whittington Club was a middle class family club in London of which Shaen was for several years Chairman and Dickens and Thackeray were members.

28. *Memorials of Two Sisters*. op cit page 128

29. GL414:p530.

30. GL162:p237. cf *The Flight from Work* by Goram Palm, C.U.P. 1978 in which the author suggests that modern industry needs to adapt some of the values of family life and that work is best done in teams of 'unequal' workers.

31. GL170:p254 and GL171:p255.

32. Louis Blanc was a French radical Politician who founded several co-operatives on the principals of Chevalier, the founder of a French religious order GL55:p90.

33. GL69:p108.

34. GL398:p510.

35. GL159:p234.

36. GL386:p494.

37. *These Eighty Years* op cit. vol 11, pages 161, 250.

38. GL509b:p927.

39. See *The Christian Socialist Revival*, 1887-1914, Peter d'A Jones, 1968, for reference to Scott Holland.

CHAPTER 9

Preface, John Ruskin, Unto This Last, reprinted in: *Unto This Last and Other Writings*, ed Clive Wilmer, Harmondsworth: Penguin 1985. *Preface, passim*

1. GL53 p88f. GL75:p124. GL79p130. GL100:p158. GL159p234. GL211:p309f see note p310. GL237:p341. GL384:p490. GL418:p538.

2. GL476a:p915f, see Appendix E, Table of Descriptions, page 963.

3. GL597:p787.

4. GL598:p787.

5. GL93:p147f.

6. *Church and People* op cit, Chapter XI, quoted.

7. e.g. GL386:p 494.

8. *Cousin Phillis, and Other Tales*: The World's Classics Edition Ed. Angus Easson O.U.P. 1981. p264. (All future references are to this edition.)

9. ibid p270.

10. ibid p271.

11. ibid p271.

12. ibid p274.

13. ibid p279.

14. ibid p285.

15. ibid p348.

16. ibid p353.

CHAPTER 10

1. See town guide to the annual *Knutsford Royal May Day Festival*, published by the Knutsford May Day Committee and printed by Hewitt, 25-29 King Street, Knutsford.

2. GL562:p747.

3. *The Letters of Mary Sybilla Holland*, Ed. Bernard Holland, 1907, letter written from Church House, Knutsford, May 1876, page 37ff.

4. 'Mrs Gaskell and George Eliot.' Barbara Hardy, *The Victorians*, edited Arthur Pollard, 1970, pages 169-179.

15. Dickens called Mrs Gaskell 'conceited' after reading this article on 'Company Manners,' see 'Dickens and Mrs Gaskell,' Annette Hopkins, *Huntingdon Public Library Quarterly* vol IX, August 1946. Dickens was, of course, unrepentently middle-class and was noted for the opulence of his dinner-parties, see GL111:p175.

6. See also HHS pp 40, 41, 72 and GLS 6p11, 7p12pp, 10p23, 11p26: a Nathaniel Gaskell also left money in the 18th century for the poor of Cross Street Chapel.

7. The poet referred to is Tennyson whose 'Locksley Hall,' published in 1842, expressed views on nature later developed further in *In Memoriam*, a work particularly admired by Mrs Gaskell, see GLS 73 and 79.

8. Such failures were common at the time when Mrs Gaskell was writing, see 'Mrs Gaskell' Mat Hompe, *The Gentleman's Magazine*, vol 279, 1895, p 134.

9. Obviously here contrasted with the commercial banks. Quotations from *Cranford*: World's Classics Ed. 1981.

CHAPTER 11

1. *A Gathered Church*, Donald Davie, Routledge and Kegan Paul, 1976, p 27.

2. Lord Kenneth Clark, *Civilisation* 1969, B.B.C. Chapter 10, passim.

3. *Howitt's Journal*, vol 2, 1847; see Sharps, p45.

4. GL418:p537.

5. *Early Victorian Novelists*, Lord David Cecil, 1934, revised 1948.

6. *My Diary* (1835-38) 50 copies privately printed by Clement Shorter in 1923, original in the possession of Mrs Trevor Jones, grand-daughter of Marianne Gaskell.

7. GL30:p62f. GL230:p334. GL141:213.

8. GL32:p64. The party included the Darbishires, Geraldine Dewsbury, author of a sensational novel Zoë, Dr Hodgson, Principal of Chorlton High School and 'Mr Green,' probably the barrister son of the Revd Henry Green of Knutsford.

9. GL499:p 675.

10. GL532:p712.

11. See Appendix 'Literary References in Mrs Gaskell's Works' to *The Woman Question in Mrs Gaskell's Life and Works*, Aina Rubenius, 1950 Upsala Harvard, a quotation, in the original French, from *An Introduction to the Devout Life*, a work on the spiritual life by St Francis de Sales appears in *North and South*, Ch XVI; a reference to Count de Sales, father of Lady de Tabley is in GL404a:p894.

12. GLS - Miscellaneous p971.

13. *Publications of the Modern Language Association of America*, vol 53, 1938, p 545.

14. GL454:p599.

CHAPTER 12

1. Sharps, p 276.

2. *Prosper Mérimée*, A.W. Raitt, 1970, p 131.

3. GL122:p186. GL129:p195. 'French Writing Today,' *Times Literary Supplement*, 26th March 1954, quoted.

4. 'Mrs Gaskell in France,' 1849-1890, *P.M.L.A.* as above, English translation of French passages by Eveleen Huggard in the possession of Anna Unsworth; for other material on Mérimée see section on his letters in *French Poets and Novelists*, Henry James, 1878 and relevant entry in the *Oxford Companion to French Literature*.

5. GL395:p508, and note 3.

6. GL55:p91. GL94:p150.

7. GL422:p545.

8. GL449:p592. The Portico was a reading-room, for gentlemen only, of which William Gaskell was chairman for many years. Ladies were only allowed to borrow periodicals after they had 'lain on the tables' for three months.

9. See 'Shams,' *Fraser's Magazine* February 1863, signed E.C.G. Tentatively defined as by Elizabeth Cleghorn Gaskell by Prof W. Houghton in the *Wellesley Index to Victorian Periodicals* and verified by Anna Unsworth and Andrew Morton in 'Mrs Gaskell Anonymous,' *Victorian Periodicals Review*, Spring, 1981, vol XIV, No. 1.

10. *Times Literary Supplement*, 16th December 1977, p 1481.

11. GL94:p 149f.

CHAPTER 13

1. 'Mrs Gaskell and George Eliot,' *The Victorians* op cit p 169.

2. Mr Gibson is clearly based on Dr Peter Holland and William Gaskell. The latter had a slight Scottish accent, presumably acquired at Glasgow University, also a 'contempt for demonstrative people' and an attraction to any woman with a pretty face (see Sharps p409 and GL25a:p57.) Mrs Gaskell's fear of her own death, her husband's probable re-marriage and its possible ill-effect on her eldest daughter's character are referred to in GL16:p46.

3. For references to members of the Darwin family, see GL99:p157. GL100:p158. GL308:p411. GL443a:p902. 484b:p9l9. GL550:p732. GL553:p736.

4. GL550:p732.

5. Valentine card reproduced in Sharps, op cit, opposite p 554.

6. 'A Biographical sketch of an Infant,' written in 1840, first published in 1877 and re-printed in *Darwin on Man*, Howard E. Grüber, Wildwood House, 1974, pp64ff.

7. MS reproduced in HHS opposite p354.

8. *Wives and Daughters*: Ed. Angus Easson, The World's Classics, O.U.P., 1987, p681.

CHAPTER 14

1. GLS 438:p567. 461:p610. 523a:p933.
2. MS letters to Mrs Gaskell 731/70, 731/71, John Rylands University Library, Manchester.
3. *Scholar Extraordinary: The Life of Professor Hon. Max Müller* - Niraud Chaud Chaudhuri, Chatto and Windus, 1974, p270.
4. Wives and Daughters, Ed. Angus Easson, The World's Classics O.U.P. 1987, p681.
5. GL500:p677.
6. GL526:p707.
7. GL546:p726.
8. GL550:p732.
9. GL543:p598.
10. *Wives and Daughters*, op cit p63. The Knutsford area is surrounded by 'meres,' i.e. small stretches of water.
11. op cit 73.
12. op cit 24.
13. op cit 61.
14. Anna Unsworth photographed Dam Head in 1974 and another photograph appears in a privately printed book, written by Swinton Holland and edited by W.F. Irvine, Edinburgh, 1902, entitled *The Hollands of Mobberley* with some account of the Holland family of Knutsford. In this book there is also a letter (p61) from Margaret Holland of Mobberley to Abigail Holland of Knutsford mentioning Sandlebridge and saying that "Mrs Gaskell and Miss Lucy Holland have just been here". The letter is dated 10th February 1838.
15. *Wives and Daughters*: op cit p112.
16. op cit p480-485.
17. op cit p197.
18. op cit p619.
19. op cit p618.
20. op cit p39.
21. op cit p74.
22. *The English Countryman, A Study of the English Tradition*, H.J. Massingham, 1942, chapters on 'The Peasant' and 'The Yeoman' passim; see also *The Rural Tradition*, W.J. Keith, Harvester Press, 1975; and *Response to Revolution* D.O. Thomas, University of Wales Press, 1989, pp55-59.

CHAPTER 15

1. Relevant entry in the *Companion to American Literature*.
2. Introduction to *The Letters of Mrs Gaskell and Charles Eliot Norton 1857-1865*, Jane Whitehill, 1932, ppxxii, xxiii.
3. op cit, pxxiii.
4. op cit, p116.
5. op cit p 98.
6. GL504:p682.
7. GL482:p642.
8. Whitehill op cit, p99.
9. GL583:p773.
10. *The Aeneid of Virgil*. Trans. C. Day Lewis, London, 1961.
11. I am much indebted to Professor Donald Davie for his article 'Hardy's Virgilian Purples', *Agenda*, Autumn, 1976, for valuable information and all quotations in this section are from it unless otherwise stated.
12. *The Divine Comedy*: Dante Alighieri, trans. Geoffrey Bickersteth, Oxford, 1972, p 483: 'Purgatorio' Canto XXX 28-33.
13. GLS166:p243. 211:p308. 401:p514. 444:p582. 493:p666f.
14. *Ruth* pages 5, 40, 65, World's Classics Ed. O.U.P., 1985.
15. *Wives and Daughters* Page 75: Page 116, World's Classics Ed. 1987. op cit.
16. *Cousin Phillis* Page 307f, World's Classics, op cit.
17. ibid Page 273.
18. ibid Page 334.
19. ibid Page 304.
20. *Shirley* - Charlotte Brontë, Chapter XVIII.
21. GL167:p248.
22. Whitehill, op cit page XIX.
23. *Cousin Phillis* page 266, World's Classics Ed. op cit.
24. ibid, Page 268.
25. ibid Page 275.
26. ibid Page 327.
27. *Cousin Phillis*, centenary edition, George Bell, London 1910, illustrated by M.V. Wheelhouse.
28. National Library of Scotland, *MS* 23181 fols 180-5.

CHAPTER 16

1. Details on The Lawn, HHS. pp430-7: brochure of The Distressed Gentlefolks Aid, the charitable organisation which now owns The Lawn: GL583:p774. GL587:p779. GL589:p780.
2. GL575a:p936.
3. GL585:p576f.
4. GL1:p1.
5. GL9:p20.
6. GL13:p34.
7. GL17:p46.
8. GL570:p758f.
9. *MSS* deposited by the Unitarian College, Manchester, with the John Rylands University Library, Woodhouse Collections A.2. The word 'gammon,' meaning nonsense, is used similarly in Trollope's *Framley Parsonage.*
10. GL490:p659f.
11. GL570:p759.
12. Sharps, op cit, page 409, footnote no 208, quoted from *MSS* 6035ff, and *MS* 6036ff 53-54, National Library of Scotland, Edinburgh.
13. GLS124:p190. 25ap57.
14. GL25a:p57.
15. 'Mrs Gaskell and George Eliot,' Barbara Hardy, *The Victorians,* op cit, page 169.
16. GL316:p419.
17. *Florence Nightingale,* Cecil Woodham-Smith, Re-Print Society 1952, pages 269ff.
18. GL69:p108.
19. GL583:p775.
20. GL581:p770.
21. 575a:p938.

CHAPTER 17

1. GL69:p109.

2. For much interesting material on Puritan women see *Puritanism in North West England*, R.C. Richardson, M.U.P., 1972.

3. GL593:p784f.

4. GL485:p647f.

5. GL69:p108.

6. *The New England Quarterly*, VI, 1933, page 627ff.

7. GL229:p332.

8. *Early Victorian Novelists: Essays in Revaluation*, Lord David Cecil, Section on Mrs Gaskell, Penguin 1948.

9. Raymond Williams, E.J.A. Hobsbawm, Steven Marcus et al.

10. 'Dickens and Mrs Gaskell' Annette Hopkins, *Huntingdon Library Quarterly*, August 1946.

11. In a recently discovered Gaskell letter, now *MS* Robberds 1 Folder 162, Manchester College, Oxford, she thanks a correspondent for a pamphlet on the Education of Pauper Children, and says that she had often heard in Scotland of "the strong attachment between decent families and the sort of foster child brought up in the midst of the family; and loving approximation of God's ordinance of a "family" is surely to be desired." (circa 1860).

12. e.g. the Carson women in *Mary Barton*, the Thornton sisters in *North and South* and Lady Harriet in *Wives and Daughters*.

13. *Literature and History*, Thames Polytechnic, March 1975, page 28.

14. *Papers of the Manchester Library Club*, LVIII, 1932, pages 13-26.

15. 'Recollections of Mrs Gaskell' *The Christian Life and Herald* 1st October, 1910, quoted by Annette Hopkins in her *Elizabeth Gaskell: Her Life and Work*, 1952, page 367.

16. *On the Constitution of the Church and State*, Samuel Taylor Coleridge, (1830), edited by John Colmer, Routledge and Kegan Paul, Princeton University Press, 1976, p43, 'Mrs Gaskell and the 'Verifiable' Landscape,' *Faith and Freedom*, Manchester College, Oxford, Summer 1989, vol 42, no. 125, part 2, page 76, Anna Unsworth.

17. GL p970, 971.

SELECT BIBLIOGRAPHY

The following is but a small selection of the books, articles and manuscript sources that have been referred to in the research for this book. Others will be found in the notes relevant to each chapter.

Arnold, Thomas, *Life and Correspondence*. Ed. Arthur Stanley, Ward and Lock, 1844.

August, Eugene, 'Tennyson and Teilhard: the Faith of 'In Memoriam.'' *Publications of the Modern Language Association of America*. March 1969.

Bamford, Samuel, *Walks in South Lancashire*, Pubd. by himself 1844, Harvester Reprint.

Batho, Edith, *The Later Wordsworth*, C.U.P. 1933.

Bennett C.R., *The Story of Knutsford*, Knutsford Society, 1976.

Beer, John, Ed., *Coleridge's Variety: Bicentary Studies*, MacMillan, 1974. 'Coleridge's Poetic Intelligence'. MacMillan, 1977. *Wordsworth and the Human Heart*, MacMillan, 1979.

Beer, Patricia, *Reader, I Married Him*, MacMillan, 1974. (Section on Mrs Gaskell).

Bland, D.S., '*Mary Barton* and Historical Accuracy', *Review of English Studies*, January 1950.

Boggs, C.G., *Reflections of Unitarianism in Mrs Gaskell's Novels*, unpublished thesis, University of California, 1958. 'Without Dogma, Without Creed; English Unitarianism during the First Two Thirds of the 19th Century'. *Unitarian Historical Transactions*, October 1966.

Bolam C.G., *The English Presbyterians*, with J. Goring, H.L. Short, and R. Thomas, Allen and Unwin, 1968.

Briggs, Asa, *Victorian Cities*, Pelican 1968. *Victorian People*, Pelican 1975.

Burney, E.L., *Mrs Linnaeus Banks, Author of 'The Manchester Man' etc* E.J. Morten, Manchester, 1969, (Isabella Banks).

Butler, Josephine, *An Autobiographical Memoir* (1909), Ed. G.L. and A. Johnson, Arrowsmith, 1928.

Carlyle, Thomas, *Past and Present* (1843) Dent, 1915.

Carpenter S.C., *Church and People 1789-1889*, London, 1933.

Chadwick, E.H., *Mrs Gaskell, Haunts, Homes and Stories*, Pitman, 1910.

Chandler, Alice, *A Dream of Order: The Mediaeval Ideal in Nineteenth Century Literature*, Nebraska University Press, 1970, London, 1971.

Clarke, M.V., *Fourteenth Century Studies*, Oxford, 1937.

Coleridge, S.T. *Collected Letters of Samuel Taylor Coleridge*, Ed. E.L. Griggs, Oxford 1966. *Confessions of an Inquiring Spirit* (1840), Scolar Reprint, 1971. *Select Poetry and Prose*, Ed. Stephen Potter, London, 1971. *Lectures on Politics and Religion* (1795) Ed. Lewis Patton and Peter Mann, Routledge, Princeton University Press, 1971. *The Collected Works. Coleridge Poems*, Ed. with Introduction by John Beer, Dent, 1974.

Crabb Robinson, Henry, *On Books and their Writers* (3 vols), Ed. Edith J. Morley, London 1938. *The Correspondence of Henry Crabb Robinson and the Wordsworth Circle*, (2 vols), Ed. Edith J. Morley, Clarendon Press, 1927.

Cunningham, Valentine, *Everywhere Spoken Against: Dissent in the Victorian Novel*. O.U.P., (section on Mrs Gaskell).

Davie, Donald, *A Gathered Church, the Literature of the English Dissenting Interest*, 1700-1900. Routledge and and Kegan Paul, 1978. *Dictionary of National Biography*.

Easson, Angus, *Elizabeth Gaskell*, Routledge and Kegan Paul, 1979.

Eckermann, John Peter, *Conversations with Göethe*, (1850) Dent, 1935.

Eliot T.S., 'The Letters of Mrs Gaskell and Charles Eliot Norton, 1855-1865.' *The New England Quarterly* vi, 1933.

Encyclopaedia Brittanica, (1877)

Engels, Prederick, *The Condition of the Working Class in England* (1848), Panther, 1969.

Erdman, David, *Coleridge, Wordsworth and the Wedgwood Fund* New York Public Library, 1956.

Fletcher, Mrs, The Autobiography of - Ed. Mary Richardson, Edinburgh, 1875.

Fox, A.J. *Annals of the Todmorden Unitarian Congregation: Centennial Sketch, Waddington*, Fielden Square, Todmorden, 1924.

Friedan, Betty, *The Second Stage*, 1982.

Galway, Margaret, 'Joan of Kent and the Order of the Garter,' *University of Birmingham Historical Journal* Vol 1, no 1, 1947.

Gaskell, Elizabeth, There is no complete edition of her works but the most complete are: *The Works of Mrs Gaskell*, Ed. A.W. Ward (8 vols), The Knutsford Edition, London *1906 (The Life of Charlotte Brontë* is omitted). *The Novels and Tales of Mrs Gaskell*, Ed. Clement Shorter (11 vols), Worlds Classics, London, 1906-19 (including *The Life of Charlotte Brontë*.) *My Diary* (1838), privately printed by Clement Shorter 1923). *The Letters of Mrs Gaskell and Charles Eliot Norton* Ed. Janet Whitehill, O.U.P., 1932. *The Letters of Mrs Gaskell* Ed. J.A.V. Chapple and A. Pollard, M.U.P., 1966. Gaskell, William, MSS letters, Woodhouse Collection A.2., John Rylands University Library, Manchester.

Gérin, Winifred, *Elizabeth Gaskell - A Biography*, Clarendon Press, 1976.

Göethe, Johann Wolfgan von, *The Sufferings of Young Werther* trans. Bayard Quincy Morgan, (1957), John Calder, 1976. *Wilhelm Meister* (1777-1829) (2 vols), trans H.W. Waidson, John Calder, 1977.

Gray, Ronald, *Göethe, A Critical introduction*, C.U.P. 1967.

Green, Henry, *Knutsford: Its Traditions and History* (1859), Smith Elder and Co, E.J. Morten, Manchester, 1969. 'The Nonconformity of the Old Parish of Rostherne, including Knutsford and the Adjacent Parishes.' English Presbyterianism Memorials no. 16, signed H.G., *The Unitarian Herald* 18.10.1862, 29.10.1862, 1.11.1862, 8.11.1862, 15.11.1862.

Greg, W.R., Mistaken Aims and Attainable Ideals of the Artizan Class, London, 1876. (Includes a reprint of his review *of Mary Barton) Edinburgh Review*, April 1849.

Grüber, Howard E., *Darwin on Man*, Wildwood House, 1974.

Hardy, Barbara, 'Mrs Gaskell and George Eliot,' *The Victorians*, Ed. A. Pollard, Sphere Books Vol 6, 1970,

Hartwell, R.H., 'The Rising Standard of Living in England 1800-1850,' *The Economic History Review*, 2nd series, xiii, April 1961.

Herford, Brooke, *Travers Madge: A Memoir*, London 1867.

Herford, Travers, Unpublished memoirs, transcribed and edited by Anna Unsworth under the title *A Unitarian Childhood in Mid-Victorian Manchester*: typescript in the editor's possession.

Hobsbawm, E.J.E., 'The Standard of Living during the Industrial Revolution,' *The Economic History Review*, 2nd series, August 1963. 'Ringing the Changes,' the *Observer*, 14.3.76 (continuing disagreement on the standard of living during the Industrial Revolution).

Hohendorf, Horst, *The Life and Times of Göethe*, trans. Salvator Attanasio, Hamlyn, 1969.

Holland, Bernard, *The Lancashire Hollands*, London, 1917 (includes extensive bibliography and pedigrees).

Holland, Sir Henry, *Recollections of Past Life*, London, 1872.

Holland, Mary Sybilla, The Letters of. Ed. Bernard Holland, London, 1908.

Hollis, Patricia, 'Engels, Manchester and the Working Class,' *Literature and History*, Thames Polytechnic, Autumn 1976. 'Mrs Gaskell and her Social Work among, the Poor,' *The Inquirer*, 8.10.1910.

Holt, R.V., *The Unitarian Contribution to Social Progress*, Allen and Unwin, 1938.

Hompes, Mat, 'Mrs Gaskell and her Social Work among the Poor,' *The Inquirer*, 8.10.1910.

Hopkins, Annette, 'Liberalism in the Social Teaching of Mrs Gaskell,' *The Social Service Review*, March 1931. 'Mrs Gaskell in France 1849-1890', *Publications of the Modern Languages Association of America* vol 53, 1938. 'Dickens and Mrs Gaskell,' *The Huntingdon Library Quarterly*, August 1946. *Elizabeth Gaskell: Her Life and Work*, John Lehman 1952.

Hunter, Joseph, *The Rise of the Old Dissent*, 1842.

Huxley, Julian and Kettlewell H.B.D., *Charles Darwin and His World*, Thames and Hudson, 1974.

Irvine, Hugh Colley, *The Old D.P.S. A Short History of Charitable Work in Manchester and Salford 1833-1933*. The committee of the Manchester and District Provident Society of Manchester and Salford, 1933.

James, Henry, *French Poets and Novelists*, (1878) Macmillan 1919. *W. Wetmore Storey and His Friends*, Blackwood, 1903.

Keith, W., *The Rural Tradition, William Cobbett, Gilbert White, and other Non-Fiction Prose Writers of the English Countryside*. Harvester Press, 1975.

Knutsford Royal May Day Procession Festival Programme (1975), Printed by Hewitts, 25-29 King Street, Knutsford.

Levere, Trevor, 'The Poetic Church,' *Times Literary Supplement* 22.10.76., (Wordsworth and Coleridge).

Lucas, John, 'Mrs Gaskell and the Nature of Social Change,' *Literature and History,* Thames Polytechnic, London, March 1975.

Magill, C.P., *German Literature*, O.U.P., 1974.

Marcus, Steven, *The Other Victorians: A Study of Sexuality and Pornography in Mid Nineteenth Century England*, Weidenfeld and Nicholson, 1966.

McClachlan, Herbert, *The Unitarian Movement in the Religious Life of England: its Contribution to Thought and Learning (1700-1900)*, Allen and Unwin, 1934. Ed. *Essays and Addresses*, (1860) M.U.P., 1950.

Mérimée, Prosper, The Letters of -, Review in 'French Writing Today,' *Times Literary Supplement*, 26.3.54.

Müller, Max, *MSS* letters to Mrs Gaskell, MSS 731/70, 731/71, John Rylands Library, Manchester.

OBITUARIES of Mrs Gaskell in *The Inquirer*, one signed W.G., 18.11.1865 (contains several errors), one reprinted from the *Unitarian Herald*, same date (Mrs Charles Herford), one reprinted from *MacMillan's Magazine*, 2.12.1865. (The above obituaries and other copies of *The Inquirer* can be seen at Manchester College, Oxford).

Oxford Companions to American, English, and French Literature.

Payne, Revd G.A. *250th Anniversary of Brook St Chapel, Knutsford*, an address given at the Town Hall, Knutsford, 20th May 1939.

Prickett, Stephen, *Coleridge and Wordsworth: The Poetry of Growth*, C.U.P., 1970, Romanticism and Religion: The Tradition of Coleridge and Wordsworth in the Victorian Church, C.U.P., 1976.

Quiller-Couch, Sir Arthur, *Charles Dickens and other Victorians*, C.U.P., 1925 (Section on Mrs Gaskell).

Raitt, A.W., *Prosper Mérimée*, Eyre and Spottiswoode, 1970.

Richardson, R.C., *Puritanism in North-West England*, M.U.P., 1972.

Ritchie, Lady Anne Thackeray, Introduction to *Cranford*, MacMillan, 1891. *Letters of Anne Thackeray* Ritchie, Ed. Hester Ritchie, Murray, 1924.

Rubenius, Aina, *The Woman Question in Mrs Gaskell's Life and Work*, Upsala and Harvard, 1950.

Ruskin, John, *Unto This Last* (1860-62), Collins, 1970. *Modern Painters (1843-1860), Selections*, Nelson, n.d.

Sanders, Gerald de Witt, *Elizabeth Gaskell*, Newhaven 1929.

Shaen, Margaret, Letters to Elizabeth Haldane in the National Library of Scotland, Edinburgh. *MS*6035 H 185-6, *MS*6036 ff 43-4, *MS*23181 H 180-5, *MS*23181 ff 190-1.

Shaen, William, *MS* letter to one of his sisters on Chartism, Symington Papers, Box 19, Leeds City Archives Dept.

Shaffer, Elinor, *Kubla Khan and the Fall of Jerusalem* C.U.P. 1975.

Sharps, John Geoffrey, *Mrs Gaskell's Observation and Invention*, Linden Press, 1970.

Shelston, A.J., '*Ruth*, Mrs Gaskell's Neglected Novel' *Bulletin of the John Rylands University Library*, Spring, 1976.

Short Revd H.L., 'The Importance of the 17th century in Unitarian History,' *Unitarian Historical Transactions*, 1950. 'The Great Ejection and its Consequences', *Tercentenary Lectures*, Pubd. by the Midland Union of Unitarian and Free Churches, 1962.

'The Founding of the British and Foreign Unitarian Association', Supplement to the *Unitarian Historical Society Transactions* Aldiss Press, Oxford, 1975.

Shusterman, David, 'William Rathbone Gregg and Mrs Gaskell' *Philological Quarterly*, April, 1957.

Smith, A. Cobden, 'Mrs Gaskell and Lower Mosley Street' *The Sunday School Quarterly*, 11.1.1911.

Solly, Revd Henry, *These Eighty Years: the Autobiography of a Unitarian Chartist* (2 vols) London, 1893.

Tatton Park, National Trust

Tillotson, Kathleen, *Novels of the 1840s*, Oxford Paperback, 1955. (Section on *Mary Barton*.)

Uglow, Jenny, *Elizabeth Gaskell, a Habit of Stories*, Faber and Faber, 1993.

Unsworth, Anna and A.Q. Morton, 'Mrs Gaskell Anonymous' *Victorian Periodicals Review*, Vol XIV, Number 1, Spring, 1981.

Ward, A.W., Introduction to *Ruth*, Knutsford Edition, 1906.

Waller, Ross D., *Sermons and Society, An Anglican Anthology*, Pelican Original, 1970.

Whitfield, S. Stanton, *Mrs Gaskell, Her Life and Works*, London 1929.

APPENDIX

A SIMPLIFIED VERSION OF THE HOLLAND FAMILY PEDIGREE

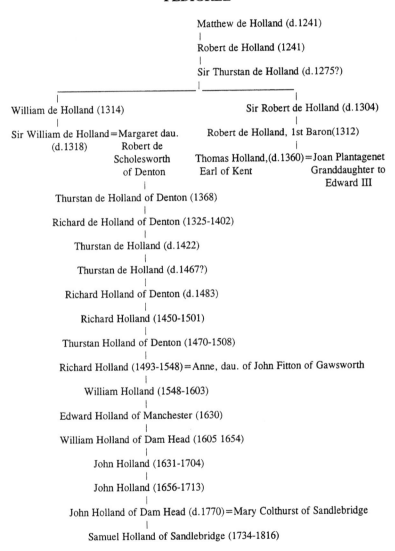

Matthew de Holland (d.1241)

Robert de Holland (1241)

Sir Thurstan de Holland (d.1275?)

William de Holland (1314)   Sir Robert de Holland (d.1304)

Sir William de Holland = Margaret dau.   Robert de Holland, 1st Baron(1312)
(d.1318)   Robert de
        Scholesworth   Thomas Holland,(d.1360) = Joan Plantagenet
        of Denton   Earl of Kent   Granddaughter to
                    Edward III

Thurstan de Holland of Denton (1368)

Richard de Holland of Denton (1325-1402)

Thurstan de Holland (d.1422)

Thurstan de Holland (d.1467?)

Richard Holland of Denton (d.1483)

Richard Holland (1450-1501)

Thurstan Holland of Denton (1470-1508)

Richard Holland (1493-1548) = Anne, dau. of John Fitton of Gawsworth

William Holland (1548-1603)

Edward Holland of Manchester (1630)

William Holland of Dam Head (1605 1654)

John Holland (1631-1704)

John Holland (1656-1713)

John Holland of Dam Head (d.1770) = Mary Colthurst of Sandlebridge

Samuel Holland of Sandlebridge (1734-1816)

243

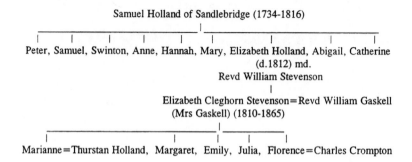

Samuel Holland of Sandlebridge (1734-1816)

Peter, Samuel, Swinton, Anne, Hannah, Mary, Elizabeth Holland, Abigail, Catherine
(d.1812) md.
Revd William Stevenson

Elizabeth Cleghorn Stevenson=Revd William Gaskell
(Mrs Gaskell) (1810-1865)

Marianne=Thurstan Holland, Margaret, Emily, Julia, Florence=Charles Crompton

244